Adapting
Instruction
to
Individual
Differences

Adapting Instruction to Individual Differences

Edited by

Margaret C. Wang

University of Pittsburgh

and

Herbert J. Walberg

University of Illinois at Chicago

●

McCutchan Publishing Corporation

2526 Martin Luther King Jr. Way
Berkeley, California 94704

Library of Congress Catalog Card Number 84–61508
ISBN 0–8211–2263–0

Cover design by Terry Down, Berkeley, Calif.
Typesetting composition by Vera-Reyes, Inc., Manila

Contents

Contributors

Lorin W. Anderson, University of South Carolina
David C. Berliner, University of Arizona
Lizanne DeStefano, Yale University
Walter Doyle, University of Texas—Austin
Patricia Gennari, University of Pittsburgh
Robert Glaser, University of Pittsburgh
Edmund W. Gordon, Yale University
Robert E. Grinder, Arizona State University
Philip W. Jackson, University of Chicago
David W. Johnson, University of Minnesota
Roger T. Johnson, University of Minnesota
Nancy Karweit, Johns Hopkins University
Herbert J. Klausmeier, University of Wisconsin
Edward A. Nelsen, Arizona State University
Stefanie Shipman, Yale University
Robert E. Slavin, Johns Hopkins University
Harriet Talmage, University of Illinois at Chicago
Sigmund Tobias, City College, City University of New York
Ralph W. Tyler, System Development Foundation
Herbert J. Walberg, University of Illinois at Chicago
Richard C. Wallace, Jr., Pittsburgh Public Schools
Margaret C. Wang, University of Pittsburgh
Hersholt C. Waxman, University of Pittsburgh

Foreword

This book deals with one of the most important and difficult tasks of education in a democratic society. Modern democratic societies have generally established equality of educational opportunity for all children as an essential goal. Yet helping all students learn what is essential for their intelligent participation in a modern democratic society has proved to be a difficult task, and many educators have given up the effort. They have lowered their goals to helping students learn *something*, even if what the students learn is not enough for responsible democratic citizenship.

In an authoritarian society, where an elite group is responsible for the decisions and actions of the nation, most youth are not expected to become intelligent and responsible citizens. Their education emphasizes memorization of the detailed picture of the world that has been formulated by the group in power, and the inculcation of habits of respect and obedience to the authority of the rulers. These are the primary educational goals for the children of the common people.

But the American nation was founded by people who visualized a society in which everyone would be both a ruler and a worker. They believed that through education all of the citizens of the new nation would learn what was necessary to be intelligent rulers. There is no doubt that, at that time, the intellectual leaders of the American Revolution knew the wide range of individual differences in human populations because some of these differences were discussed by the Greek, Roman, and English philosophers whose writings furnished the

x   **Foreword**

texts of English secondary schools in the eighteenth century. Nevertheless, they believed that the desire for a democratic community and the dedication of effort to build such a nation would ensure that each citizen acquired the necessary knowledge, skills, and attitudes.

This belief in democratic education has inspired American educational leaders for two centuries, and it appears from the reports in this volume that substantial progress is being made toward realizing these goals. In 1776, the prevailing opinion was that the common man could be trained but that he was not capable of the kind of learning required for intelligent judgments when new situations developed and new problems were encountered. Even as late as this century, children were viewed by many psychologists as having different degrees of educability, and those with low IQs were thought incapable of abstract learning. Slowly, we have become aware of the fact that so-called intelligence tests, or aptitude tests, have usually taken the behavior of the middle-class educated person as the norm of intelligence and have not investigated the intelligent behavior of the children and youth in other American cultures. This new view was the subject of the ground-breaking experimental work of Allison Davis and Kenneth Eels, reported in their book *Intelligence and Cultural Differences* (1951), which verified that many more children and youth could be educated than had previously been believed.

As theoretical concepts are developed that help us understand the ways in which children are capable of intelligent learning, experience and experiments teach us what instructional procedures and supportive environments are helpful to students of different backgrounds. This volume reports some of the more promising ones. But, as American schools come to grips with the problems of dealing constructively with differences in children's learning, new complications emerge as society becomes more complex. What was required in 1776 to participate intelligently and responsibly in that society was relatively simple. Social problems were largely encountered in local communities among neighbors whose mutual involvements were frequent. These problems of family and neighborhood were generally understood and modes of attacking them were recognized and acceptable to most adults in the community. Economic problems were also thought to be simple and conceived in common terms, although the influence of taxation and accessibility to credit was not then well understood. Nevertheless, most educators at that time believed that five to eight years of schooling provided an adequate foundation for the citizen of a democratic society.

Since then, economic, political, and social life has grown increasingly complex. Furthermore, many of the contemporary activities of mankind are dependent upon the utilization of plants, animals, inert materials, and energy. The intelligent citizen now must deal with problems that can be understood fully only by drawing upon the developments of science and technology. Children and youth today must learn much more in order to be intelligent and responsible citizens than was required of earlier generations. As we discover how to adapt elementary school instruction in reading, writing, and arithmetic to the differences among learners, we are facing somewhat different problems in the secondary school. Yet, all youth need to learn to use the resources of scholarship that are being developed by the major fields of inquiry, if they are to be able to grapple constructively with the increasingly complex problems of modern society. This calls for continued experiments and experience, going beyond those of earlier years.

Finally, the development which makes research and practice in this field most challenging and difficult is the growing appreciation of the value of variety in the composition of a democratic society. The early pioneers in America developed a culture—practices, beliefs, attitudes, and appreciations—which enabled them to survive, expand, and prosper. New immigrants and native mavericks were inducted into this earlier culture under the prevailing view that all of the major elements of that culture were essential for the nation to survive and maintain its continued viability. More recently, this view of Americanization has been modified. The point has been cogently made that a democratic society can benefit from the variety of its membership. Such a society is more interesting and less drab than one in which the features of only one cultural group predominate, and it has greater potential for survival and strength when it embodies the positive features from the various cultural groups. This line of thinking has led to a request that schools identify constructive features of the several cultures from which their students come and help the students learn the skills, attitudes, and appreciations that have been found.

To do this, and at the same time to help students learn those things required for community, where all persons are respected and appreciated and all spend some of their time sharing in a common life, would be a new and heavy responsibility for America's public schools, and there are very few validated examples that could guide a widespread program development. But the recognition of the desirability of such a goal is stimulating both research and development. One of the major problems is to select the positive features in different cultures that can enhance the community without tending toward divisiveness or isolation.

This brief background statement is intended to suggest the importance of the work reported in this book. It deals with both educational theory and practice in schooling that seeks to be responsive to the differences in students. It provides an exposition of the major approaches being employed. The chapters were written by leading researchers and developers of adaptive instruction programs who then came together for a working conference to discuss, clarify, and revise what they had written in the light of criticism. This helped to create a degree of unity among the chapters and to give emphasis to the major generalizations derived from the experiences of the authors.

Ralph W. Tyler

Preface

Finding effective and practical learning environments that meet students' individual needs has been a continuing challenge for researchers and practitioners. Efforts aimed at helping schools to meet this challenge can be traced back to the last century, or even earlier. The underlying premises of this work are that individuals learn in different ways and at different rates, and that a major responsibility of schools is to accommodate these differences in order to maximize each student's education. Major research theories concerning individual differences and schooling have remained relatively constant, but there are a number of significant theoretical and substantive developments. The purpose of this book is to examine several approaches to adaptive instruction, the psychological theories underlying their design, and the implications for school improvement.

New views of individual differences, combined with recent developments in cognitive-instructional psychology and research on classroom processes, have had a major impact on how individual differences in learning are examined and described. Teachers now require more information on student learning differences when planning instruction. Rather than being viewed as static, such differences in learning have come to be considered alterable.

In addition, growing research evidence suggests a wide range of variability in the ways that students acquire, organize, retain, and generate knowledge and skills. Thus, learner differences are less likely to be identified through traditional tests. Instead, differences are identified and described according to the manner in which students process information and the knowledge and competence they possess for specific learning tasks. As a result of these developments, researchers and teachers are giving increased attention to instruction that is based on the specific learning needs of individual students. These needs are identified through analysis of the processes by which students acquire and retain knowledge and skills.

In addition to the evolution in psychological concepts and educational principles, adaptive instruction in regular school settings has been aided by current efforts to provide high-quality educational opportunities for every student. The passage of the Education for All Handicapped Children Act (Public Law 94-142), in particular, has mandated support systems to accommodate the diverse needs of individual students in regular classrooms. For these reasons, school administrators and teachers are more supportive of individualized instruction that combines direct assessment of student capabilities with direct instruction that builds each student's competence in the basic skills.

We can therefore be optimistic about the utility and timeliness of adaptive instruction programs. Along with the technical advances, adaptive instruction is establishing a strong theoretical base. Research has produced the knowledge and technical skills for providing adaptive instruction and for motivating school personnel to implement new programs. The opportunities seem better now than ever before to respond constructively to individual differences in learning and to increase the effectiveness of instructional practices. In this context, this book was conceived to provide a forum for discussions of the "state of the art" of the theory, research, and practice of adaptive instruction.

This book is organized in two parts. The first focuses on the theory and research underlying efforts to provide instruction that is adaptive to the learning needs of individual students. The second part consists of descriptions of the design, development, implementation, and evaluation of selected adaptive instruction programs and practices.

The first part includes five chapters. In Chapter 1, Herbert J. Walberg reviews theories of instruction and learning differences of the last three decades and summarizes recent research that bears upon these theories. A historical perspective is provided in Chapter 2 by Robert E. Grinder and Edward A. Nelsen, who review earlier strategies for dealing with individual differences in learners and discuss their value in terms of current programs. In Chapter 3, Edmund W. Gordon, Lizanne DeStefano, and Stefanie Shipman summarize and analyze research on the special needs of students in relation to features of adaptive and nonadaptive instruction. Philip W. Jackson, in the fourth chapter of this part, critically reviews research on the problems involved in accommodating individual learning needs through conventional teaching and learning and assesses the potential of adaptive instruction for providing solutions to these problems. In their comments, Robert Glaser and Walter Doyle analyze the preceding chapters in this section from the perspective of fundamental research on adaptive instruction, cognitive psychology, and the tasks of teaching and learning.

Chapters in the second part of the book are concerned with the practice of adaptive instruction. The first six focus on the design and supporting research of specific instructional approaches; the next two chapters deal with more general issues related to the practicality of adaptive instruction and the implementation of this approach in regular school settings.

David W. Johnson and Roger Johnson present a review of evidence on the effectiveness of the cooperative learning groups approach in Chapter 6 and discuss classroom operation and the planning of adaptive strategies for the accommodation of student differences in the execution and evaluation of a national implementation program. In Chapter 7, Sigmund Tobias describes computer-assisted instruction and new software programs that go beyond the electronic flash card approach of the past to tailor instructional cues, correctives, and reinforcement more specifically to the cognitive and motivational needs of individual learners. In Chapter 8, Herbert J. Klausmeier outlines strategies for relating instructing and advising practices to the educational needs of individual students, and he describes features of secondary schools as unique social organizations that facilitate implementation of the practices.

The theoretical and research bases for the design, implementation, and evaluation of an approach to adaptive instruction that combines a highly structured diagnostic-prescriptive curriculum for basic skills instruction with more open-ended, student-planned, and student-managed, exploratory learning options are discussed in Chapter 9 by Margaret C. Wang, Patricia Gennari, and Hersholt C. Waxman. In

Chapter 10, Robert E. Slavin describes the rationale, plan, operation, and evaluation of an adaptive instruction program that incorporates both cooperative teams and individualized learning. The research basis and history of the "learning for mastery" approach are treated by Lorin W. Anderson in Chapter 11, along with a report on very recent research related to the implementation, optimization of components, and large-scale evaluation of this approach.

In the final chapters of the second part, Richard C. Wallace, Jr. discusses adaptive instruction in Chapter 12 in light of the administrative problems, needs, and opportunities facing large urban school systems. In Chapter 13, Nancy Karweit reviews the implications of school time for educational policy decisions as well as for individual differences in the instructional learning process and in student achievement. The discussants for the chapters in the second part of the book, David C. Berliner and Harriet Talmage, compare and contrast the various approaches described in the chapters from the perspectives of contemporary educational psychology, curriculum design, classroom instruction, and program evaluation.

Much of the material in this volume was originally presented at an invitational conference held at the Learning Research and Development Center of the University of Pittsburgh. Appreciation is expressed to the National Institute of Education for the funding to sponsor the conference. Many individuals have made significant contributions to preparation of the book. We are especially grateful to Professors Robert Glaser and Lauren B. Resnick, Co-directors of the Center, for their encouragement, advice, and critiques, and to Rita Catalano, who played a major role in coordinating the conference activities and provided editorial assistance in each stage of our efforts to finish the book.

Margaret C. Wang
University of Pittsburgh

Herbert J. Walberg
University of Illinois at Chicago
January 1985

PART I

The Content of Adaptive Instruction

CHAPTER

1

Instructional Theories and Research Evidence

Herbert J. Walberg

Adaptive education, in brief, is intended to make learning more effective by suiting instruction to the needs of students. The first purpose of this chapter is to define adaptive education more explicitly and to indicate the psychological theories and models of instruction on which it draws. The second purpose is to present syntheses of research on adaptive instruction.

THEORIES OF ADAPTION AND INDIVIDUALIZATION

Adaptive programs make use of a variety of techniques that have been found to be effective in different classroom settings. These techniques include mastery learning, cooperative teamwork, and individualized instruction (Walberg 1984). Adaptive programs make use of these techniques in the ways that seem most suitable for each teacher, class, and student, so there may be considerable variety among the programs.

Despite varying applications, adaptive education has features that distinguish the approach from traditional or nonadaptive education. These features are not like rigorous Boolean logical descriptors, but are more similar to family facial features that only collectively set one group noticeably apart from another. Wang and Lindvall (1984) provide seven such distinguishing descriptors that have proved useful in identifying thirty-eight studies of adaptive education from hundreds of studies found through computer and other citation searches of educational research literature (Waxman, Wang, Anderson, and Walberg 1984):

1. Instruction based on the assessed capabilities of each student.

2. Materials and procedures that permit each student to make progress in the mastery of instructional content at a pace suited to his or her abilities and interests.

3. Periodic evaluations of student progress that serve to inform the student concerning mastery.

4. Student assumption of responsibility for diagnosing present needs and abilities, for planning individual learning activities, and for evaluating mastery.

5. Alternative activities and materials for aiding student acquisition of essential academic skills and content.

6. Student choice in selecting educational goals, outcomes, and activities.

7. Students' assistance of one another in pursuing individual goals and cooperation in achieving group goals.

From another standpoint, however, theoretical models of individualized instruction can be considered partly adaptive in certain respects. Both traditional and contemporary theories and practices of educational individualization are intended to suit lessons to groups or individual students; but, as the next section suggests, they might best be considered elements or components of adaptive education that employ a more comprehensive approach.

Traditional Individualization Models

Enrichment and acceleration are presently the most common methods for individualizing learning. Both models require a series of activity units and tests, and generally a final examination. Students move through the same course of instruction in the same sequence;

students must, in most cases, repeat the entire course if judged as failures.

In enrichment programs, every student spends roughly the same amount of time learning. Individual variability, to the distress of radical egalitarians, is evidenced in normally distributed test scores on unit tests and final examinations that correlate with measures of aptitude and home environment. Often combined with whole–group lessons, recitation, and seatwork, enrichment has been the dominant method of American schooling since the turn of the century.

In sharp contrast, acceleration ideally means that satisfactory performance is fixed at, say, 80 percent; since all students are expected to attain that criterion, time spent by each student varies. Oddly, two extensive reviews of early classroom research by Strang (1937) and by Stephens (1968) conclude that there is little correlation between time spent in instruction and achievement. Recent quantitative syntheses, however, show consistently positive correlations between time spent and amount learned (Walberg 1984). The major assumption of acceleration is that time can compensate for deficiencies in quality of instruction, student aptitude, and home environment.

Recent Diagnostic Models

In two contemporary models of individualized learning, diagnostic pretests are given before beginning courses of instruction. The hierarchical model is based on the idea that it is necessary to learn the content elements of one unit of instruction before going on to the next and that some students will have already mastered some units before beginning a new course. Pretests serve, therefore, to place individual students at the most appropriate point in the sequence of instruction. Their progress is measured after each unit, and if they fail any unit, they must repeat that unit before proceeding on to the next.

The random model assumes that units need not be presented in a hierarchy or sequence; a student, for instance, may need instruction in the first and fourth of five units but not in the others. Diagnostic pretests show which units to assign to students so that they all master the corpus of units and avoid studying those they have already mastered.

Multimodal and Multivalent Models

Recent experimental models of individualized instruction require multiple courses of instruction. In the first model, the multimodal, several courses of instruction or sequences of lesson units lead to the same achievement goals. Students are administered a pretest to determine their level of aptitude (which may be measured in terms of prior achievement, learning styles, and motivational preferences) and then are assigned appropriate courses of instruction. Students may also be allowed to select their own courses.

Multimodal individualization assumes that aptitudes interact with educational treatment, that is, that some forms of instruction are better than others for a particular student or group. Despite much research in the last few years in this area, "aptitude-treatment interactions" have been difficult to replicate. In a 231-item review, Bar-Yam (1969) found some replicated evidence that bright, flexible, and assertive students perform better when instructional methods are flexible and require independence than do their opposites, who may do better in more structured settings.

Aptitude-instruction interactions appear to account for little replicated variance in achievement compared to the main effects of aptitude, instruction, and environment, and it is likely that, if such interactions are indeed powerful, their influence would have been uncovered by now. Nevertheless, much theorizing about individualization seems to be based on the premise of their ubiquity (Cronbach and Snow 1974), and they may deserve further research.

The multivalent model assumes not only that there should be different sequences of instruction but that they should lead to different goals for different students. Harvard Project Physics was deliberately based on these premises. It was felt that different teachers and students might elect to pursue different goals in physics, for example, mathematical mastery or understanding the nature and history of scientific methods. To permit cooperative planning, guides for teachers and students describe the course organization, various objectives, and alternative instructional activities. Open education represents a still more radical alternative, since students are expected to find or create their own learning materials to suit their educational purposes (Walberg 1984).

The success of contemporary models of individualized learning may depend on efficient monitoring as well as on an effective system for quick summarization of data for decision making and student feedback. The continuing pervasiveness of enrichment with whole-group lessons and recitation, and, to a lesser extent, acceleration with seatwork, may be attributable to the lack of well-developed management systems for more suitable instruction. To be feasible over the long term, adaptive education may require school reorganization, extensive staff support, and computer processing of data on student progress so that lessons may be conveniently tailored to individual needs.

EDUCATIONAL PRODUCTIVITY AND INSTRUCTIONAL MODELS

This section analyzes eight multidimensional instructional models within the framework of a theory of educational productivity encompassing eight factors that consistently predict affective, behavioral, and cognitive learning (Walberg 1971, 1984). The theory holds that classroom learning is a multiplicative, diminishing-returns function of four essential factors (student ability and motivation, and quality and quantity of instruction) and possibly four supplementary or supportive factors (the morale or social-psychological environment of the classroom, education-stimulating conditions in the home and in the peer group, and exposure to mass media, particularly television).

Each of the essential factors appears to be necessary but insufficient for classroom learning, that is, all four of these factors appear to be required at least at minimal levels for classroom learning to take place. It also appears that the essential factors may substitute, compensate, or trade off for one another at diminishing rates of return. For example, immense quantities of time may be required for a moderate amount of learning to occur if motivation, ability, or quality of instruction is minimal. Within this theoretical perspective, adaptive educators seek to modify the amount and quality of instruction to make it more suitable to the ability and motivation of each student to (a) raise the average class achievement, (b) bring each student to at least a minimum, (c) diminish the variability of outcomes, or (d) optimize a combination of these three goals.

The roles of the four supplementary factors are less clear. Although morale, home environment, peer group pressures, and television exposure predict classroom learning outcomes (Walberg 1984), they may supplement as well as support classroom learning. If, for example, eighteen-year-old students attended school six hours a day for 180 days for twelve years and required ten hours a day on average for sleep and meals, then they spent only 21.2 percent of the potentially educative hours in school. If the first six years of life are counted as potentially educative, and if half the hours in school are subtracted because of absences, disruptions, noneducative activities, and inattentiveness (Walberg and Frederick, in press), then only 7.1 percent of the potentially educative time was spent learning in school. If it is true, as Aristotle held, that experience, not just the teacher, teaches, then, for several reasons, blocks of time devoted to potentially educative but nonschool activities must also be evaluated.

First, much instructional research employs standardized tests that cover knowledge that may be acquired within or outside school. Selecting or refining items on the basis of discrimination (that is, correlation of items within the total score), as is often done, tailors the performance measure to generalized verbal ability rather than to specific elements of the curriculum or what is taught. Curriculum-relevant outcomes can be recommended, but whether they are used or not, indications of the supplementary and supportive factors can serve as powerful covariates that increase the precision and sensitivity of experiments (that is, randomized assignment to treatment in general field trials) and raise the validity of quasi-experiments and other observational studies by helping to discount rival hypotheses. Although ability, prior achievement, and motivation may partly control for the less proximal factors, it has not been shown that they can completely mediate their influence.

Second, the less proximal factors may support classroom learning by influencing the more proximal factors such as ability and motivation, which may in turn influence the quality and quantity of instruction, since teachers may perform more efficiently in responsive classes. Learning may also take place in the home, within the peer group, and through exposure to mass media. Such learning may substitute for what is missed in school, but it will still be represented on outcome tests. Although treatment randomization helps to rule out such rival hypotheses of causal influence, experiments may also sacrifice the external validity of the observed influence since the randomization may make for unnatural, contrived conditions of classroom instruction. Results that are robust across experimental, observational, and case-study research, and that take comprehensive and explicit account of the full set of factors, would be most convincing with respect to chains of causal influence.

Third, from a theoretical point of view, the classroom can be viewed as an open system that is not isolated from external influences. Even if our main interest is in improving instruction, learning in the home and in the peer group outside of school need not differ in kind from that in school. Theoretical models or regression equations that estimate the weightings of all major factors in the determination of educational outcomes provide: (a) an overall accounting of learning processes, (b) multivariate diagnostic assessments of each student's profile, and (c) quantitative indications of better allocations of learning resources and predictions of outcomes. In short, a more comprehensive approach to assessment provides a more realistic basis for prescription.

The purposes of this section are to explicate the specific common constructs in contemporary models of instruction, to compare and contrast their roles in the models, and to relate them to the general productivity factors. Voluminous research and opinions regarding the eight models could be cited. This section, however, is confined to theoretical issues, since much empirical research on instruction is atheoretical; and the research that has sought to prove the validity of the models has been confined to a single model in any given study without comparing the validity of two or more models. It can be hoped that the analysis may (a) show the commonalities and distinctions among the models, (b) suggest transcendent and unique theoretical constructs among them that deserve consideration in future instructional models, and (c) identify causal paths that differ across the models and may be empirically investigated.

Psychological Models of Educational Performance

To specify the productivity factors in further theoretical and operational detail and provide a more explicit framework for future primary research and synthesis, Haertel and others (1983) compared eight contemporary psychological models of educational performance. As explained before, each of the first four factors in Table 1.1—student ability and motivation, and quality and quantity of instruction—may be essential or necessary but insufficient for classroom learning (age and developmental level are omitted because they are unspecified in the models).

The other four factors in Table 1.1 are less clear. Although they consistently predict outcomes, they may support, or substitute for,

Table 1.1

Classification of Constructs According to the Model of Educational Productivity

Theorist	Ability	Motivation	Quality of Instruction	Quantity of Instruction	Social Environment of Classroom	Home Environment	Peer Influence	Mass Media
Carroll (1963)	Aptitude Ability to comprehend instructions	Perseverance	Clarity of instruction Matching task to student characteristics	Opportunity to learn (time)				
Cooley & Leinhardt (1975)	General ability Prior achievement	Motivators (internal)	Motivators (external) Structure Instructional events Attitude toward teachers	Opportunity to learn (time)	Attitudes toward school		Attitudes toward peers	
Bloom (1976)	Prior achievement Reading comprehension Verbal IQ	Attitude toward subject matter Self-concept as learner	Use of cues Reinforcement Feedback and correctives	Participation in learning task (time)	Attitudes toward school			
Harnischfeger & Wiley (1976)	Pupil background	Intrinsic motivation	Teacher activities	Pupil pursuits (7 time categories)				

Bennett (1978)	Aptitude Prior achievement	Implicit	Clarity of instruction Task difficulty and pacing	Total active learning time Quantity of schooling Time allocated to curriculum activity
Gagné (1977)	Internal conditions of learning	Implicit	Activating motivation Informing learner of objective Directing attention Stimulating recall Providing learning guidance Enhancing retention Promoting transfer of learning Eliciting performance and providing feedback	
Glaser (1976)	Task learnings already acquired Prerequisite learnings Cognitive style	Implicit	Materials, procedures, and techniques that foster competence (e.g., knowledge structures;	

Table 1.1 (continued)
Classification of Constructs According to the Model of Educational Productivity

Theorist	Ability	Motivation	Quality of Instruction	Quality of Instruction	Social Environment of Classroom	Home Environment	Peer influence	Mass Media
	Task specific aptitudes General mediating ability		learning-to-learn; contingencies of reinforcement) Assessment of effects of instruction					
Bruner (1966)	Task relevant skills	Predispositions	Implanting a predisposition toward learning Structuring knowledge Sequence of materials Specifying rewards and punishments					

Source: Geneva D. Haertel, Herbert J. Walberg, and Thomas Weinstein, "Psychological Models of Educational Performance: A Theoretical Synthesis of Constructs," *Review of Educational Research* 53 (Spring 1983): 75-92. © 1983 American Educational Research Association. Reprinted with permission.

classroom learning. At any rate, it would seem useful to include all factors in future primary research to rule out exogenous causes and increase statistical precision of estimates of the effects of the essential and the other factors.

Table 1.1 shows that the constructs of ability and quantity of instruction are widely and relatively richly specified among the models. Explicit theoretical treatments of motivation and quantity of instruction, however, are largely confined to the Carroll (1963) tradition represented in the first four models; and the remaining factors are largely neglected.

The table poses theoretical questions that can be empirically researched. The tension between theoretical parsimony and operational detail, for example, suggests several: Can the first four constructs mediate the causal influences of the last four? Would assessments of Glaser's (1976) five student entry behaviors allow more efficient instructional prescriptions than would, say, Carroll's, Bloom's (1976), or Bennett's (1978) more general and more parsimonious ability subconstructs? Would less numerous subconstructs than Gagné's (1977) eight instructional qualities or Harnischfeger and Wiley's (1976) seven time categories suffice?

The theoretical formulation of educational performance models, in the past two decades since the Carroll and Bruner papers, has advanced rapidly. The models are explicit enough to be tested in ordinary classroom settings by experimental methods and production functions. More comprehensive and better formulated research and syntheses should help us reach a greater degree of theoretical and empirical consensus on effective educational practice.

RECENT SYNTHESES BEARING UPON ADAPTIVE EDUCATION

Recent quantitative syntheses of research on systems, constituents, and constructs of adaptive education (Walberg, Schiller, and Oh 1983) show consistently positive results. Table 1.2 shows results of many studies and syntheses grouped under the following categories: quantity, methods, systems of instruction; classroom social environment; and peer group. Also shown are the number of studies, a brief definition of the independent and dependent variables, the average effect size of correlation, and the percentage of studies showing positive results.

Table 1.2
A Summary of Research Syntheses on Instruction

Author	Number of Studies	Subjects	Independent/ Dependent Variables	Effect Size	Percent Positive	Comments
Quantity						
Fredrick and Walberg (1980)	35	Elementary Secondary College	Instruction time and achievement	0.38	86	
Methods						
Cohen, Kulik, and Kulik (1982)	38	College	Tutoring versus conventional teaching and achievement	0.40 0.29 0.09 0.33 0.42 0.18	87 100 78 87 80 75	Tutee achievement on final exam Tutee attitude toward subject Tutee self-concept Tutor achievement on final exam Tutor attitude toward subject Tutor self-concept
Horan and Lynn (1980)	15	Elementary Secondary College	Sequentially structured lessons and achievement	0.44 0.07 0.21		Elementary Secondary College
Kavale (1980)	34	Average age: 7.5	Psycholinguistic training and achievement	0.39	95	
Luiten, Ames, and Ackerson (1980)	135	Grade 3 to Graduate School	Advance organizers (subject matter overviews) and learning	0.21		Effects larger for higher achievers; college students; and oral presentation
			Advance organizers and retention	0.26		Effects largest for 22+ days

Study	N	Level	Focus	Effect size	%	Category
Slavin (1980)	28	Grades 2-12	Cooperative learning and achievement attitudes		81 78 95 65	Curriculum specific tests Standardized tests Race relations Mutual concern
Lysakowski and Walberg (1981)	39	K-College	Positive reinforcement on learning	1.17		
Smith (1980)	47	Elementary Secondary	Teacher expectations and learning Teacher expectations and student attitudes Teacher expectations and student achievement	0.16 0.31 0.38		Ability Attitudes Achievement
Yeany and Miller (1980)	28	Grade 5 through College	Effects of diagnostic prescriptive instruction on science achievement Effects of diagnostic prescriptive instruction on science attitudes	0.49 0.18		Diagnostic feedback only Diagnostic feedback and remediation
Systems Ariello (1981)	115	Secondary and College	Individualized instruction and science achievement	0.35		

Table 1.2 (continued)
A Summary of Research Syntheses on Instruction

Author	Number of Studies	Subjects	Independent/ Dependent Variables	Effect Size	Percent Positive	Comments
Athappilly (1978)	134	Elementary through College	Innovative mathematics curricula and learning	0.24 0.12		Achievement Attitude
Bangert, Kulik, and Kulik (1983)	51	Grades 6 through 12	Individual instruction and learning	0.38 0.27	65 64	Achievement Attitude
El-Nemr (1979)	59	Secondary and College	Inquiry method for teaching biology and learning	0.16 0.54 0.20 0.47		Achievement Process skills Critical thinking Laboratory skills Attitudes
Hartley (1977)	153	Elementary and Secondary	Individually paced math instruction and learning	0.41 0.60 0.11 0.16		Computer-assisted instruction Tutoring Programmed instruction Industrial learning packets
Kulik, Kulik, and Cohen (1979)	75	College	Personalized system of instruction and learning	0.69 0.46	94 91	Achievement Attitude

Study	N	Level	Topic	Effect size	Percentile	Outcome
Kulik, Kulik, and Cohen (1980)	59	College	Computer-based instruction and learning	0.25 0.24	69 73	Achievement Attitude
Kulik, Cohen, and Ebeling (1980)	56	College	Programmed instruction and achievement	0.24	71	
Kulik, Shwalb, and Kulik (1982)	47	Secondary	Programmed instruction and learning	0.08 -.14	49 44	Achievement Attitude
Pflaum, Walberg, Karegianes, and Rasher (1980)	96	K-College	Experimental reading instruction and achievement	0.60		
Weinstein, Boulanger, and Walberg (1982)	33	Junior and Senior High School	Innovative science curricula and achievement	0.31	79	
Classroom Social Environment Johnson et al. (1981)	122	Elementary through Adult	Cooperative, competitive, and individualistic goal structures on achievement	0.00 0.78 0.37 0.76 0.50 0.03	54 76 68 83 81 47	Cooperative Cooperative Group Cooperative Group Competitive

Table 1.2 (continued)
A Summary of Research Syntheses on Instruction

Author	Number of Studies	Subjects	Independent/ Dependent Variables	Effect Size	Percent Positive	Comments
Kulik and Kulik (1981)	51	College	Homogeneous grouping of students of similar abilities and achievement	0.10	71	
Peer Group Ide, Parkerson, Haertel, and Walberg (1981)	10	Elementary and Secondary	Peer-group characteristics such as aspiration and socioeconomic status of friends outside of school and learning	r = 0.24	76	

Note: Effect sizes are indexes of the average comparative effects of educational methods; the larger the effect size, the greater the effect on learning. Percent positive is the percentage of all studies or results that showed positive effects on learning (in most cases experimental groups compared to control groups—the exception being peer group which is the percentage of positive correlations). See Walberg (1984) for additional technical information.

The amount of instructional time shows a moderate relation to learning and consistently positive results. In addition, however, many methods of instruction in Table 1.2 show small to large and consistently positive results. Depending on definition, many of these methods may be classified as components or aspects of adaptive education, for example, tutoring, sequentially structured lessons, cooperative learning, and diagnostic-prescriptive instruction.

Instructional systems may be thought of as systematic organizations of instructional methods and subject matter. Nearly all of these show positive effects on average. Some produce substantial effects of more than a third of a standard deviation, for example, individualized instruction, individual pacing by computer and tutoring in mathematics, personalized system of instruction (in college studies), and experimental approaches to reading instruction. The moderate results for computer-assisted instruction (about a quarter of a standard deviation) should not be taken as indicative of the computer's potential since much of the research concerned the outdated use of computers for repetitive, nonadaptive purposes.

Work at the Johns Hopkins University and the University of Minnesota shows substantial advantages of cooperative over competitive and individualistic goal structures. Such cooperative-learning programs appear to harness the social energies of students and channel them into constructive efforts. By comparison, the effects of homogeneous grouping, though positive, are small and less consistent. (See chapters by the Johnsons and Slavin in this book.)

Full-Scale Systems of Adaptive Education

Research on full-scale systems of adaptive education that meet the seven criteria set forth by Wang and Lindvall (1984) and mentioned in the introduction of this chapter has recently been synthesized. Waxman and others (1984) calculated 309 effects from statistical data on about 7,200 students in kindergarten through grade twelve in thirty-eight studies of adaptive systems. Seventy-seven percent of the comparisons favored adaptive over control groups on learning outcomes; and the average effect, .45 standard deviation, is substantial.

The average effect of adaptive education, however, is not as large as some of its component parts shown in Table 1.1, such as reinforcement. Such components of adaptive education are typically evaluated on narrow measurements that directly reflect the immediate lessons rather than on more general learnings and nationally standardized achievement tests. Adaptive programs have more often been evaluated according to multiple, comprehensive criteria. Thus, educators, in selecting adaptive programs, may be faced with a trade-off between narrow components that efficiently maximize the attainment of a few, narrow goals and full-scale systems that substantially raise a greater variety of outcomes.

CONCLUSION

Instructional theory and research of the past decade have made rapid strides. The major determinants of school learning, including extramural factors, are clearly identified; and their operational characteristics can be specified in considerable detail. (See the references cited and, further, the primary studies cited in these reviews and syntheses). Reasonably consistent results can be found in narrowly focused studies of cues, reinforcement, content, and timing as well as broader studies of systems of support, instruction, and content. Educational theories appear to be converging on central constructs of instruction, although many value issues, such as the relative balance of individual excellence and group equality and of teacher control and learner autonomy, are subject to a range of opinion. Subsequent chapters of this book illustrate a variety of successful programs of adaptive education.

It may be premature to state precisely how components of adaptive education contribute to the accomplishment of learning and other goals, particularly long-term outcomes. Nor can it be said that empirical research has been geared satisfactorily to the adjudication of rival educational theories. Nonetheless, research sets forth useful theories and systematic evidence that cannot only lead to more effective research, but can also serve as an important basis for improving the productivity of educational practice.

REFERENCES

Ariello, Nancy C. "A Meta-analysis Comparing Alternative Methods of Individualized and Traditional Instruction in Service." Doct. dissertation, Virginia Polytechnic Institute and State University, 1981.
Athappilly, Kuriakose K. "A Meta-analysis of the Effects of Modern Mathematics in

Comparison with Traditional Mathematics in the American Educational System." Doct. dissertation, Western Michigan University, 1978.

Bangert, Robert L.; Kulik, James A.; and Kulik, Chen-Lin C. "Individualized Systems of Instruction in Secondary Schools." *Review of Educational Research* 53 (Summer 1983): 143-58.

Bar-Yam, Miriam. "The Interaction of Student Characteristics with Instructional Strategies: A Study of Students' Performance and Attitudes in a High School Innovative Course." Doct. dissertation, Harvard University, 1969.

Bennett, S. Neville. "Recent Research on Teaching: A Dream, a Belief, and a Model." *British Journal of Educational Psychology* 48 (June 1978): 127-47.

Bloom, Benjamin S. *Human Characteristics and School Learning*. New York: McGraw-Hill, 1976.

Bruner, Jerome. *Toward a Theory of Instruction*. New York: W. W. Norton, 1966.

Carroll, John B. "A Model of School Learning." *Teachers College Record* 64 (May 1963): 723-33.

Cohen, Peter A.; Kulik, James A.; and Kulik, Chen-Lin C. "Educational Outcomes of Tutoring: A Meta-analysis of Findings." *American Educational Research Journal* 19 (Summer 1982): 237-48.

Cooley, William W., and Leinhardt, Gaea. *The Application of a Model for Investigating Classroom Processes*. Pittsburgh, Penn.: Learning Research and Development Center, University of Pittsburgh, 1975.

Cronbach, Lee J., and Snow, Richard E. *Instructional Methods and Aptitudes*. New York: Appleton-Century-Crofts, 1974.

El-Nemr, Medhat A. "Meta-analysis of the Outcomes of Teaching Biology as Inquiry." Doct. dissertation, University of Colorado, 1979.

Fredrick, Wayne C., and Walberg, Herbert J. "Learning as a Function of Time." *Journal of Educational Research* 73 (March/April 1980): 183-94.

Gagné, Robert M. *The Conditions of Learning*. New York: Holt, Rinehart & Winston, 1977.

Glaser, Robert. "Components of Psychology of Instruction: Toward a Science of Design." *Review of Educational Research* 46 (Winter 1976): 1-24.

Haertel, Geneva D.; Walberg, Herbert J.; and Weinstein, Thomas. "Psychological Models of Educational Performance: A Theoretical Synthesis of Constructs." *Review of Educational Research* 53 (Spring 1983): 75-92.

Harnischfeger, Annegret, and Wiley, David E. "The Teaching-Learning Process in Elementary Schools: A Synoptic View." *Curriculum Inquiry* 6 (Fall 1976): 5-45.

Hartley, Susan S. "Meta-analysis of the Effects of Individually Paced Instruction in Mathematics." Doct. dissertation, University of Colorado, 1977.

Horan, Patricia F., and Lynn, David D. "Learning Hierarchies Research." *Evaluation in Education* 4, no. 1 (1980): 82-83.

Ide, Judith K.; Parkerson, JoAnn; Haertel, Geneva D.; and Walberg, Herbert J. "Peer Group Influence on Educational Outcomes: A Quantitative Synthesis." *Journal of Educational Psychology* 73 (August 1981): 472-84.

Johnson, David W.; Maruyama, Geoffrey; Johnson, Roger; Nelson, Deborah; and Skon, Linda. "Effects of Cooperative, Competitive, and Individualistic Goal Structures on Achievement: A Meta-analysis." *Psychological Bulletin* 89 (January, 1981): 47-62.

Kavale, Kenneth. "The Efficacy of Psycholinguistic Training." *Evaluation in Education* 4, no. 1 (1980): 88-90.

Kulik, Chen-Lin, and Kulik, James A. "Effects of Ability Grouping on Secondary School Students: A Meta-analysis of Evaluation Findings." Unpublished paper, University of Michigan, 1981.

Kulik, Chen-Lin C.; Shwalb, Barbara J.; and Kulik, James A. "Programmed Instruction in Secondary Education: A Meta-analysis of Evaluation Findings." *Journal of Educational Research* 75 (January/February 1982): 133-38.

Kulik, James A., and Kulik, Chen-Lin C. "Individualized College Teaching." *Evaluation in Education* 4, no. 1 (1980): 64-67.

Kulik, James A.; Cohen, Peter A.; and Ebeling, Barbara J. "Effectiveness of Programmed Instruction in Higher Education: A Meta-analysis of Findings." *Educational Evaluation and Policy Analysis* 2 (November/December 1980): 61-64.

Kulik, James A.; Kulik, Chen-Lin C.; and Cohen, Peter A. "A Meta-analysis of Outcome Studies of Keller's Personalized System of Instruction." *American Psychologist* 34 (April 1979): 307-318.

Kulik, James A.; Kulik, Chen-Lin C.; and Cohen, Peter A. "Effectiveness of Computer-Based College Teaching: A Meta-analysis of Findings." *Review of Educational Research* 50 (Winter 1980): 525-44.

Luiten, John; Ames, Wilbur; and Ackerson, Gary. "A Meta-analysis of the Effects of Advance Organizers on Learning and Retention." *American Educational Research Journal* 17 (Summer 1980): 211-18.

Lysakowski, Richard S., and Walberg, Herbert J. "Classroom Reinforcement and Learning: A Quantitative Synthesis." *Journal of Educational Research* 75 (November/December 1981): 69-77.

Pflaum, Susanna; Walberg, Herbert J.; Karegianes, Myra; and Rasher, Sue P. "Methods of Teaching Reading." *Evaluation in Education* 4, no. 1 (1980): 121-25.

Slavin, Robert. "Cooperative Learning." *Review of Educational Research* 50 (Fall 1980): 315-42.

Smith, Mary Lee. "Meta-analysis of Research on Teacher Expectations." *Evaluation in Education* 4, no. 1 (1980): 53-55.

Stephens, John M. *The Process of Schooling: A Psychological Examination.* New York: Holt, Rinehart & Winston, 1968.

Strang, Ruth. *Behavior and Background of Students in College and Secondary School.* New York: Harper and Row, 1937.

Walberg, Herbert J. "Models for Optimizing and Individualizing School Learning." *Interchange* 2, no. 3 (1971): 15-27.

Walberg, Herbert J. "Synthesis of Research on Teaching." In *Handbook of Research on Teaching,* edited by Merlin C. Wittrock. Washington, D.C.: American Educational Research Association, 1984.

Walberg, Herbert J., and Fredrick, Wayne C. "Instruction Time and Learning." In *Encyclopedia of Educational Research,* edited by Harold E. Mitzel. New York: Macmillan, forthcoming.

Walberg, Herbert J.; Schiller, Diane S.; and Oh, Sung S. "Educational Research as Applied Science." Unpublished manuscript, University of Illinois, Chicago, 1983.

Wang, Margaret C., and Lindvall, C. Mauritz. "Individual Differences and School Learning Environments: Theory, Research, and Design." In *Review of Research in*

Education, vol. 11, edited by Edmund W. Gordon. Washington, D.C.: American Educational Research Association, 1984.

Waxman, Hersholt C.; Wang, Margaret C.; Anderson, Kenneth A.; and Walberg, Herbert J. *Adaptive Education and Student Outcomes: A Quantitative Synthesis*. Pittsburgh, Penn.: Learning Research and Development Center, University of Pittsburgh, 1984.

Weinstein, Thomas; Boulanger, F. David; and Walberg, Herbert J. "Science Curriculum Effects in High School: A Quantitative Synthesis." *Journal of Research in Science Teaching* 19, no. 6 (1982): 511-22.

Yeany, Russell H., and Miller, P. Ann. *The Effects of Diagnostic/Remedial Instruction on Science Learning: A Meta-analysis*. Athens, Ga.: University of Georgia, 1980. ED 187 533.

Individualized Instruction in American Pedagogy: The Saga of an Educational Ideology and a Practice in the Making

Robert E. Grinder and Edward A. Nelsen

Adaptive education today refers mainly to matching instructional objectives and activities to the experiences, aptitudes, and interests of individual pupils (Bangert, Kulik, and Kulik 1983; Glaser 1977, 1983). It is one of the more venerable practices in pedagogy. Our forebears who taught children to draw hieroglyphics on the walls of caves, to hunt the prairies for their supper, to respect their elders, and so forth, surely taught according to children's individual abilities.

Plato, in his *Republic* (Jowett 1942), urged that children be directed toward philosopher, guardian, or artisan roles depending on whether they possessed "golden, silver, or brass" talents. In contemporary American pedagogy, the practice of adapting instruction to individual differences has oscillated between intuitive accommodation or benign disregard and enthusiastic advocacy.

During colonial times, instructional activities were individualized because circumstances and expediency demanded it. As industrialism gained momentum, mass or group instruction became the norm. Then, early in the twentieth century, individualized instruction again became common, but for new reasons and under new conditions.

In matters of schooling generally, and in the tribulations of individualized instruction particularly, educational practices have always been shaped by ideological, administrative, and economic issues. First, at the ideological level, educators have wrestled with beliefs and questions about the inherent goodness or badness of human nature, the significance of mental faculties in learning, and the role of education in shaping citizenship. Second, at the administrative level, educators have had to deal with such practical matters as class size, age differences, teacher competencies, and availability of curriculum materials. These varying circumstances have affected the choices administrators have made to concentrate on custodial duties and instructional routines or on the individual needs of pupils. Third, at the economic level, educators have had to consider cost efficiencies and benefits. Costs are usually minimized when facilities, curricula, materials, and teacher work loads are standardized; they must often be increased to enable teachers to deal with pupils individually.

Undoubtedly, every educational undertaking has faced the problems mentioned here. Different solutions have surfaced and disappeared as a consequence of their interplay with current religious, political, and fiscal concerns. For example, colonial educators appreciated neither the ideological nor the fiscal benefits of individualized instruction, but they practiced it anyway. During the early industrial period, educators were beginning to see the rationale for individualized instruction, but endorsed mass instruction for economic reasons. Later in the industrial period, however, their successors enthusiastically supported individualized instruction; they were convinced of its merits ideologically and they were certain that with the new marvel of the day, educational testing, they had the technological tools to implement individualized instruction cost effectively. These educators introduced individualized instruction to revolutionize education, teach the "whole" child in both basic skills and citizenship, and in the process, revitalize schooling in America. Yet the extraordinary did not happen! The early programs waned, and since then, except for heroic experimental efforts here and there (Bangert et al. 1983; Pressey and Janney 1937; Reavis and Mahoney 1940; Spaulding 1983; Wang, Gennari, and Waxman in this volume), individualized instruction has counted for little more than a few yahoos in the wilderness.

Our purpose in this essay, then, is to investigate the conjunctures of pedagogical and social factors that have made individualized instruction fluctuate within American pedagogy. We have divided our discussion into three roughly defined historical periods that correspond to the tribulations in individualized instruction that we noted above. Specifically, we examine the following question: What transpired to affect individualized instruction in each period? Since the early twentieth-century programs failed to live up to their promise, we comment briefly in conclusion about what, in hindsight, appear to have been their significant limitations.

COLONIAL EDUCATION: INDIVIDUALIZED INSTRUCTION BY DEFAULT

Colonial parents hated idleness. Puritan virtue made the employment of children and youth as low-paid servants, helpers, or apprentices to older, experienced workers a righteous undertaking. But the informal training of young people for useful labor was not viewed as sufficient to thwart sinful impulses and temptations. The times called for formal schooling; young people must learn to read in order to understand principles of religion. The American revolution inspired new levels of nationalism and heightened concern that young people also learn to appreciate the principles of democracy. Most communities before the war had established "dame schools," in which neighborhood women who could read assumed teaching responsibilities; now many of these schools were joined with the private, relatively select grammar schools to make provisions for publicly supported education (Johnson 1963).

Living conditions were harsh in colonial America, and poverty was widespread. Schooling was a necessity, not an extravagance. Prudent construction practices of the day dictated one-room log schoolhouses, about thirty feet square. Sticks were inserted between the logs along the sides of the building, and boards were nailed to them to serve as desks. Adolescents faced the walls, sitting on long, backless benches in order to work at the desks. Younger children had no desks; they faced the center of the room squeezed together on another set of benches that were placed parallel to those of the adolescents. As many as 100 pupils might be packed into the single room, depending on how closely they could be seated on the benches, but no matter how many pupils there were, no thought was ever given to providing more than a single teacher.

Pupils were seldom at the same level of academic development, so schooling was ungraded. A dozen or more relatively learned young men and women might be well along in adolescence, a large proportion of the younger children might be unable to read, and several of them probably would not know the alphabet. Everyone would study with different materials. Books were scarce, and family heirlooms often were pressed into service as texts, to be passed on as long as they held together. Lucky pupils possessed "primers," so named because they contained both the alphabet and devotionals—proverbs, catechisms, and short narratives retold from the books of the Bible. Other subjects—writing, arithmetic, geography, and spelling—were taught without textbooks. Teachers simply replicated exercises that had been passed on to them when they had been students. Young people were drilled and indoctrinated. The psyche or soul had been described since antiquity as being comprised of mental functions or faculties, like memory, judgment, imagination, and attention. Philosophers and theologians subsequently had reified these faculties, holding that each of them possessed independent psychic energy. Colonial educators thus sought to teach young people subject-matter skills via training that would explicitly discipline the faculties. Teachers were largely indifferent to children's developmental levels. Spelling words, for example, were chosen for difficulty rather than children's capabilities; the greater the challenge, so much the better. Hard words would strenuously exercise the memory faculty.

Religious orthodoxy governed the colonial perspective on human nature and learning. The Puritan religion recognized an irrevocable conflict between desire to enjoy worldly pleasures and desire to obey church dicta. Innate sinfulness surely would lead to indulgence and depravity unless obedience was instilled, so discipline by the rod was the rule. Pedagogues did not acknowledge that young people had intrinsic interest in learning; motivation came from the rod. Parents were uneasy when schoolmasters shied away from applying it, and plenty of severe punishment was regarded as a teaching virtue. Most schools had a whipping post set firmly in the center of the school floor, and offenders of both sexes and all ages were frequently tied and whipped in the presence of their schoolmates. Sometimes, however, the older, stronger boys resisted. When they sensed that a schoolmaster lacked courage or physical strength, school violence might ensue.

Teaching in colonial schools thus was individualized in certain respects, but less by design than by necessity. Teachers had no alternative, and their work load was horrendous. Practical matters dictated that teachers must keep fifty to one hundred pupils in line if instructional activities were to be kept from degenerating into chaos. No wonder that so much as a giggle or wiggle meant swift retribution. Teachers had little time to reflect about their pioneering work; indeed, the demands of managing a group of such diverse pupils forced them to compromise their practice of individualized instruction. Examinations, for example, were conducted by recitation. The young people usually memorized lessons from different sources, which meant that each pupil had to be summoned before the teacher individually. Presumably, it was an exhausting process, and it took teachers out of contact with the rest of the class. So they began to organize pupils into recitation groups, where lessons in spelling, arithmetic, geography, and the like could be recited in unison. The process marks the beginning of rough systems of grading, and it led directly, whenever common curriculum materials were available, to placing young people with others their own age for purposes of both study and recitation. Why not? The attempts to be efficient and cut costs in colonial schools were paradoxically hostile to the individualized instructional practices that were badly needed when pupils were so diverse and curriculum materials so primitive.

THE EARLY INDUSTRIAL REVOLUTION AND THE ADVENT OF MASS INSTRUCTION

Coastal cities grew to become great seaports, and inland communities emerged as centers of trade, transportation, and communication during the eighteenth and nineteenth centuries. A new urban, indus-

trial society was rising in the United States. Few doubted that
individual initiative, hard work, and self-discipline—metaphysical
inspiration notwithstanding—were responsible for technological progress and economic expansion. Secularism was rising, too, as theologi-
cal influence waned. Why, then, should not the schools foster
citizenship and encourage social mobility as well as teach basic
subjects? Why not develop the personal and social skills that would be
useful to young people in a dynamic, changing society? Schooling
practices needed to adapt to industrialism. Colonial schools had
grown in size, perhaps to two rooms, and graded textbooks had
appeared by mid-nineteenth century, but religious texts still dominated the curricula, and pupils still memorized and recited. Moreover,
urban school buildings were prohibitively expensive to construct
because of corruption among influential politicians, who bought and
sold teaching and administrative posts. Early in industrialism schooling had lost touch with society, and in many instances, schools
functioned with little organization and supervision (Johnson 1963;
Cremin 1964).

The circumstances called for reform, and distinguished forerunners
of change in American education began to make themselves heard.
Horace Mann, for example, struggled to fashion a fresh ideology of
education. He would continue to stress basic subjects, but in contrast
to the premises of religious orthodoxy and faculty psychology, he
sought to attain two seemingly contradictory objectives simultaneously: to inculcate in young people an unfettered sense of exploration and initiative and, in deference to the ideals of industrial society,
to shape in them civic loyalty, respect for property, and social conformity. A pedagogical solution to the dilemma of educating for both
individual freedom and social conformity eluded Mann; however,
William Torrey Harris had an answer. Harris had begun his career in
education about the time of Mann's death. He became a highly
regarded school superintendent of St. Louis, a distinguished philosopher, and later, United States Commissioner of Education. The
writings of Georg Wilhelm Friedrich Hegel, an early nineteenth-
century philosopher, had convinced Harris that human development
and societal growth constituted a dialectical, interactive process in
which cycles of alienation and conciliation repeated themselves. As
Harris saw it, the natural instincts and impulses of children would be
melded with the expectations of civilized society as young people

learned to take responsibility for their own behavior. Schooling would thus direct young people away from primitive, self-centered motives to a world in which freedom and responsibility eventually attained balance (Cremin 1964; Travers 1983).

Harris, of course, had to be practical. Urban schools were bursting at the seams; a surging hoard of young immigrants and farm children pressed against their doors. Harris and the nation's superintendents knew that traditional schooling practices were inadequate. Harris's administrative answer was the graded school, where pupils would receive promotions regularly on the basis of their work. He envisioned that basic subjects, initiative, and self-constraint could be learned within a disciplined framework, and he emphasized economy, efficiency, and, especially, standardization. School textbooks by now had become relatively uniform and age-graded; in the hands of the teachers of the day they were used to classify and systematize classroom activities. But Harris's ideology did not really fit mass instruction. The practices that he introduced were functional from the standpoint that they enabled teachers to adapt instructional activities to large numbers of pupils, but they reduced to shambles his aim to integrate the individualistic and social objectives of pedagogy. He sought, as did Mann, to extricate learning from the doctrines of faculty psychology; for example, he pleaded for making history exciting and meaningful, and he urged that geography be learned through use of practical examples. To Harris, "education was not a matter of doing things to pupils, but rather a matter of encouraging the pupils to do things for themselves" (Travers 1983, p. 35). Under pressure simply to provide schooling for the masses, however, order rather than freedom, external coercion rather than self-discipline, and passivity rather than initiative characterized classroom learning.

LATE INDUSTRIALISM AND THE REBIRTH OF INDIVIDUALIZED INSTRUCTION

In colonial schools young people had learned basic skills in order to master principles of religion and civil obedience. Pupils were taught initiative, self-discipline, leadership, and so forth, not at school, but by participating in family, community, church, and workplace functions. Subsequently, industrialism separated young people from easy contact with agents of socialization. William Torrey Harris, therefore, had urged that schooling must provide preparation for the larger, wider responsibilities of life (Cremin 1964). The curriculum, he said, should be the basis for carrying out the activities necessary for rounding out life. Harris and his followers, however, had overestimated the capability of teachers and the educational system to reconcile pupils' self-interests with the demands of the curriculum. The young people who became alienated seemed less likely to strive for conciliation among their conflicts, as Hegelian logic would predict, than to become even more alienated. Problems associated with grade repetition, nonpromotion, boredom, apathy, and dropping out of school grew widespread. Educators responded by setting standards so low that as many as two children out of ten in every grade had already achieved the standards for that grade at the opening of school (Caldwell and Courtis 1925).

Circumstances called for a dynamic new perspective on the methods of schooling. Since the early industrial period, the conviction had been growing among leading educators like Mann and Harris that the school should assume increasing responsibility for the growth of the "whole" child. Educators now insisted more stridently that schooling should be responsible, not only for teaching basic skills (reading, writing, arithmetic, and so forth), but also for developing good citizenship, capacity to handle the affairs and problems of everyday life, knowledge of scientific and social facts that govern practical aspects of living, and perspective on the arts.

How, then, were these splendid objectives of schooling to be achieved? By reviving individualized instruction, of course. However, whereas instruction in colonial times had been individualized simply out of expediency, it now could be individualized systematically on the basis of new developments in educational technology and theory. On the one hand, educators drew upon the emerging field of measurement for new methods of classroom testing. These tools of testing, in turn, seemingly would enable a single teacher to manage relatively large numbers of pupils. They provided starting points for instructional activities, feedback and check points along the way, and a final accounting of achievement. Testing thus allowed pupils to grow in basic skills at their own rate, and as a consequence of the greater efficiency in teaching basic skills, pupils could be provided time during the school day for citizenship development through social activities. On the other hand, educators drew upon fresh perspectives in philosophy and psychology for a new developmental theory that conceptualized instructional learning as an intrinsically rewarding process. It refocused the curriculum on the needs of the child. Accordingly, let us examine more closely how the changes in the fields of both measurement and developmental theory shaped practice in individualized instruction.

Miracle of Measurement: Educational Testing

After Sir Francis Galton published *Hereditary Genius* in 1869, he said that he wished that he had named the book "Hereditary Ability" (Galton 1978). Galton intended to emphasize primarily the ranges that individuals reveal in their inherited abilities or mental traits. He argued persuasively that persons differed from each other in general abilities by measurable amounts, and he described an imaginary scale for charting the differences. His insights were of immense significance. They suggested to educators that bases for such matters as grade classifications, grouping within grades, and promotions could be determined objectively, reliably, and economically. Tests would supplant recitation for purposes of evaluation. Although Galton did not devise any specific tests, by 1890 an American psychologist, James McKeen Cattell, had published an article entitled "Mental Tests and Measurements," in which he called for standardized testing and establishment of norms (Cattell 1890).

The floodgates opened swiftly. Educational psychologists believed themselves to be on the threshold of developing instruments for appraising all the significant differences among pupils: Ebbinghaus, Cattell, Jastrow, Bolton, Norsworthy, Kirkpatrick, Thorndike, Binet, Terman, and many others produced a tidal wave of tests in which they revealed convincingly that variability in human behavior was an empirical reality. For example, Bolton (1892) administered digit-memory tests to children, and then compared his findings with teacher judgments of "intellectual acuteness." Kirkpatrick (1900) sought to determine whether tests were indicative of progress in school work; he administered tests of counting aloud, making vertical marks, sorting cards, interpreting ink spots, and the like to 500 children. He compared his results with grades that teachers had assigned these children for schoolwork. Norsworthy (1906) subsequently developed group tests for mentally deficient children, and importantly, was first to demonstrate empirically that the standing of a child on a test could be expressed in terms of the variability of the group.

Alfred Binet, the French psychologist, published in 1908 the first version of an intelligence test for use in the schools. Binet was interested primarily in a general ability measure; however, his pioneering work provided tremendous impetus not only to the study of individual differences but to that of patterns of intraindividual abilities. Binet advanced the idea of selecting different attributes or functions that could be isolated for study, establishing a range and distribution for each attribute within the population, and then determining degree of covariation between the functions. Binet's research led eventually to the practice of "psychography," whereby the scores that individuals might make on separate, measurable traits were plotted as a profile. The psychograph soon became the basis for plotting progress in individualized instruction. A psychograph might indicate a child's standing in respect to several basic skills, and thereby reveal to teachers the levels at which the child should begin work in different subject-matter areas.

Proponents of testing prophesied far-reaching benefits for individualized instruction. Starch (1919), an author of a leading textbook of the day in educational psychology, thus declared: "this enormous range of ability . . . is probably the most important single fact discovered with reference to education in the last decade" (p. 39). And Caldwell and Courtis (1925) were moved to assert: "as a result [of developments in testing], teachers are at last beginning to act on the belief that children differ, and to invent methods of classroom teaching which will enable a teacher to deal with a large group of children and yet allow a child to grow at his own rate and to study in his own way" (p. 124).

The early measurement specialists saw in psychological measurement three important pedagogical advantages. First, tests would provide ways of determining the kinds of opportunities children would require if they are to develop to the limit of their capabilities. Second, tests would promote cost-effectiveness; they could reveal the precise point at which given learning opportunities should be presented— never again would pupils be either so far ahead or so far behind that they were wasting their time (Starch 1919). A subsidiary outcome of cost savings would lead also to a revival of the ungraded school, for if children could be grouped according to capacity and ability, an indicator of educational progress as gross as grade placement would lose its meaning (Caldwell and Courtis 1925). Third, tests were viewed as sources of motivation. For example, Lang (1930) pointed out that children found it stimulating to experience the results of tests, to graph them on a learning curve, and to rival their own best efforts in subsequent testing. A test setting, therefore, was thought to foster development of intellectual power. It provided opportunity to apply previously learned knowledge in a context that required diligence, concentration, and persistence. These advantages inspired educators to inundate their pupils with practice tests. This feature of instructional activity was believed to transfer responsibility for learning from teacher to pupil. Self-scoring procedures, daily individual records, and psychographs put young people in charge of their own development. Testing made it possible for them to become partners in schooling. Moreover, when young people did take charge of their own development, a single teacher could presumably administer adequately to the needs of as many as fifty children, yet completely individualize their instruction (Caldwell and Courtis 1925).

Developmental Theory and Child-centered Curricula

Whereas testing provided the tools for implementing programs in individualized instruction, new perspectives on child development and learning provided a rationale for centering the educative process around children's activities (Mossman 1929). The new approach held essentially that children learned best when they could integrate new information with that previously learned. Schoolwork should be introduced, therefore, on the basis of detailed, firsthand understanding of the experiences children bring to the classroom. To accomplish this step in the practice of individualized instruction, teachers must know every child's background—interests, aptitudes, community and family life, and so forth—and ensure that instructional activities are presented in a fashion that relates them closely to this background. Activities with concrete materials, for example, would lead into geography, nature study, and elementary science; activities with peers would direct attention to the meaning of history and social studies; activities associated with work would bring into perspective industrial, agricultural, and commercial aspects of life. Since young people would soon realize that they needed basic skills—reading, spelling,

arithmetic, language, and writing—if they were to advance in knowledge, they would be drawn naturally to these subjects, too. Learning,
then, was conceived of as the outcome of activities in which children
were engaged. Basic subjects were not taught as ends themselves, but
were integrated with the activities that interested students.

Whereas pedagogy in colonial times had been derived from the
premise that human nature was in bondage to sin, pedagogy in early
industrial America was based on the Hegelian premise that people
were in bondage to nature. Instead of religious orthodoxy, the dialec-
tic of bringing individualistic impulses into harmony with the requirements of citizenship constituted the new rationale for schooling.
Pedagogy in the later industrial period, however, freed young people
from concepts of moral or instinctual bondage. The French romanti-
cist, Jean Jacques Rousseau (1712-1778) had been among the first
pedagogues to challenge the venerable doctrines. In his *Emile*, the
Magna Carta of individualized instruction, Rousseau wrote that
"everything is good as it comes from the hands of the author of
nature." He idealized the role of the pure state of nature in developmental processes; he insisted that children were fundamentally virtu-
ous, not creatures fallen from grace. Rousseau saw the primary
impetus for learning in the spontaneous, natural impulses of.children.
Children are only beginners, he argued, and they should not be
expected to learn as if they possessed the logical structures of the adult
mind. Schooling, therefore, should be organized around the budding
capabilities of children.

But how should it be organized? Early twentieth-century proponents of individualized instruction needed an appropriate theory of
learning to supplant faculty psychology, and they found it in the
reasoning of Johann Friedrich Herbart (1776-1841). Herbart had
formulated John Locke's views on the association of ideas into a
theory of learning known as "apperception." He said that ideas and
sensations that enter the mind remain there as an "apperceptive
mass" to influence later learning; moreover, those that maintain
themselves in consciousness exert the most influence. Interest develops when strong and vivid ideas are hospitable toward new ones, since
a pleasant feeling arises from the association of old and new ideas.
Since past associations could be used to facilitate the apperception of
new ones, interests were given credence as sources of motivation.
Herbart's work thus contributed to individualized instruction in three

significant ways. First, it predicted that learning follows from building up a sequence of ideas important to the individual, and thereby gave teachers a semblance of theory about cognitive development and motivation. Second, by emphasizing the influence of past experiences, Herbart directed the attention of teachers to the importance of commencing the learning process at a point commensurate with a child's readiness. Third, he reinforced the belief that interest in constructive activities was more effective than corporal punishment in fostering learning.

Ideology into Practice: Early Programs in the Making

Preston Search, superintendent of schools in Pueblo, Colorado, was the first educator to reject completely the lockstep method of mass instruction. Search implemented the "Pueblo Plan" between 1888 and 1894. He determined that children should progress in school at rates that they set for themselves, and he abolished all class instruction, substituting instead teaching according to the individual needs of pupils (Starch 1919). Search was well ahead of his time, and his comprehensive program of individualized instruction could not be well implemented, given the state of school curricula, teacher preparation, and educational testing; consequently, despite Search's administrative innovations, the Pueblo Plan evaporated shortly after he left the superintendency.

The next major innovation in individualized instruction occurred in 1912, when Frederic L. Burk organized all classes from kindergarten through eighth grade in the training school at San Francisco State Teachers College to enable pupils to progress in each school subject as rapidly as their individual abilities permitted. Burk's program became known as "The Individual System" or "Burk's Plan of Individual Instruction." Burk's system called for self-instructional texts, strictly individual progress in the "common essentials" or basic skills, and group activities to ensure development of social skills. Each child was given an outline of study for each of several subjects; provisions were made for testing and promoting the child as soon as the work outlines were completed. Mary A. Ward, an associate in the program, reported that the faculty worked enthusiastically writing self-instructional textbooks. She also indicated that pupils were so interested in their activities that problems of discipline and inertia disappeared (Ward, Carter, Holmes, and Anderson 1925).

Burk's practices were extended from a small private school to an entire school district when Carleton W. Washburne, in 1919, exported them to Winnetka, Illinois (Washburne and Marland 1963). The Winnetka Plan, however, placed greater emphasis on group and creative activities than had Burk's. Curricula were divided into two parts. One part dealt with the basic knowledge and skills that all children were expected to acquire. Children were allowed to take as much time as they needed to master a unit of work, but they were required to master it. Time at work, not quality of work, was permitted to vary. The other part provided for children's self-expression among their peers. These activities did not emphasize mastery of specific skills or knowledge. In Winnetka, half of the morning and half of the afternoon were given over to individual work in the common essentials while the other half was given over to group and creative activities. During the time devoted to individual work, a child might be given fourth-grade arithmetic during one period, but a few minutes later, in the same room, might be doing fifth-grade reading. Each child prepared a unit of work, checked the results against an answer sheet, and then went on to the next unit. After completing a small group of units, which might have taken three or four days or two weeks, the child self-administered a test. If the child found that the materials had been mastered (100 percent on the practice test), the teacher was asked for a "real" test. The teacher corrected this test, and if it was not 100 percent correct, the child would be expected to practice on his or her weak points, and then ask for a retest. The Winnetka plan allowed teachers to spend their time in management and remedial instruction rather than in routine group instruction such as listening to recitations. Teachers helped individuals here or a group there, encouraging and supervising. Teachers were among the children as they worked, not at their desks. During the part of the day devoted to group and creative activities, children might dramatize a part of their history work, perhaps by putting on an informal impromptu play or by preparing a more elaborate one to be presented to the school during an assembly. Every child at Winnetka also participated on committees comprised of peers, which managed pupil social activities like assemblies and plays. For more creative endeavors, children might take field trips, work on the school newspaper, entertain one another, and so forth.

Perhaps the most innovative of programs in individualized instruction was the Dalton Laboratory Plan, which was first introduced in the public schools of Dalton, Massachusetts, a few months after the program in Winnetka began. Proponents of the Dalton Plan used the uniform curricular materials of the day, but they wholly revised the instructional climate of the school. They rejected the order, coerciveness, and passivity that they saw as characteristic of mass instruction, and they questioned the wisdom of dividing the school day partly into individualized and partly into group activities. So they reorganized the life of the school to give pupils more freedom in how they tackled the learning of basic subjects and greater opportunity to build up from day to day the sort of habits that they would need for participation in "true community life." Under the Dalton Plan teachers worked with each pupil to outline a series of jobs to be completed within a school year. The time for each job was set by the teacher to be completed within a twenty-day (school month) period. Pupils were given "work norms," to help them determine appropriate rates of activity. The Plan substituted laboratories for classrooms, and pupils were permitted to go from one to another, "*mingling and living,*" just as they might in the community at large. The Dalton Plan was designed particularly to encourage pupils to manage their own time efficiently and to become responsible for their assignments. Whenever pupils completed a unit of work or participated in a laboratory activity, they recorded the results of their work on both "individual" and "class progress" graphs. To its proponents, then, the Dalton Plan represented a perfect balance between individual freedom and pedagogical definitiveness. It was a plan that presumably put young people in command of the resources they would need to become masters rather than servants of their destinies (Parkhurst 1925).

CONCLUSION: IDEOLOGY, PRACTICE, AND REALITY

The establishment of pioneering programs in individualized instruction at the turn of the century was a remarkable contribution to educational ideology and practice. Colonial schools had indeed practiced individualized instruction, but only as a consequence of necessity. Authoritarian control, drill, and recitation provided bases for training the general faculties of the mind. Subsequent developments in mass instruction during the industrial revolution—uniform textbooks, grade placements, and promotions—brought a semblance of factory-like efficiency to schooling. The new approach standardized educational practices at lower per-pupil costs, but young people of widely varying capability and social, language, and ethnic backgrounds were streaming into the schools. Teachers were unable to cope with students' individual needs. The dilemma was solved after the turn of the century by reinventing individualized instruction. The new pedagogy now included an ideology for developing in young people the requisite skills for responsible participation in a democratic community, and, importantly, a technology for dealing with individual differences. Caldwell and Courtis (1925) made the point in this way: "Enrichment of the curriculum [via individualized instruction] means something more than the mere addition of more subjects to the required list. It means a social revolution as complete and as far-reaching as the progress of democracy itself" (p. 118). Unfortunately, however, the ideology of individualized instruction promised more than the educational bureaucracy could deliver. The state of the art of individualized instruction was primitive at the turn of the century. Neither ideology nor technology was sufficiently developed to sustain widespread practice. We remember the pioneer programs today chiefly because they command passing reference in a review of educational history. What went wrong?

Limitations in Ideology

Educational reformers sought to produce well-trained, healthy, ethical, responsible citizens. They were aware that a knowledge base to accomplish their aims could not be drilled into children. So they chose the other extreme. They provided social experiences that were vaguely conceived and unsystematically executed. As Caldwell and Courtis noted, "To speak in striking terms, we may say that the modern school has ceased to be a prison and is becoming a childish utopia" (p. 118). Consequently, schools were eventually accused of "antiintellectualism" as a result of their preoccupation with social activities. For example, as Marland has observed, society began to demand a definition of educational fulfillment more specific and concrete than the early reformers had taken time to describe (Washburne and Marland 1963).

The reformers assumed that children were capable of setting goals and taking responsibility for their daily activities. These presuppositions were derived, in turn, from beliefs that most children possessed sufficient intrinsic interest and perspective to strive for abstract goals of achievement and citizenship. The reformers also entertained the romantic notion that group activities would somehow reconcile conflicts between competitive impulses and cooperative tendencies. However, children in the programs seldom functioned as competently as the educators envisaged (Sutherland 1925; Washburne and Marland 1963). Further, the instruction, despite its adaptation to different learning rates, may have fit poorly the cultural expectations of many young people. The reformers, for example, held an ethnocentric view of democratic life: "They were convinced of the appropriateness of their middle-class 'American' values . . . [and they intervened], with an arrogance that was typically unwitting, in the lives of people different from themselves" (James and Tyack 1983, p. 403).

Limitations in Practice

Educational testing proved to be essential to large scale implementation of programs in individualized instruction. Testing provided a technology for establishing the starting points of instruction, providing feedback during learning, and monitoring progress. Testing also heightened consciousness of need for instructional objectives, for after all, testing is of little avail unless it measures what pupils are supposed to be learning. However, the potential of testing was not realized. First, the process of setting objectives seemed initially to be an easy matter, but in practice, the effort turned out to be vastly more complex and impractical than anticipated. Tests of mathematics, reading, and language mechanics were fairly easy to develop (Starch 1919). But educators could not develop tests that assessed achievement of insight and creativity, transfer of training, application of skills to everyday life, and logical reasoning. The available measures thus focused teachers on objectives that were both fewer in number and narrower in scope than they had originally intended. As in colonial times, individualized learning activities often focused on drill, memorization, and recitation. Second, testing became rampant. Pupils were incessantly examined on aptitude tests, interest tests, placement tests, practice tests, and achievement tests. Although pupils usually scored their own practice tests, this information was recorded on progress sheets kept by the teacher. Teachers were required to administer, score, record, and interpret test data. These tasks probably drove many teachers batty. Yet additional demands associated with testing that were equally overwhelming were placed on teachers. Once the tests were interpreted in the context of the children's total background, including home life, peer relations, and personal interests, new learning tasks had to be formulated to suit each child. Then, the teacher faced the question of keeping the young people motivated and oriented toward their work. As the pupils carried on their activities, teachers were expected somehow to provide remedial help separately to a few dozen children at once. Third, testing activities may have discouraged pupils, too. When young people take tests and continuously fail to improve, eventually they attribute their failure not just to lack of effort but to lack of ability, and they withdraw from the learning situation. However, there is little evidence that proponents of individualized instruction systematically considered how such factors might influence the motivation and aspirations of young people.

Apart from testing, teachers also faced the difficult problems of adapting to the different personalities and coping styles of their pupils. Some pupils probably were independent, some may have been aimless, and others may have been uninterested. For example, Spaulding (1983) has recently described eight coping styles that he has found in several hundred classrooms, kindergarten through grade twelve. Individualized instruction appears to work only for students who initiate independent, self-directed activity. Spaulding notes, too, that individualized instruction is unsatisfactory for pupils who are overly aggressive, dependent, and manipulative. Teachers were presumably more comfortable dealing with pupils who best fulfilled their expectations, and probably distributed their attention in remedial activities differentially on the basis of their favoritism.

What, then, sustained the educators who confronted all these problems? The early programs in individualized instruction had been initiated on the basis of inspired leadership and collegiality. The participants believed themselves to be part of a revolution in education. They volunteered or were recruited on the basis of their enthusiasm for the ideology and their commitment to the programmatic goals of inspirational leaders. But unfortunately, later-generation educators were not caught up in the same spirit of invention. Whereas initial participants were carried forth by the momentum of innovation, subsequent participants were confounded by inadequacies in ideology and contradictions in practice. The dependency of the pioneer programs upon inspired leadership and collegiality may explain partially why they were not more widely exported across the nation. Although many of the experimental programs excited the imaginations of thousands of teachers, and hundreds of districts attempted to adopt them, the adaptations were often made in name only. Neither the ideology nor the practice was clearly understood, and when the promised structure and outcome failed to emerge, order, as always, supplanted freedom, and routine replaced initiative.

REFERENCES

Bangert, Robert L.; Kulik, James A.; and Kulik, Chen-Lin C. "Individualized Systems of Instruction in Secondary Schools." *Review of Educational Research* 53 (Summer 1983): 143-58.

Bolton, Thaddeus L. "The Growth of Memory in School Children." *American Journal of Psychology* 4 (April 1892): 362-80.

Caldwell, Otis W., and Courtis, Stuart A. *Then and Now in Education 1845:1923*. New York: World Book Co., 1925.

Cattell, James M. "Mental Tests and Measurements." *Mind* 15 (July 1890): 373-81.

Cremin, Lawrence A. *The Transformation of the School*. New York: Vintage Books, 1964.

Galton, Francis. *Hereditary Genius*. London: Julian Friedmann Publishers, 1978.

Glaser, Robert. *Adaptive Education: Individual Diversity and Learning*. New York: Holt, Rinehart & Winston, 1977.

Glaser, Robert. *Education and Thinking: The Role of Knowledge*. Pittsburgh: Learning Research and Development Center, University of Pittsburgh, 1983.

James, Thomas, and Tyack, David. "Learning from Past Efforts to Reform the High School." *Phi Delta Kappan* 64 (February 1983): 400-6.

Johnson, Clifton. *Old-time Schools and School-books*. New York: Dover, 1963.

Jowett, Benjamin. *Plato: Five Great Dialogues*. New York: Walter J. Black, 1942.

Kirkpatrick, E. A. "Individual Tests of School Children." *Psychological Review* 7 (May 1900): 274-80.

Lang, Albert R. *Modern Methods in Written Examinations*. Boston: Houghton Mifflin, 1930.

Mossman, Lois C. *Principles of Teaching and Learning in the Elementary School*. Boston: Houghton Mifflin, 1929.

Norsworthy, Naomi. *The Psychology of Mentally Deficient Children*. In *Archives of Psychology*, No. 1. New York: Science Press, 1906.

Parkhurst, Helen. "The Dalton Laboratory Plan." In *Adapting the Schools to Individual Differences*, edited by Carleton W. Washburne, Twenty-fourth Yearbook of the National Society for the Study of Education, Part 2. Bloomington, Ill.: Public School Publishing Co., 1925, pp. 83-94.

Pressey, Sidney L., and Janney, J. Elliott. *Casebook of Research in Educational Psychology*. New York: Harper & Brothers, 1937.

Reavis, William C., and Mahoney, Lewis H. "The Organization of Education at Various Levels." *Review of Educational Research* 10 (October 1940): 315-30.

Spaulding, Robert L. "A Systematic Approach to Classroom Discipline, Part Two." *Phi Delta Kappan* 65 (October 1983): 132-36.

Starch, Daniel. *Educational Psychology*. New York: Macmillan, 1919.

Sutherland, A. H. "Factors Causing Maladjustment of Schools to Individuals." In *Adapting the Schools to Individual Differences*, edited by Carleton W. Washburne, Twenty-fourth Yearbook of the National Society for the Study of Education, Part 2. Bloomington, Illinois: Public School Publishing Co., 1925, pp. 1-30.

Travers, Robert M. W. *How Research Has Changed American Schools: A History from 1840 to the Present*. Kalamazoo: Mythos Press, 1983.

Wang, Margaret C.; Gennari, Patricia; and Waxman, Hersholt C. "The Adaptive Learning Environments Model: Design, Implementation, and Effects." Chapter 9, this volume.

Ward, Mary A.; Carter, Grace E.; Holmes, Hilda M.; and Anderson, Cecelia. "Individual System as Developed in the San Francisco State Teachers College." In *Adapting the Schools to Individual Differences*, edited by Carleton W. Washburne, Twenty-fourth Yearbook of the National Society for the Study of Education, Part 2. Bloomington, Ill.: Public School Publishing Co., 1925, pp. 60-82.

Washburne, Carleton W., and Marland, Sidney P., Jr. *Winnetka: The History and Significance of an Educational Experiment*. Englewood Cliffs, NJ: Prentice-Hall, 1963.

Characteristics of Learning Persons and the Adaptation of Learning Environments

Edmund W. Gordon
Lizanne DeStefano
and Stefanie Shipman

One of my most vivid recollections as a child is of my country doctor father standing next to a seriously ill old black woman, who was lying on her sickbed with a stream of blood arching from the blood vessel in her left arm that my father had just lanced. The cuff from his sphygmomanometer was still attached to her right arm, and he was watching its gauge as closely as he watched her. After what seemed like an eternity, he stopped the bleeding and placed a cool, wet towel on her head. Her breathing became easier. The mild jerk in her right foot subsided and she slowly opened her eyes. The crisis had passed. Later that day, as we drove back home, my father explained that the woman's blood pressure was dangerously high, and that he had to let some of the blood out to relieve the pressure. "If we could have gotten her to a hospital, we might have tried something else, but out here we have to be adaptive," he explained.

I often think of my father travelling through the countryside, adapting what he knew about the healing art to the needs and conditions he encountered in his patients. I think about the other country doctors of that period, letting blood to get rid of impurities in the system and performing other procedures we now know to be useless if not dangerous. And I think about us, their counterparts in education, as we seek to practice the art of teaching, adapting what we know—often under less than optimal conditions—to the needs of our pupils. I dream about the day when we shall know more about teaching and learning and be able to look back with amazement that we were able to do as much good and as little harm as we did, in a profession that has yet to establish its bases firmly in the sciences of behavior and pedagogy.

I have been asked to write about adaptive learning environments from the perspective of the learner. Most teachers recognize that learners differ greatly in their learner-relevant and learner-non-relevant characteristics. Good teachers go to great lengths to try to make adjustments in the learning experiences of children whom they know to be unlike other learners. A sizable body of research has developed around concerns for the individualization of instruction and for the exploration of the potential of attribute-treatment interactions (ATIs). Yet the range of variance in curriculum design and instructional practice is far less rich than is the diversity to be found in the populations of learners. Only modest complementarities exist between our emerging knowledge of the characteristics of learners and our knowledge of curriculum development and pedagogy. Our best developed adaptations to individual differences are concerned with learning rate, interests, or combinations of developed abilities, achievement, and background experiences.

In the United States, the oldest and most common approach to dealing with individual differences is homogeneous grouping by age, sex, race, and general ability in school, grade, classroom, and activity units. Although grouping by age remains the norm, grouping by sex, race, and general ability has become less common at the school, grade, and classroom levels. This is partly due to democratic concerns regarding the unequal allocation of resources and academic stimulation among such groupings. It·is recognized that grouping by these latter categories into classroom units does not result in homogeneous groups; it simply reduces variation in a classroom on one dimension. Lately, grouping by ability into autonomous classes has come under attack because most of the research on grouping practices has shown no universal academic benefits to low-, medium-, or high-ability groups over what they would have achieved in similar but mixed-ability classes. In addition, some of the affective outcomes from such groupings have been rather insidious, stemming from the social-class character of the resulting structure, especially when confounded with race and sex segregation (Esposito 1971). Thus, education programming has turned to individualized learning systems that serve children of a wide variety of ability groupings in the same classroom.

Gagné's (1974) system of identifying the hierarchical cognitive requirements of an educational task has had a tremendous impact on the best of these individualized learning systems. In stressing the importance of a careful analysis of the steps in learning, he laid the groundwork for teaching a child any concept or skill for which prerequisites can be carefully identified. In learning hierarchically arranged information and skills, it is presumed that the individual characteristics of importance are achievement of the prerequisite skills and information. Gagné recognized different kinds of learning (signal, stimulus-response, chaining, verbal association, discrimination, concept and role learning, and problem solving), each requiring different modes of presentation and teacher prompts and/or direction to be most effective.

This process, then, is an example of transforming the task to meet the demands of both the kind of learning involved and the student characteristics considered most relevant to the task at hand, regardless of the child's performance on some measure of intelligence or a more global type of achievement measure. The assumption is that children fail at an educational task only because it is inappropriately presented or it is mistakenly assumed that the children have the identifiable prerequisites. Thus children take a pretest on the material to be mastered and, according to the information received regarding their acquisition of the prerequisites, they follow the universal sequence of steps for that material, although they may start at earlier or later steps than their peers. Gagné has formed highly precise but generalizable rules for teaching particular "bits" of learning within any hierarchically structured topic relative to the particular "bits" of learning the child has already acquired, thus creating a system for individualizing education on the basis of prior achievement.

A few centers have used this concept of individualizing education according to prior achievement as the basis for large-scale federally supported individualization programs (many of which are mentioned in this book) that are implemented in school systems across the nation. Although the emphases of these programs differ with regard to the different ages of the target group, all lean heavily on the goal of individual mastery of behaviorally prescribed objectives, the choice of alternative presentations of instructional material, frequent pre- and post-testing with regard to achievement level, the special training of teachers, administrators, and support personnel for data management and for counseling and diagnostic services, and integrated teamwork in administrative and management procedures. The intent of each program is to improve student achievement outcomes and interest in schooling. After the two or more years required to complete im-plementation and adjustment, all programs appear to do very well, especially in regard to the achievement of their low- and middle-ability groups. Cost varies, since many of the testing and data-processing functions require the use of computer terminals for the efficient use of personnel time (Talmage 1975). But despite the relative success of many of the programs that plan learning experiences based on prior achievement, findings from a three-year study conducted by Wang and her associates suggest that further delineation of student learning characteristics is a critical need in individualizing instruction and adapting learning environments (Nojan, Strom, and Wang 1982). Ideally, in addition to prior achievement, learning environments that are truly adaptive should be systematically sensitive to a variety of learning behaviors associated with individual pupil characteristics such as affective response tendencies, cognitive style, motivation, and identity.

Periodically, articles by teachers appear in applied education journals describing how they have met the call for individualization within their classrooms. A hodge-podge of methods and theories has emerged out of the pragmatic quest to deal adequately with the obvious range of individual pupil characteristics with which teachers are confronted. Presumably these are highly sensitive and conscientious teachers who, whether they do or do not read the educational psychology journals, are making systematic observations and judgments concerning their pupils that are congruent with the findings of educational research. Hunt (1975) is convinced that good teachers have an intuitive sense for the differential characteristics of their pupils and adapt their teaching behavior to their perceptions of those characteristics. Unfortunately, we must conclude that these teachers depict rather uncommon classroom procedures, and that most public education in this country is individualized only to the extent of providing readers with texts on a few different reading levels, combined with some separate instruction for small reading groups within a classroom unit.

It is not surprising that educators have put into practice so little of their knowledge regarding learner characteristics. Not only is this knowledge complex and contradictory, but the major recent efforts at systematizing, clarifying, and interpreting the many related studies have provided little empirical basis for optimism and no guidelines for its application. Bracht's (1970) extensive review led him to conclude that the empirical evidence does not support the expectation that the matching of learner traits and learning experiences will result in significantly improved learning. After some twelve years of exploration and contemplation, Cronbach and Snow (1977) go to great lengths in their most recent book to report the limited utility and the complicated problems of the empirical evidence in support of attribute-treatment-interactions (ATIs) as an approach to the improvement of education. But there continues to exist a persuasive logical relationship between learner characteristics (attributes), learning experiences (treatments), and learning outcomes (interaction results). Several of us, including Cronbach and Snow (1977), Endler and Magnusson (1976), Glaser (1977), David Hunt (1975), J. McV. Hunt (1961), and Messick (1970), find it hard to dismiss the promise of the paradigm despite the missing evidence of its validity. But the tenuous nature of the paradigm does help explain why it is not more strongly represented in curriculum development.

ATI research has been *the* expression of concern regarding the importance of individual differences for learning and teaching. It is best characterized statistically as the comparison of the regression slopes of a variable from individual behavior onto an educational outcome variable under two or more contrasting educational treatments. Two kinds of interaction are defined by plotting the calculated slopes, for the range of the ability measured, on the same graph. In the *ordinal interactions*, one treatment is associated with significantly higher criterion scores than the other treatment for a section of the aptitude range, with an insignificant difference between the two treatments at another part of the range. In the *disordinal interactions*, the slopes actually cross so that at one section of the aptitude range, one treatment produces significantly higher results, whereas the other treatment produces better results at a different part of the aptitude range.

Cronbach and Snow (1977) presented a thorough review of the substantial amount of research conducted over the last decade that attempted to discover ATIs using this, and less powerful, statistical methods. They moderated Bracht's (1970) and others' conclusions that there was no evidence for meaningful ATIs with the observations that, for the great majority of the studies they reviewed, (a) small sample sizes militated against respectable power in the statistical tests and encouraged chance effects; (b) person and treatment variables were paired speculatively without a sound theoretical background for generating hypotheses; and (c) treatments were usually short, ill-defined, or unnaturalistic. Moreover, they pointed out that inconsistencies across "replications" are likely because of unanticipated interactions with variables considered too irrelevant to document and, therefore, are unresearchable or unexaminable.

Why is the Attribute-Treatment-Interaction knowledge base so confused? In a very provocative article, Messick (1970) suggested that one of the problems is that we are trying to tally up the score before we have learned the rules of the game. The interactions that have so far been studied are sometimes based on human traits for which the assessment technology is quite limited. Treatments are used that may be too simplistic in their design, and that therefore provide an insufficient complement to the trait under study. Our conceptions of the interactions studied are usually tied to methodological or programmatic constraints rather than based on comprehensive theoretical models.

One of the most serious problems produced by the ATI scoreboard approach is the assumption that studies using the same independent and dependent variables are studying the same interactions between independent variables. The crucial distinction is that ATIs are dynamic, multiply determined events only partially describable or investigatable by present statistical methods. Even recognizing that some factors may be more crucial than others in determining (or predicting) a particular behavioral event, the one-on-one independent and dependent variables model is inadequate to explain specific behaviors in complex, partially controlled, real-life situations or settings. The major problem in treating these studies as multiple replications is that although we know that many factors affect school performance, this often overlapping interaction of identified factors or variables is not controlled or accounted for when the findings of these research studies are aggregated and compared.

When looking for main effects, it is legitimate to expect that the effect isolated should be operative in every instance that exemplified the unhampered operation of that effect. On the other hand, when investigating interactions, that is, the complicating or mediating influences of independent variables on dependent variables, the door is open to numerous *unmonitored* independent variables to affect either the action of the monitored variables or the mediating effects of their own interactions. This possibility of unmonitored variables in the research situation affecting observed interactions between monitored variables leads to what Snow (1977) called "locale specificity of effects," which without further experimental controls on environmental factors, restricts our generalizations concerning either main or interaction effects to the particular sample studied. Several situations can affect the results in this way. Study samples, students, teachers, or classrooms can differ in their overall categorization on some dimension on which there is no or little variability within samples (for example, classroom climate, teacher characteristics, neighborhood median income, and so forth); student characteristics can vary in range, standard deviation, or shape of distribution, as well as by their mean values (each of these affecting the likelihood of statistically significant results); and, perhaps most unfortunately, researchers may differ in their conceptions and measurements of the variables presumably under their common investigation.

A basic limiting factor in ATI research is that it forces a search for techniques that produce flattened regression lines over the range of variability of concern. The model allows conclusions about interactions to be drawn only from comparing the slopes of simple regression lines, using one input and one outcome variable per comparison. Unfortunately, this glosses over some important sources of interactions. The model should be considered as a simple methodological application of the basic principle accepted by most educators: if outcome variability is highly related to input variability and is of a similar range, then education has had little effect other than that of maintaining rank position from entry. Reducing the relationship between input and outcome variables reduces the caste character of achievement level and allows schooling a stronger influence, but it does not guarantee optimization of school learning for the individual.

There are other factors that limit the usefulness of what we know about individual differences and the design of learning experiences. These include the following:

1. ATIs are far more complex than the study of them so far would indicate. The study of these interactions has failed to take into account such factors as teacher and treatment interactions, the complexity of educational tasks as phenomena, the fact that tasks can be approached and solved with differing strategies and combinations of traits, or that the traits may function differentially across subjects and situations.

2. A part of the complexity of which we speak is to be found in situational variance. Relatively little work has been done on characterizing environments and situations and their functional properties. In addition, a few of us are only beginning to talk about the interpenetration of ecologic, personologic, and existential phenomena in situational variance. Environments, traits, and treatments have their characteristics, but they also have their meanings. It is, in part, the neglect of the influence of situations and attributions that makes difficult a better understanding of ATI.

3. Psychological and scientific works in general are based on a search for laws applicable in most instances; but in the behavioral and social sciences, and education in particular, we do not know enough about the nature and function of the specific instances to generate laws with respect to how the larger constructs, of which they are a part, operate. We may be prematurely copying the hard sciences as we try to bring comparable precision to our work, forgetting that those sciences developed over hundreds of years. During those developing years, much

time was devoted to the generation of descriptions and taxonomies. ATI may be in need of better descriptions and taxonomies before we proceed with further tests of its validity and utility in education.

4. We have not yet developed appropriate categories and labels by which to study ATI. We tend to identify people by qualities such as socioeconomic status, developed intellect, ethnicity, language, and sex, rather than characterizing them by such functional characteristics as specific manifestations of cognitive style, temperament, and motivation, the dynamic patterning of which tells us much about how individuals approach certain tasks or respond to specific stimulus situations.

The above factors, and still others, make difficult our understanding of individual and group differences and ultimately our appreciation of the value to pedagogy of the ATI paradigm. These same factors help explain why there appears to be little empirical support for the very logical and commonsense notion that differences in human characteristics should be associated with differences in the effectiveness of various educational treatments. In addition to these methodological, operational, and technical reasons for the lack of clarity in this area, one of the reasons why the empirical evidence in support of this notion is so limited may be that the conceptual work in support of the logic of the relationship has not yet been done. As Rothkopf (1978) has observed, "It would be a mistake to expect too much from methodological reform alone. Both hands, the statistical and the conceptual, are needed to plow the field of aptitude x treatment interactions in teaching. The reasons for weak studies and incoherent results derive chiefly from our inadequate conception of the learning person. We need more psychological insights to provide us with working hypotheses about significant aspects of teaching and how they interact with personal abilities" (p. 708).

Glaser (1977) in some ways anticipated the Rothkopf criticism in a little book that is pregnant with pedagogical ideas. In his *Adaptive Education*, Glaser recognizes that the combination of available alternatives provided in systems of schooling and the decision-making procedures used to place individuals in these alternatives are the fundamental characteristics by which educational enterprise can be described and analyzed. He then uses these characteristics to describe the ways in which aspects of teaching can be adapted to individual diversity.

Glaser outlines five models of educational enterprise, which are not mutually exclusive and which are combined in a variety of ways at different levels of education.

Model One: Selective with Limited Alternatives

Individuals come to an educational setting with an initial state of competence. Through informal and formal means, this state is assessed and on the basis of that assessment a decision is made to place the student in the standard educational environment or to designate the student as a poor learner for which some special treatment is required. The activities carried out in the standard learning environment are generally limited in the alternative modes of learning provided and emphasize the particular abilities addressed in the initial assessment, to the exclusion of other abilities. Because the selection process is geared to include those students with a relatively high performance in the abilities required to succeed in the given educational environment, the environment can remain fairly rigid.

Model Two: Development of Initial Competence

The second model has the same characteristics as Model One: selection procedures and a learning environment. In Model Two, however, not only are individuals assessed with respect to presence or absence of abilities that allow participation in the program, but some diagnostic decision is made about the nature of those abilities. For individuals whose initial state of competence is not sufficient for selection, an educational environment is provided to develop their competence to a point where participation in the program is maximized. In this way, through some combination of prior and continued monitoring and instruction, entry abilities are modified so that the number of individuals who succeed is maximized. A student is forced to adjust to the standard program with the help of supplemental instruction, implying that the deficit lies in the learner rather than in the learning environment.

Model Three: Accommodation to Different Styles of Learning

Model Three attempts to respond to the limitations of Model Two by providing alternative, flexible educational environments and in-structional methods that accommodate to different learners' abilities at entry into the program and throughout the course of learning. As information is obtained about the learner, decisions are made to enhance probabilities of success in alternative instructional environments with various learning opportunities. The procedures by which instructional methods are altered for different students is based largely on teachers' intuition and expertise. This process can be improved by increasing the range of diagnostic, instructional, and organizational resources available to teachers.

Model Four: Development of Initial Competence and Accommodation to Different Styles of Learning

The fourth Model considers the combination of the second and third Models. In this case, achievement is maximized both by improving the initial state of competence and by providing multiple environments so that abilities and instructional environments can be matched and there can be movement across the alternate environments as the individual develops the skills useful to learn in each context.

Model Five: Alternative Attainment Possibilities

In the previous four Models, the educational goal reflected the emphases of the elementary school, that is, to teach basic literacy to all students. Model Five contains a variety of educational outcomes usually associated with higher education. Multiple goals encourage the development of different constellations of human abilities and reward many different ways of succeeding.

It is not unreasonable to identify the selective, limited-alternative Model One with past and prevailing educational practice. Currently, intelligence and aptitude have emerged as the significant entering abilities that are assessed to the exclusion of most other individual characteristics. The assessment instruments used are not designed to determine different ways in which students learn best or to identify basic competencies necessary to learn various kinds of tasks in various environments. Model Two attempts to introduce flexibility and seeks success for a greater number of students by developing initial competence.

It is not until Model Three, however, that the concern for the interaction between instruction and individuals, which is the crux of the Rothkopf criticism, becomes apparent. Glaser indicates that Model Four—providing for development of initial competence and accommodation to different ways of learning—offers maximum adaptability of aspects of teaching to individual diversity in the elementary years, while Model Five—offering multiple educational outcomes —maximizes success in the upper grades. A cognitive psychologist who is uniquely sensitive to many of the practical concerns of classroom teachers, Glaser goes on to describe and give specifications for the design, delivery, and management of teaching and learning transactions consistent with these models. However, even Glaser's very advanced concepts fail to provide adequate conceptions of the learning person.

Human learners are more than cognitive beings. Human behavior is also influenced by affect, by motivation, by identity, by environmental press, and, indeed, by various manifestations of status, for example, sex and gender, social and economic status, ethnicity and race, and language and culture. An adequate conception of the learning person requires that we understand each learner from each of these dimensions of human diversity as well as from the collectivity of the dimensions. Our efforts at isolating significant treatment effects in relation to differential aptitudes or attributes, as well as the limited effectiveness of adaptive and individualized education, may simply reflect our continuing insensitivity to such single and collective dimensions of the person whose learning we seek to affect. What do we know about these dimensions of human diversity in learners, and what relevance have they for the design and management of teaching and learning transactions?

Socioeconomic status accounts for that component of subjective recognition of shared similarities that is related to income, style of life, education, occupation, and the acquisition of corresponding modes of life, or prestige of birth, for an aggregate of individuals. The realization that socioeconomic status dictates class in a hierarchical society is an essential component of human history. For Marx, much of human history is rooted in the class struggle. It is this struggle that gives rise to class consciousness. This concept allows for changes in the individual, since the subjective component of consciousness of socioeconomic status makes class an active, emergent force in history. Empirical sociologists concerned with the relationship between class and educational achievement do not give emphasis to this notion of class. Rather, they use class to designate a relatively fixed set of assumed characteristics and social hierarchical positions. This latter use of the term has made for rather dubious causal assumptions since class as an indicator of social hierarchical position points to how one is likely to be perceived and treated but provides little information about the functional dimensions of one's experience and behavior. The works of Mercer (1973) and Wolf (1966) suggest that it is the functional dimensions that make differences in educational achievement, and socioeconomic status is not a reliable indicator of these dimensions.

Sex and gender are often colloquially used interchangeably but are used here to refer to the biological (sex) and social role (gender) characteristics by which distinctions are made in the identification and socialization of females and males. In discussing sex differences, we refer only to those characteristics that can be directly linked to the biological structures and functions of one of the two sexes, whereas gender is used in the discussion of socially assigned or adopted role functions. There appear to be few if any educationally relevant behaviors that can be traced to the biological aspects of sex. However, several of the behavioral differences observable in the learning behavior of boys and girls can readily be attributed to differences in gender. In addition, these differences in sex-related, socially assigned or adopted role functions also serve to influence the ways in which boys and girls are treated, what is expected of them, and what is allowed. Thus the educationally relevant characteristic is gender rather than sex.

Ethnicity is used to refer to one's belonging to and identification with a group that is characterized by such attributes in common as physical characteristics, genetic and cultural history, belief systems, and sometimes language. Although often used synonymously with race, it does not specify biological race (Caucasian, Mongolian, or Negro) but may be used to refer to a group that shares, among other things, a common gene pool. Ethnicity may be assumed, inherited, or assigned. As used in this report, ethnicity includes the growing concern with the self-interest of a group as a manifestation of ethnicity. As Ogbu (1978) has indicated, ethnicity often functions like caste, in that it determines a position in the social order from which its members cannot escape. Since ethnicity is so often associated with status, it is the status phenomenon that has the greatest implications for education. In the United States, ethnic status determines in large measure the nature of one's access to educational opportunities. Because of stereotypic thinking, it influences what is expected of the ethnic group member and, because of biases born of the caste-like nature of ethnicity, how one is treated in educational settings is significantly influenced by one's ethnicity. Thus, although ethnicity provides us with few leads for pedagogical intervention, it does strongly suggest the nature of some aspects of educational conditions and circumstances.

Culture is that complex experiential whole that includes knowledge, belief, art, morals, custom, and any other capabilities and habits acquired by humans as members of society. The total pattern of human behavior and its products embodied in thought, speech, action, and artifacts are dependent upon man's capacity for learning and transmitting knowledge to succeeding generations through the use of tools, language, and systems of abstract thought. As a descriptive concept, culture is a product of human action; as an explanatory concept, it is seen as a dialectical cause of human action. In a more colloquial sense, culture is the mores and way of life of a people. Cultures differ. Some are more influenced by technological developments than others and some are more complex; but no people is without its culture. The culturally "deprived" is a misnomer. With respect to education, the culture of the school may complement or be alien to that of some of its students. Bridging and second-culture learning present the largest challenge for education; failure to achieve an effective level of complementarity is the greatest threat.

Motivation has been traditionally defined as a personalistic variable reflecting the ability of a person to sustain effort in the absence of extrinsic rewards, or as a prompting force or an incitement working on a person to influence volition and action. It is the second definition, which gives emphasis to forces acting *on* a person, that better reflects the definitional emphasis utilized here. We see the prompting force as residing *within persons* and *within stimuli*. The process is reinterpreted to refer to the acquired *ability of stimuli* contained within situations to sustain the performance capability of certain individuals. It is in the nature of human organisms to act and react. The ability of stimuli to arouse and sustain human action is the motivating force. In the context of this definition, in education it is the responsibility of the learning experience to be motivating and not of the learner to be motivated. Obviously, the conditions and sources of motivation differ for different learners.

Language, conceptually defined, is a systematic means of communicating ideas or feelings by the use of conventionalized signals, sounds, gestures, or marks having understood meanings. In a deeper sense, however, languages are collections of symbolic, representational repertoires and their appropriate milieu (setting, topic, social status of participants) for realization in speech or other communication modes. The language system or systems used are thus the vehicles for expressive and receptive communication. In addition, the language system provides the schemata around which mental functions gain meaning. Language competence, then, is a necessary condition for effective education. Educational experiences are more effective when there is congruence between the language of the school and that of the learner. However, learning is not rendered impossible simply because there is a lack of congruence.

Identity, in common parlance, refers to what stands out about a person and how the person defines himself or herself. It has been defined as the unity and persistence of personality reflecting the individual comprehensiveness of a life or character. Here a distinction is drawn between basic and qualitative identity. Basic identity is the nonreflective state in which existence is taken for granted, or in which the sense of existence leads to feelings that all is well. Qualitative identity refers to the sense of completeness, synthesis, and continuity by which persons perceive in themselves a character of a particular kind. Of the characteristics that learners bring to learning situations, it is, perhaps, identity by which most of the components of individuality are integrated. To the extent that one's characteristics are consciously orchestrated in the interest of learning, it is probably around identity that such patterning occurs. Operating at the core of sense of self, identity is the wellspring for sense of efficacy and ultimately for effort applied to learning.

Cognitive response tendency, usually called cognitive style, is used to refer to relatively consistent patterns characteristic of an individual in the manner and form rather than the level of perceiving, remembering, and thinking. The most commonly utilized categories are abstract and concrete functioning and field-independent and field-dependent styles. Since style connotes a higher degree of stability than is supported by the evidence, the term *tendency* is frequently used in preference to the term *style*.

Affective response tendency, identified generally as temperament, is used to refer to relatively consistent patterns, characteristic of an individual, of emotional responses to a specific stimulus situation. Aspects of temperament such as characteristic tempo, rhythmicity, adaptability, energy expenditure, mood, and focus of attention are most often referred to in the literature, and are given emphasis in most discussions. However, affective responses also include stylistic variation in processes such as attribution, personalization, projection, and cathexis. Cognitive response tendency and temperament speak to the how of behavior, defining for the most part the manner in which behavior is deployed in response to stimulus situations. It is the relative consistency in these response tendencies that leads us to type individuals and to anticipate reactions. In learning and other developmental situations, it is thought that the complement between response tendency and situational demands facilitates development while conflict and contradiction tend to challenge and may distort the course of development. Shipman and Shipman (in press) argue that one of the purposes of education is to extend the repertoire of response tendencies available to the learning person.

Health and nutrition refer to the status of the biophysiological equilibrium of the organism in its environment. Often underestimated as variables of importance to education, health and nutrition influence attentional behavior, available energy, and stability of response potential, as well as such ordinary factors as school attendance and availability for instruction.

Environmental press refers to the influence of living and nonliving phenomena that surround the individual. Specifically, press is what these phenomena can do *to the subject* or *for the subject*—the power that they have to affect the well-being of the subject in one way or another. There is a distinction between the press that exists objectively for a subject (alpha press) and the press that a subject perceives (beta press). The environment may be thought of as objective or subjective. The objective environment can be defined to include, but not necessarily be exhausted by, the alpha press. However, it may be the attributed character (beta press) that is projected onto the environment by the perceiver that gives environmental press its special role as a determinant of the individual's engagement in and response to educational intervention. Thus, the ecology of learning situations is being increasingly viewed as important. However, it is the social and personal dimension that may be of greatest importance to the learning person.

In a recent National Institute of Education report (Gordon 1985), the knowledge base relevant to understanding these dimensions of diversity was explored and the possible implications for education were explicated. In the course of the completion of this work, it became clear that, as important as each of these learner characteristics may be, it is not in their unilateral but in their multilateral impact that their importance for teaching and learning resides. Learners do not bring their unique characteristics singly to bear on teaching and learning transactions. Rather, they bring these characteristics to bear on learning behavior in dynamically orchestrated patterns or clusters. It appears that it is these orchestrations, and not the individual attributes, that influence the learner's approaches to learning problems, the strategies and skills that are developed in response to learning task demands, the directional deployment of effort, and, ultimately, the nature and quality of task engagement, time on task, goal-directed deployment of energy, resource utilization, and efficacious behavior. Thus, it may be important that the teacher know the dominant features of each pupil's cognitive style, temperament, sources of motivation, identity, and so forth, but even more important that the teacher be sensitive to the stimulus conditions and situational constraints under which aspects of each of these domains change.

One could say that we are dealing with learner attributes at three levels: traits (cognitive style or temperament), instrumental behaviors (strategies, directed effort, skills), and intermediate outcome behaviors (time on task, resource utilization), the product of all of which is achievement. Instead of focusing on a specific manifestation of cognitive style, for example, it may be necessary to study several components of cognitive stylistic preference as they are orchestrated in learning strategies and to focus the manipulation of educational treatment on these strategies rather than on style. We have earlier suggested (Gordon, Wang, and DeStefano 1982) that it should be noted that even single-domain clustering or patterning may reflect too limited a conceptualization. Messick (1982) suggests that human traits in learning behavior may be best understood as encompassing cross-style and cross-domain (for example, affective or cognitive) patternings that are not necessarily constant across situations. What is being suggested here is the real possibility that preoccupation with the learner's tendency to utilize a specific manifestation of a single domain or even the learner's utilization of multiple expressions from a single domain is counterproductive. Rather, a better conceptualization of the principle of behavioral individuality must include dynamic and dialectical relationships, within and between domains, selectively integrated into response tendencies.

It is entirely possible that multiple manifestations of styles or response capabilities may be present simultaneously, with some expressions more readily available, some more actively incorporated into habit patterns, or some attached by prior experience to specific stimuli or situations. Specific instances of learner behavior may then be the product of deliberate or fortuitous selection from the repertoires of possible responses. Leona Tyler (1978) has written: "The core idea is that each individual represents a different sequence of selective acts by means of which only some of the developmental possibilities are chosen and organized. . . . As Whitehead pointed out, the fundamental realities are actual occasions in which indeterminate possibilities are transformed into determinate actualities." Our learner behaviors are examples of Whitehead's "determinate actualities." They are the results of selective acts through which multiple manifestations of diversity (Tyler would say individuality) are orchestrated. To seize upon unitary components of those orchestrations may be an error. But the adaptation of instruction to those orchestrations may pose a greater challenge than the pedagogical sciences foundational to education currently enable us to meet. In what directions, then, do our current knowledge and experience enable us to move?

In answering this question, let us examine three issues: (1) What needs are served by existing models? (2) To what should education be adaptive? and (3) What are the demands placed on teachers of an appropriately adaptive education?

1. What needs are served by extant models of adaptive education?

The spirit of adaptive education seems to provide greater support for humanistic approaches to instruction. Its focus on individuals rather than on groups seems to insure that individual pupils are less likely to be ignored, whether their individual learning needs are addressed or not. The customization that we have achieved does seem to serve the needs of some pupils, since individualization tends to broaden the achievement spectrum.

Yet extant models are still too narrowly prescriptive in that they are sensitive singly to pupil characteristics. In many cases, diagnostic information on pupil characteristics reflects a concern for curriculum rather than for the functional nature of the learning person. We have not fully exploited the area of cognitive psychology that addresses the affective and cognitive processes by which pupils mediate their own learning or by which learning can be mediated. This knowledge base may offer us a greater understanding of the learning person and, through that understanding, the development of an appropriately adaptive education.

2. From the perspective of learners, to what should education be adapted and for what purpose?

Clearly, these questions cannot be answered independently. That to which education should be adaptive depends upon the purposes to be served and the characteristics of the learner.

One can use current theory and common sense to hypothesize about the relative importance of different learner characteristics as the purpose of educational tasks changes. For example, when the primary purpose is to enable mastery of content and skills, adaptation to developed abilities and prior achievement may be most important. Interest, motivation, and affective response tendency may not be as salient, but probably should not be ignored. Adaptation to sex, ethnicity, and social class may be marginally helpful but probably would not be crucial. On the other hand, when the purpose is to learn how to learn and to systematize mentation in problem solving, adaptation to affective response tendencies and cognitive style may be highly important while prior achievement, developed abilities, and status characteristics may be less important. When the purpose is to develop appreciations and a sense of efficacy, it may be that interests, motivation, and identity are the salient learner characteristics to which adaptation must be responsive and that, in some cases, such as when the purpose is to develop understanding of process, relationships, and meanings, blending of all learner characteristics may be required.

Unfortunately, it is unlikely that the matching process is that simple. What is to be adapted to as well as the purposes for which education should be adaptive are not static phenomena. They can change over time and across learning situations, making it essential that adaptive education be recognized as dynamic, dialectical, and transactional in response to Whitehead's "determinate actualities."

3. What are the demands on teachers of an appropriately adaptive education?

If adaptive education is to serve learners rather than teachers and if, to do so, it must be dynamic, dialectical, and transactional, to deliver adaptive education may place responsibilities on teachers that are far greater than they are currently prepared to assume. It becomes necessary to speculate about the qualities such teachers should possess and what regimen of training might facilitate these qualities.

Let us return to the example of the "country doctor," the best of whom were prepared in the tradition of the Viennese physician— broadly educated, richly cultured, with a good knowledge of human anatomy, some appreciation of physiology and biochemistry, and a keenly attuned medical intuition. Using limited diagnostic technology, they had to depend upon judgment and wisdom informed by considerable experience. It may be that the teachers we need for adaptive education must be broadly educated, sensitized to diverse cultures, with a good knowledge of human behavior and its development, some appreciation of the science of pedagogy, and a keenly attuned pedagogical intuition. Using limited diagnostic technology, they may, like country doctors, have to depend on their judgment and wisdom informed by experience.

But, given the requirements of a truly adaptive education, these professional practitioners of the art of teaching may not be good enough. They may now stand where the country doctor stood, soon to be replaced by scientifically educated pedagogues. For while teaching will forever be in part an art, its foundations can and should rest on the sciences of human behavior. Pedagogical practice and adaptive education in particular must be informed by those foundational sciences. The orchestrations that we have suggested as being at the core of adaptive education cannot otherwise be systematically arranged.

REFERENCES

Bracht, Glenn H. "Experimental Factors Related to Aptitude-Treatment Interactions." *Review of Educational Research* 40 (December 1970): 627-45.

Cronbach, Lee J., and Snow, Richard E. *Aptitudes and Instructional Methods*. New York: Irvington, 1977.

Endler, Norman S., and Magnusson, David, editors. *Interactional Psychology and Personality*. New York: Wiley, 1976.

Esposito, Dominick. *Homogeneous and Heterogeneous Groupings: Principal Findings and Implications of a Research of the Literature*. New York: Teachers College, Columbia University, 1971. ED 056 150.

Gagné, Robert M. *Essentials of Learning for Instruction*. Hinsdale, Ill.: Dryden Press, 1974.

Glaser, Robert. *Adaptive Education: Individual Diversity and Learning*. New York: Holt, Rinehart & Winston, 1977.

Glaser, Robert, and Rosner, Jerome. "Adaptive Environments for Learning: Curriculum Aspects." In *Systems of Individualized Education*, edited by Harriet Talmage. Berkeley, Calif.: McCutchan, 1975.

Gordon, Edmund, editor. *Human Diversity and Pedagogy*. Pomona, N.Y.: Ambergis Family Press, 1985.

Gordon, Edmund; Wang, Margaret C.; and DeStefano, Lizanne. "Temperament Charateristics and Learning." Pittsburgh: Learning Research and Development Center, University of Pittsburgh, 1982. Mimeographed.

Hunt, David E. "Person-Environment Interaction: A Challenge Found Wanting Before It Was Tried." *Review of Educational Research* 45 (Spring 1975): 209-30.

Hunt, J. McVicker. *Intelligence and Experience*. New York: Ronald Press, 1961.

Mercer, Jane R. *Labelling the Mentally Retarded: Clinical and Social System Perspectives on Mental Retardation*. Berkeley, Calif.: University of California Press, 1973.

Messick, Samuel. "The Criterion Problem in the Evaluation of Instruction: Assessing Possible, Not Just Intended, Outcomes." In *The Evaluation of Instruction: Issues and Problems*, edited by M. C. Wittrock and David W. Wiley. New York: Holt, Rinehart & Winston, 1970.

Messick, Samuel. "Cognitive Styles in Educational Practice." Paper presented at the annual meeting of the American Educational Research Association, New York, 1982.

Nojan, Mehran; Strom, Charles D.; and Wang, Margaret C. "Measures of Degree of Implementation and Program Evaluation Research." Paper presented at the annual meeting of the American Educational Research Association, New York, 1982.

Ogbu, John U. *Minority Education and Caste: The American System in Cross Cultural Perspective*. Carnegie Council on Children Monograph. New York: Academic Press, 1978.

Rothkopf, Ernst Z. "The Sound of One Hand Plowing." *Contemporary Psychology* 123 (October 1978): 707-8.

Shipman, Stefanie, and Shipman, Virginia. "Cognitive Styles: Some Conceptual,

Methodological, and Applied Issues." In *Human Diversity and Pedagogy*, edited by Edmund Gordon, in press.

Snow, Richard E. "Individual Differences and Instructional Theory." *Educational Researcher* 6 (November 1977): 11-15.

Talmage, Harriet, editor. *Systems of Individualized Education*. Berkeley, Calif.: McCutchan, 1975.

Tyler, Leona E. *The Psychology of Human Differences*. New York: Appleton-Century-Crofs, 1978.

Wolf, Richard. "The Measurement of Environments." In *Testing Problems in Perspective*, edited by Anne Anastasi. Washington, D.C.: American Council on Education, 1966.

Private Lessons in Public Schools: Remarks on the Limits of Adaptive Instruction

Philip W. Jackson

Human beings differ from one another in many ways, as any pair of eyes can plainly see. Save for the rarity of identical twins, no two people look alike, much less act or think or feel the same. Although we may share characteristics with others, each of us, when studied closely, turns out to be utterly unique, a nonrecurring event in the history of our species.

What is the significance of that uniqueness for education in general and for teachers in particular? What does it mean for pedagogical aims and methods? Does it call for a matching idiosyncrasy in the teacher's response to each pupil? Is that possible, given the demands of mass education and the human resources available to accomplish it? If so, how?

Over the centuries educators, including a few famous philosophers, have pondered these questions. Almost all who have done so have concluded that some accommodation to differences among students was not only highly desirable within a system of mass education but was utterly inescapable if such a system was to work at all. Not until this century, however, have the practical consequences of that conclusion been pursued with as much zeal as has been witnessed in this country (and possibly England as well) over the past fifty or sixty years. The result has been a bewildering array of educational policies and practices, all aimed at coming to grips in one way or another with the fact of human diversity.

The practice of grouping students on the basis of one or more characteristics and then teaching each group differently is, as we all know, the most common approach to the problem. The graded school system, with its different levels of instruction in the various school subjects, is the most widespread attempt at a solution. Not far behind are various forms of ability grouping, the creation of "special" programs for handicapped students of one sort or another, an elective system, allowing students to choose their own curriculum on the basis of interests or career plans, and special provisions, sometimes including separate schools, for the gifted and the talented.

An additional set of policies and practices focuses on the school system's points of entry and exit and the speed with which students move from one point to the next. Admissions criteria, promotion and retention policies, and graduation requirements are the major categories under this heading. By varying these practices we can make some allowance for individual differences. These allowances include double promotions, failing a grade and having to repeat it, early admission or early graduation, earning advanced placement for the study of certain high school subjects, and suspending or expelling students for academic or other reasons. As these examples indicate, provisions for differently timed movement through the system are commonplace in American schools, though obviously variable from school to school and from region to region.

A third class of strategies includes various schemes for allowing students to work on their own for all or part of the school day, with the teacher monitoring their progress and intervening when help is needed. From both a theoretical and practical point of view, these schemes are the most interesting, for they press the goal of adapting to individual differences to its limits by attempting to incorporate "private" lessons within the crowded conditions of the classroom. The generic term for all such efforts is "individualized instruction," but every scheme is usually given a name or an acronym of its own to distinguish it from others. Names were common in the past; acronyms are more so today. Thus, in the early decades of this century there emerged the Dalton Plan, the Winnetka Plan, the Gary Plan, the Batavia System, Burk's Individual System, and the Decroly Method, to name but a few. Today we have IGE, IPI, PEP, NRS, CAI, and more.[1]

What most of these schemes have in common, beyond the goal of individualizing instruction, is a way of looking at teaching and learning that provides a model, so to speak, for how instruction should proceed. The elements of that model, including its assumptions and presuppositions, yield a *modus operandi* that has come to typify efforts to individualize instruction in this country from the early twenties to the present day. Its essence is a closely coordinated interaction among its parts in the form of what we would today call a series of "feedback loops," a notion drawn from the newly emergent science of cybernetics. In skeletal form what this model entails is an arrangement whereby the teacher (or some surrogate device, such as a computer program) initiates a "move" of some kind, monitors the ensuing response on the part of the student, and responds accordingly, thereby completing one cycle while at the same time initiating another.

Let us consider in greater detail how such a system works and why it is so appealing to developers of schemes for individualizing instruction. The essential features of the model are most easily revealed when what is to be learned is a skill of some kind, such as reading or mathematical computation, though the teaching of factual information—what epistemologists call "propositional knowledge"—would do as well. What is crucial in all such instances of skill development and in the learning of most factual information as well is that the form of both the finished performance and the steps leading to it are known in advance. This knowledge has two functions. It makes it possible for the teacher to judge the accuracy or inaccuracy of what the student

---

[1] In the order listed, these acronyms stand for: Individually Guided Education, Individually Prescribed Instruction, Primary Education Project, New Primary Grades Reading System, and Computer-Assisted Instruction.

does and it also enables the teacher (or, again, some surrogate device) to determine what should happen next. In his book, *Adaptive Education*, which discusses the application of such a model to a variety of educational settings, Glaser (1977) says it this way:

> The primary role of the student's current performance in determining the subsequent nature of the educational setting and the constant evaluation of the match between individual performance and the educational environment are the defining characteristics of an adaptive mode. (p. 62)

To picture the system in action, imagine an instance of what used to epitomize private instruction and still does in the minds of many—a piano teacher and her pupil. How does such a situation work? To start, the teacher knows what good piano playing looks like and sounds like. She can do it herself. She also knows (or, should she forget, possesses instructional material that will remind her) the steps or stages by which accomplished performance can be reached. She knows or can quickly learn what comes before what in the repertoire of skills and she dutifully follows such a sequence when deciding what her student is to learn at any given time. Armed with that knowledge (self-discovered or prepackaged), she initiates instruction by finding out what her pupil knows about piano-playing to begin with. On the basis of that information she selects the appropriate "level" at which to enter the repertoire of piano-playing skills. Either by words or by actions she models what is wanted, making it clear what her student is to do. She next observes the student's subsequent performance, noting how well it conforms to what she has asked for. If it is very far off, she corrects it by telling the student what is wrong, by demonstrating again, or perhaps by manually positioning his fingers on the keys. If her pupil's performance is flawless or close to it, she offers praise and moves on to the next skill or calls for a session of practice in order to habituate what has been learned. Once she is satisfied that a particular skill has been mastered, she moves on to the next higher level and the cycle begins again.

This is an overly simplified sketch, of course. It does not begin to reveal all the teacher might be attending to or seeking to accomplish at any given moment. Nor does it acknowledge the possibility of unforeseen difficulties, such as a pupil's unwillingness to follow the teacher's directions. But the addition of these and other considerations, though it might make the model more lifelike, does not alter the fundamental maneuver that marks the continuous operation of such a system. Reduced to its simplest terms, that maneuver calls for comparing the student's performance with some standard of what is desired—evaluating the "match" between that performance and the educational environment, as Glaser puts it—and then deciding what to do on the basis of that comparison.

Now let's extend this model to a situation in which many students are present at once—a reading class, for example. What arrangements will such a class call for?

We must first acknowledge that the teacher cannot be in two places at once. (Though very skillful teachers sometimes come close to creating the illusion that such a feat is possible!) This means that while she is working with one student the others must be doing something else. Since sheer idleness during those periods when the teacher is busy elsewhere would be a colossal waste of time, we must see to it that the students are productively engaged in doing something ("seatwork," it is commonly called), even when the teacher is not at their side. Also, because the time spent with the teacher is limited, her interventions, when they finally occur, must be propitiously timed. We next must anticipate that not all students will be at the same take-off point at the start. Some will enter the class highly skilled for their age, some with skills only partially developed, and some perhaps with no skills at all. Finally, we might expect our classful of pupils to encounter a variety of difficulties along the way, each requiring a slightly different remedial action before normal progress can be resumed. Thus, though all students in the class may be said to be headed toward the same goal—proficiency in reading, broadly speaking—the paths along which they travel to get there are bound to be numerous, coming close perhaps to the upper limit of there being a separate path for each student in the class.

What does this state of affairs call for in the way of instructional materials? To start, those materials need to be easily accessible and sufficiently clear to enable students to work with them on their own much of the time. Given the anticipated variety of (a) different starting points, (b) working habits, and (c) possible difficulties to be encountered along the way, the materials must be capable of being flexibly assembled. Metaphorically speaking, what is wanted is a map of curricular terrain that can be entered at different points and traversed in several ways. Anticipating that students will not always be able to extricate themselves from the difficulties they encounter along the way, we must build into such a system some procedure whereby individual progress is periodically monitored, enabling the teacher to respond as quickly as possible to distress signals of one form or another. Another comparison that these conditions call to mind for me is that of an auto store or a TV repair shop housing an inventory of small parts. What is wanted, in brief, is an educational warehouse chock-full of tasks that can be easily located and assembled in a variety of ways, depending on the needs of each student as determined by his teacher or as made evident by directions that accompany the materials themselves. Such would be the ideal classroom when properly equipped for "adaptive education." Glaser applies the term "modular" to the inventory of such a warehouse. He has this to say about it:

> An adaptive environment requires curriculum material that is highly modular; there should be many distinct, separable components rather than monolithic, linear sequences that permit little opportunity for extension and exploration off the main track. Modular materials with varied points of entry, several means of access, and explicit relationships to what the students have already learned, what they should practice, and what they are interested in can provide necessary options in the course of learning. With modular curriculum materials, students can move ahead rapidly if they choose, skip certain aspects, easily go back to certain items when necessary, explore available opportunities for additional perspective and additional depth of information, and take advantage of different approaches to learning. (Glaser 1977, p. 74)

These material and procedural *desiderata* for a system of individualized instruction are by no means new. They have remained pretty much the same from the days of Frederic Burk's Individualized System, which was unveiled at the San Francisco State Normal School in about 1913, to the latest schemes emanating today from places like the Learning Research and Development Center at the University of Pittsburgh and the Research and Development Center at the University of Wisconsin. The modern versions are more up to date in certain ways, as we well might expect them to be. Thus, for example, the language of cognitive psychology has all but replaced the earlier talk of stimulus and response that was used to undergird the rationale of such efforts in generations past. Moreover, the developing disciplines of systems analysis and information processing, from which have emerged the notions of "flow charts,"

"decision matrices," and other ways of graphically depicting complex processes, afford a detailed blueprint of a model individualized system that would not have been possible a generation or so ago. But for all that, the fundamental principles remain the same. These are:
- divide a complex learning task into its component parts,
- get the student to work on each part sequentially,
- monitor his performance, matching it against some standard of what is desired, and
- make such corrections as are necessary to bring the performance in line with the model (the latter set of actions being accomplished by a variety of means, sometimes involving the teacher and sometimes not.)

The most rudimentary form of these adaptive principles I shall call "mimetic," meaning imitative. I do so because, when stripped of all their embellishments—as in the piano teaching example—their fundamental aim is to get the student to *reproduce* or to *imitate* in his own actions or words a form of behavior that has already been settled upon as a standard, even if only imaginatively, in the mind of his teacher. This does not mean that the student need be aware of his being asked to copy something. Nor need his teacher necessarily view the matter in that way. But a copy, a faithful reproduction, is what is being sought all the same, even if it is not spoken of in those terms. How generalizable is the mimetic model of teaching? As a depiction of how teachers ought to behave, whether they currently do so or not, how broad is the range of its applicability? If it does not cover all of teaching, what does it leave out?

To speak first of where it does apply, we must begin by acknowledging an extremely wide range of learning outcomes that conform exactly to the mimetic model. For example, in the learning of most motor skills—from ballroom dancing to operating a computer terminal—what is wanted is as precise a replica as possible of the performance as demonstrated by the teacher or as depicted in the instructional materials. All deviations from the prescribed way of behaving are counted as errors.

The same model applies to many verbal skills as well. Consider, for instance, the learning of a foreign language. Though it may never be expressed in these terms, the tacit goal of all such instruction is to imitate as closely as possible a native speaker. This learning includes vocal inflections and the imitation of the spoken word but also the replication of a lot of what the foreign speaker knows about his language, its vocabulary, its major grammatical rules, and so forth.

As the latter example makes clear, the mimetic model applies not simply to skills of one kind or another but also to much of what is commonly referred to as the "content" of the various school subjects. Facts and figures, principles and laws, rules and regulations, historical names and dates, plot outlines, musical melodies and lyrics, these and countless other items that might appear on a list of educational objectives are taught in a way that seeks to make them reproducible on demand by the successful student.

Lest the mimetic model as portrayed here seem too rigid and mechanical, it is important to point out that the copying does not have to be exact—a "range of acceptability" is quite within the confines of the model—nor need it be mindless aping or parroting without understanding as it is sometimes caricatured by critics of this form of teaching. It is perfectly possible for the teacher to be liberal in his definition of what is right and wrong and for the student to understand or "see why" the prescribed behavior is the most desirable.

Having established through these brief examples that the mimetic principle is widely applicable to teaching in general, we are now ready to ask what its limits might be. Are there any teaching situations in which it does *not* apply? If so, what might they be?

The usual approach to the answer to such questions begins by pointing out that the aims of education are notoriously diverse. Exactly what those aims are said to be will vary, depending on who is making the argument, but beyond factual knowledge and rudimentary skills they typically include things as the development of attitudes, values, interests, and other dispositional states; personal qualities of a global sort, like strength of character, honesty, and civic-mindedness; social attributes, such as cooperativeness and a willingness to share things with others; and a special category of human abilities having to do with the so-called "higher mental processes," which would include problem solving, creative activities of one kind and another, and possibly even thinking itself.

Having compiled a list of this kind, the next step in the argument is to contend that not all of these diverse aims fit within a mimetic conception of what teaching and education are all about. If that contention can be made to stick, the limits of the mimetic principles will have been established.

In his treatise on adaptive education, Glaser (1977) puts forth an argument somewhat along the lines outlined here. Borrowing on a discussion of educational objectives contained in a report of a federally sponsored Panel on Youth, he distinguishes between what the report refers to as "self-centered" and "other-centered" objectives. The former chiefly refer to "the acquisition of skills that expand the resources of a young person," the latter "center on others rather than self, and (are) concerned with the social maturity that is characteristic of mutually responsible and mutually rewarding involvement with others" (p. 19).

Though Glaser does not come right out and say so, he strongly hints at the start that his model of adaptive education, which relies almost exclusively on mimetic principles, is better suited to one set of objectives than to the other. This causes him to point out that the discussions in his book "will focus on the first class of objectives—the acquisition of self-centered personal resources and 'skills' " (p. 21).

While acknowledging the importance of the "second class of objectives" and arguing briefly for the inseparability of the two, Glaser makes clear where his own interests lie and, by implication, where our major energies as educators ought to be invested. (I take it to be no accident that Glaser's two categories of objectives bear the labels "first class" and "second class.") In any event, the impression gained throughout the book is that mimetic principles are especially well-suited to the pursuit of "self-centered objectives," first among them being "the cognitive and noncognitive skills necessary for occupational opportunities and economic independence. This . . . includes fundamental capabilities—the use of language and numbers, verbal and quantitative comprehension, and problem-solving and thinking skills—which are the objectives of elementary education" (p. 19).

The trouble with Glaser's version of the "other aims" argument, insofar as establishing the limits of mimetic principles is concerned, is that he never directly addresses the question of limits and thus leaves it begging. Indeed, his very brief discussion of "other-centered" objectives contains hints that the same model of teaching that covers basic knowledge and skills might well apply in this domain as well. He expresses concern about such goals being "accomplished haphazardly" at present. He sees no reason why that must be so. The school environment for young children, as Glaser sees it,

can be designed to provide simple experiences that they
can manage and also more complex situations which they
can learn to manage through observation of appropriate
models provided by older children and adults. (Glaser 1977, p. 21)

Phrases like "simple experiences" and "appropriate models" echo the language used to describe the working of a mimetic model. Glaser's hints in this direction come as no surprise, for they are quite in line with the legacy of advice passed on to the teaching profession by prominent educators throughout much of this century. "Define your objectives in behavioral terms," they have been told since the days of Professor Franklin Bobbitt, who well might be credited as being the inventor of such advice. "Describe your student as you would like to see him behave. Only then have you achieved the degree of precision that will allow you to proceed with maximum pedagogical efficiency."

What the "behavioral objectives" advice asks for is that we do for broad goals, like "character development" or "civic-mindedness" what has been done with such apparent success for things like initial reading instruction and the teaching of mathematics. Break these into their component parts, in sufficient detail to picture what their successful achievement looks like each step of the way, arrange the parts sequentially and pursue them one by one. In other words, adhere to mimetic principles.

From this point of view, what the acknowledgment of multiple educational aims most readily reveals is that not all of those goals that might be named have yet been subjected to the detailed analysis each requires. Those yet to be defined in behavioral terms, so the argument goes, do not differ from the others in any qualitative sense. What they stand for is, in a phrase, "unfinished business," categories of work awaiting completion.

Carried forth in this direction, the "multiple goals" argument leads inexorably to the precise conclusion it started off seeking to avoid. Multiple goals? Yes. Multiple perspectives on their meaning for teachers? No. When all is said and done, this line of argument prompts us to conclude that the mimetic principles reign supreme after all.

But do they really?

To see why they may not we need to return to the multiplicity of educational goals with an entirely different set of questions in mind.

Instead of worrying about how teachers will know when their students have mastered this or that objective—an orientation that causes our thoughts to flow naturally in the direction of behaviorism and associated ideologies—we need ask whether there may not be some desirable outcomes of schooling that are not particularly well served by being translated into precise terms. In the behavioristically inspired move from language that is sometimes vague and ill-defined to language that describes exactly what we want our students to say and do, is anything ever lost? Indeed, might there be some educational goals that are in a sense ineffable, utterly indescribable in terms of the immediately observable, no matter how hard we try?

Another way of asking these same questions is in terms of the feedback model with which we began. To state matters in language borrowed from that model, what we want to know is whether there are some teaching situations in which the *ideal* is *not* a closely coordinated interaction between teacher and student but is, instead, something like a loose coupling or a remote connection, a feedback loop that is intermittently shortcircuited perhaps.

In other words, are there normally occurring pedagogical situations in which a teacher does not know in advance what to expect a student to say or do or think in response to what has been presented, at least not in any detail and not even within some prespecified range? We might also want to ask whether there might be circumstances in which a teacher does not particularly care to find out what, if anything, his or her students have gained from their instruction, without that absence of caring being interpreted as a dereliction of pedagogical responsibility. Finally, we might consider the possibility of there being some legitimate educational goals whose realization lies outside the framework of any model that embraces the teacher and the student as interacting components in some sort of a functional unit. As a teacher, I have experienced all of these various arrangements and I am confident that most other teachers have as well (including, it must be said, most advocates of individualized instruction).

Let us consider, first, the middle situation, the one in which the teacher presents material to students but does not follow up with an attempt to discover how much has been learned. The reason for starting with this one is that, of the three that have been mentioned, it presents the least challenge to the supremacy of mimetic principles.

The most common instance of what might be call "nonmimetic"

teaching occurs during public lectures and other teaching situations in which the lecturer or the teacher is seeking to inform and enlighten and perhaps to entertain as well, but without particularly caring to discover how well his material is getting across (save perhaps by monitoring audience reaction in a most informal manner). Shall we accuse him of being a poor teacher for his lack of interest in such matters? We might wish to do so under certain circumstances, but normally, I think, we would not. We might grant that in most such situations the teacher typically *assumes* he is being understood by all or most members of his audience and, therefore, a process like that depicted in the mimetic model is *assumed* to be in operation, even though the teacher does not bother to "switch on" the evaluative mechanism, so to speak. But the important point is that there *are* situations in which pedagogical wisdom dictates that the mechanism by which student responses are matched against a standard of right or wrong are kept "off." In schools as well as in public lecture halls there are many times when teachers might for good reason decide to refrain from making judgments about the correctness or incorrectness of a student's performance or the adequacy of his understanding, even though he possesses both the knowledge and the technique for doing so. Such instances say nothing about the *intrinsic* limits of mimetic principles, but they do reveal one aspect of their limited applicability.

A more interesting situation arises when the teacher's principal goal is not that of transmitting knowledge *per se* or developing a particular skill, but is, instead, that of effecting in his students a change whose precise form cannot be determined in advance and whose "rightness" or "wrongness" cannot be judged even when the change is made manifest. To give a name to such an activity, let us call it "transformative teaching," thus differentiating it from teaching of a more "mimetic" type.

In terms of the cybernetic model, what the teacher lacks under such circumstances is a standard of correctness against which to match the student's response. This typically happens in classes where the focus is on the student's understanding and appreciation of a complicated piece of writing, such as a work of literature, or where the students have undergone some other kind of experience that they are to make personal sense of. Though there may be specific things to be learned in a reproductive sense in such situations, the chief concern from a pedagogical standpoint is to discover what the students "make" of what they have read or experienced. How do they tie it to what they already know? What sense do they make of it? The teacher's role in this process is that of an attentive listener and probing questioner. It is also that of a sympathetic companion.

In certain respects such a situation resembles the cybernetic model with its emphasis on feedback; therefore, it appears to be one in which mimetic principles would apply. There is, however, the major difference that the teacher does not possess ahead of time a set of directions telling him precisely how to respond when the student says or does this or that. He lacks a standard against which to judge the student's response. In fact, with respect to several of the questions in which the teacher is interested, there is no right or wrong; there are only answers that are puzzling or interesting—or both. To respond in any way to what the student says under such circumstances is always a gamble. Just as the teacher could not have predicted how his students would finally respond to the assignment (though he may have hoped they would do so in some ways and not in others), so can he not predict how his own response as a teacher will take hold and become transformative. Moreover, that uncertainty is not simply a matter to be settled by further observation and questioning in the here and now, for the truth is that many of the things the teacher hopes for with respect to his students lie so far in the future that in all probability the teacher will no longer be there to witness them, even if they should occur. It was certainly such a possibility that led Henry Adams to declare, "A teacher affects eternity; he can never tell where his influence stops."

All of which brings us to the third possibility, that of goals whose realization lies outside the temporal confines of the teacher-student relationship. Consider, in this regard, the loftiest of all educational goals—those having to do with character or virtue or openmindedness or a shared sense of human integrity. Until they are moored to behavioral outcomes, are such goals nothing more than pious hope, better left to commencement speakers? Or do they, despite their loftiness or perhaps because of it, have a genuine role to play in the guidance of teachers' actions?

I want to argue that ideals do have a role to play, and a crucial one at that, but before doing so it is necessary to acknowledge that in the past a lot of high-sounding talk about educational purposes has turned out to be little more than hot air. Educators have often spoken eloquently about the importance of teaching virtue or citizenship or character building, when what was going on in schools was unrelated, if not antithetical, to those ideals. These kinds of contradictions, which seem to have been more prevalent a generation or two ago than they are today, caused a lot of people to distrust all talk of lofty educational goals. The result has been a marked diminution in the level of our educational vision over the years—a more realistic and less starry-eyed outlook—which is probably a change for the better over-all.

At the same time, we well may wonder if such a change can go too far. The hypocrisy of those whose actions do not match their words is undeniable, and such persons have been known to exist within educational circles from time to time. But do such abuses warrant the discarding of ideals entirely? That would hardly seem justifiable. So the real question becomes how such ideals might function in a teaching situation. If, for some reason, they resist translation into behavioral terms—as I shall contend they do—how can we incorporate them into teaching?

My answer is that the teacher who genuinely believes that virtue or character or openmindedness is an important outcome of instruction is a radically different person from one who lacks that conviction. What the difference means insofar as the teacher's actions are concerned is impossible to say in any detail, but it is not hard to imagine the form that such convictions might take.

The teacher who believes that what he does might make a difference—a big difference—in the lives of his students would be inclined to take his work more seriously than would a person who had never given thought to such a possibility. This does not mean that he need be ponderous, always wearing a furrowed brow. But it does imply a kind of thoughtfulness, an attitude of wonder about the significance of his teaching and about what he observes his students saying and doing. Such an attitude can be sustained only by the conviction that teachers often *do* make a difference far beyond the substantive scope of the lesson at hand.

We might also expect such a teacher to be concerned about the kind of model he presents to his students. This is so because many of the more enduring outcomes of schooling, particularly those having to do with character traits, seem to be, as the saying goes, "more caught than taught." Yet the fact that he is, after all, a teacher and not just a model of such virtues as he may possess, leads us to anticipate that the teacher attuned to the possibility of far-reaching influence would be alert to the opportunities to inject a "lesson" about such matters when the occasion presented itself, and would not hesitate to do so. This does not mean that he need sermonize at the drop of a hat, for if he is wise he also knows that a little of such activity usually goes a long way. But it does require that he possess an eye and an ear sensitive to the deeper dimensions of events.

The best analogy to the differences between teachers whose actions are animated by higher educational purposes and those who are not might be two sets of parents who are similarly differentiated. Parents who have high expectations of their children may not always act wisely in pursuit of those goals, but they might not act at all were it not for their lofty vision.

Think of all a concerned parent may do in the process of raising a child—all the casual remarks, the examples set, the object lessons, the long talks and the short ones—and then transfer that attitude of vigilance and concern to a teacher who has thought about the wider purposes of teaching and who is determined to do everything in his power to fulfill them. The parallels are not exact, of course, for the teacher's contacts with his students are much more limited in both time and space than are those of the parent with the child. The scope of the parent's responsibility in moral terms is far greater, as we well know. Nonetheless, the similarities are sufficient to make us mindful of the fact that teachers, like parents, are often in a position to have a profound influence on the lives of those in their charge. Of course they have more mundane matters to attend to as well, as do parents. In fact, such matters may consume the bulk of their time, as wage-earning and housekeeping often do for parents. But let the mundane take over completely, let it blind them to the deeper significance of their task, and they become teachers in only the narrowest sense of the term.

What has all this talk of transformative teaching and of educational goals that transcend the boundaries of the teacher-pupil interaction to do with the notion of alternative education with which we began? Just this: mimetic principles, with their goal of matching what the student does against some standard of what the teacher wants done, do not begin to cover all the teaching situations that exist. Moreover, it is not just that they fail to address certain aspects of teaching. What they leave out are the most important of all, those in which teaching is viewed from the broadest and most humane perspective. Modular materials that students can work with on their own are indeed desirable, so long as we understand their limits. So too are procedures for constant monitoring and continuous feedback. Make them central to what teaching is all about, and a would-be profession remains no more than a trade. More serious than that, if our notions of teaching should ever become confined to what has herein been described as mimetic principles, the ultimate losers will not be the teachers, but those taught.

REFERENCE

Glaser, Robert. *Adaptive Education: Individual Diversity and Learning.* New York: Holt, Rinehart & Winston, 1977.

Comments on Part One

A. Cognition and Adaptive Education

Robert Glaser

The three papers on which I comment, Walberg's, Gordon's, and Jackson's, share two themes. The first is that learning and teaching abound in complexities because of an almost unmanageable range of variables. These authors are persuaded that it is impossible for any single line of inquiry to capture the full array of phenomena involved in teaching and learning. They suggest that the necessarily highly specific findings of researchers should be synthesized in multivariate analyses and built into inquiries on the intricate artistry of teaching.

Their second major theme is that the noncognitive or the nonintellectual aspects of human life and learning are neglected by educational research, although they are essential to school learning. Affect, motivation, self-concept, and status all shape learning and performance, and each is influenced by the school, the surrounding environment, and the larger culture. Though supremely influential, these factors remain poorly understood by researchers and are obscured in the transmitted lore of teaching practice.

I will comment in passing on Walberg's and Gordon's provocative observations on these matters before turning to the criticisms Jackson levels. Walberg directly addresses the issue of the huge range of variables in learning and teaching with his detailed synthesis of research evidence. In his conclusion, he says, "It may be premature to state precisely how components of adaptive education contribute to the accomplishment of learning and other goals. . . . Nor can it be said that empirical research has been geared satisfactorily to the adjudication of rival theories." But he shows optimism in saying that his synthesis of research has displayed regularities that "cannot only lead to more effective research, but can also serve as an important basis for improving the productivity of educational practice." In a word, Walberg's scholarly pursuits have made him aware of the complexity of the enterprise. He sees in this not an insurmountable obstacle, but a challenge.

Gordon speaks eloquently to the second issue, that is, our lack of understanding of the many ways learners adapt to their environments. Programs of adaptive instruction have "yet to achieve systematic sensitivity to a variety of learning behaviors associated with individual pupil characteristics . . . Human learners are more than cognitive beings. Human behavior is also influenced by affect, by motivation, by identity, by environmental press, and, indeed, by various manifestations of status, . . . and [by] language and culture. . . . What do we know about these dimensions of human diversity in learners, and what relevance have they for the design and management of teaching and learning transactions?" As a possible channel of approach, Gordon reflects on the ATI problem, indicating its present inadequacies, but acknowledging its persistent importance. He is aware that, in the past, the study of individual differences and the psychology of learning were distinct disciplines—separated by history, theoretical background, and methodology; only rarely did one person work in both fields. In recent years, however, cognitive psychologists have begun to investigate, from a common theoretical base, measures of individual differences in aptitude and the cognitive processes that lead to learning. This new approach should contribute to better understanding of the relations between a wide range of human capacities and the design of various learning environments.

Jackson also is concerned with the complexity of education and personal uniqueness, and the difficulty they impose for teaching and teachers. He phrases a set of questions that outlines what he sees as a central dilemma for research: "What is the significance of... uniqueness for education in general and for teachers in particular? What does it mean for pedagogical aims and methods? Does it call for a matching idiosyncrasy in the teacher's response to each pupil? Is that possible, given the demands of mass education and the human resources available to accomplish it? If so, how?" He blames our failure to handle these issues on our lack of understanding and neglect of the higher-level processes of the human mind; of the lofty ideals of educational goals—character, virtue, openmindedness; and of a shared sense of human integrity. Teachers must believe in these higher educational purposes; these ideals must become a profound part of their artistry; and so tools for achieving them must be a concern of researchers. I agree.

In introducing a chapter in *Adaptive Education* (Glaser 1977), I quoted one of John Ruskin's dictums: "When love and skill work together expect a masterpiece. In fine art, the heart, the head, and the hand go together." I firmly believe that the artistry of the teacher is an exercise of the heart and the head, that is, values as well as skill and knowledge. The best artists and professionals excel because they submit to the knowledge, skills, and rules of their field, but know them so well that they can proceed to carry them out with outstanding competence (which can mean bending the rules) and an attention to values. A good painter is extremely skillful and precise in mixing paints and a good musician is adept at understanding music and its production; only on the basis of this discipline can artistry and feeling be given its full and true expression. So it is with teaching. Unfortunately, my own research, like that of my colleagues, has concentrated on the skill and knowledge aspects of learning and instruction, but hopefully not to the detriment of possible explanations of what can and will emerge under appropriate conditions for good teaching. For a number of reasons, the science of psychology most referred to by educators has focused on the cognitive aspects of the human mind; questions of affect and value have been left primarily to the practice and beliefs of the teacher. As we understand more about noncognitive affective aspects of the human mind, then surely we shall strike an appropriate balance, and design school environments that consider human proficiency, intellectual activity, *and* human character.

Let me turn now to details, by giving some account of how current research can contribute to an understanding of the area Jackson correctly sees as being neglected—the higher level processes—and then speculate on how adaptive education might accommodate his educational ideals. First, I would like to give an account of a theoretical structure in which learning and teaching can be conceived. It has all the earmarks of the matching that Jackson worries about, but little of his mimetic properties. Yet it is a form of individualization and it can foster thinking and discovery.

Cognitive psychologists, in accounting for various phenomena in comprehension, problem solving, and understanding, have found it useful to appeal to the notion of schemata. Schema theory attempts to describe how acquired knowledge is organized and represented, and to explain how cognitive structures facilitate the use of knowledge. A schema is conceived of as a modifiable information structure that represents generic concepts stored in memory. Schemata represent knowledge of what we experience—interrelationships between objects, situations, events, and sequences of events that normally occur. Schemata represent both culturally shared and individualistic interpretations.

A schema can be thought of as a theory or internal model that is used and tested as individuals instantiate the situations they face in learning. As is the case for a scientific theory, a schema is compared with observations and, insofar as it accounts for its various aspects, the schema can be accepted, rejected, modified, or replaced. Like a theory, a schema allows prediction, enabling individuals to make assumptions about common patterns of events so that the knowledge they infer goes beyond the observations made in any one instance. Such prototypical structures play a central role in thinking and understanding, and in learning. The assumption, then, is that the problem solving and comprehension that lead to learning are based on individual knowledge structures and available schemata, and that people continually try to understand and think about the new in terms of this information. If this is indeed the case, then it seems best to anchor teaching to the knowledge domains in which an individual has some competence. Abilities to make inferences and to generate new information can be fostered by ensuring maximum contact with prior knowledge, which can be restructured and further developed.

The notion of schemata as theories that are a basis for learning suggests several important pedagogical principles. First, the teacher must understand the student's current state of knowledge in a domain related to the topics to be learned. Second, the teacher should specify a transitional theory that is different from, but close to, the theory held by the learner. Then third, by examining this transitional theory, a student can test, evaluate, and modify his or her current theory to achieve resolution between the two. Thus, the teacher sets the stage for further progression of schemata changes as the student works with, debugs, and generates new theories. These temporary models, or transitional pedagogical theories, as I have called them, are regularly devised and matched to student abilities by ingenious teachers (Glaser 1984). Such structures, when they are interrogated, instantiated, or falsified, help organize new knowledge and offer a basis for problem solving that leads to the formation of more complete and expert schemata. The process of knowledge acquisition can be seen as the successive development of structures that are tested and modified or replaced to facilitate learning and thinking.

The pedagogical implication that follows from this is that an effective strategy for instruction includes interrogation and confrontation. Expert teachers do this effectively, employing case method approaches, discovery methods, and various forms of Socratic dialogue. Such methods of inquiry instruction have been analyzed (Collins and Stevens 1982), and the findings suggest a useful approach to the design of adaptive instructional systems. A major goal, in addition to teaching facts and concepts about a domain, is to teach particular rules or theories for the domain. This is done, in part, by helping the learner to make predictions with and debug his or her current theory. A second goal is to teach ways to derive a rule or theory for related knowledge. The student learns what questions to ask to construct a theory, how to test one, and what its properties are. The protocols of effective teachers analyzed by Collins and Stevens show recurring strategies that teachers use for selecting cases and asking questions that confront the student with counterexamples, possibilities for correct and incorrect generalizations, and for locating ways students can apply and test their knowledge.

Such interactive adaptive methods are powerful tools for teaching thinking in the context of subject matter. Used with skill, they encourage conceptual understanding, involve and therefore motivate students, and can be adapted to the needs of different students. If used without skill, however, as Collins and Stevens point out, an inquiry approach can become an inquisition. The method requires that a teacher be continually vigilant and keep in mind the current limits of each student's thinking.

Such theory-targeted approaches to teaching are adaptive. As students acquire knowledge and skill, they can reason about implications of their own theories and then compare the events of their current level of learning to the predictions of other theories at more advanced levels, and so they learn both information and thinking processes. I submit, then, this description to indicate the possibilities of adaptive teaching that encourage the higher order mental processes that Jackson may overlook in his description.

Now, let me look more closely at Jackson's remarks and examine his key extrapolations. Although he may be accurate when he pushes the limits of separate ideas, he is in error because he does not imagine what might occur in a proper balance of things. He is wonderfully eager to correct the imbalance between intellectual proficiency, and affective, value-sensitive attitudes. And I agree, a student must learn the formalities that permit creativity, but these need to be taught as tools and not as inert knowledge that confines the capacity for creative problem solving.

Jackson says that the concept of "feedback loops" is misguiding. How can this be? If we know anything about human achievement, we know that it is influenced by information that is consequent upon a person's actions. Feedback of information is a primary mechanism of human growth, development, and evolution. In fact, it is the non-cybernetic models of learning we have most to fear, because they are insensitive to making teaching adaptive to the style and intellect of students. Educators who rely on them teach without regard to student growth and are likely to depend heavily on initial-state information provided by aptitude measures or on stereotypes including those of race and class.

Jackson says that the adaptive model centers on teaching factual information, that is, propositional knowledge. If so, then the adaptive approach is misguided in the light of modern psychology. It is quite clear that people who possess high levels of competence in various fields cannot get by with mere propositional knowledge. Propositional knowledge is only a core; it must be embedded in other forms of knowledge—particularly knowledge of the conditions and procedures for its use—so that what students learn is accessible for creative problem solving and thinking. The aspiration of adaptive education is to enable students to acquire knowledge embedded in the kind of meta-knowledge that facilitates its use. This requires teaching "when" and "if," as well as "what."

Teaching mere propositional knowledge leads to mere right-wrong or accurate-inaccurate forms of instruction, Jackson asserts. This certainly can be true, but I have tried to show in my account of schemata and knowledge structures that knowledge, in the context of learning, exists on a continuum from inaccurate and partial to accurate and more complete knowledge. A fact is not merely right or wrong, but right or wrong in regard to the particular structure in which knowledge is embedded. Just as a scientist is right or accurate until his theory is overthrown, so a student is accurate until he must account for new data. Adaptive instruction certainly must tune itself to the theories students work with, and give them practice in modifying or overthrowing their beliefs when they confront and acquire new information. Perhaps too many teachers think in terms of the absolutely right and wrong, but many others attempt to devise transitional situations so that their students can develop the ability to manage new complexities in the course of learning.

Jackson points out that the concept of modularity in curricula, which permits students to start at different places, at different times, and with materials of different characteristics, reminds him of an auto parts store. It brings to his mind the picture of the curriculum as an educational warehouse. In such a warehouse, he says, learning gets divided into parts: students have to work on things sequentially as their performance is matched against some standards. But the flexibility of a modular curriculum can be conceived in another way. Consider the warehouse not as a warehouse, but as a world that the students can explore, examining its parts and how they fit together, finding effective sequences for efficient search and points for reflection, and discovering how people, whose talents they admire, carry out this kind of exploration. Students, then, can integrate this information into their own understandings and their own forms of competence. So, rather than a warehouse model, a modular curriculum can be thought of as conforming to a world of discovery model—a world in which expertise is modeled, but in which the goal is individual expression. In Jackson's analogy to a warehouse, all deviations from a prescribed way of behaving are counted as errors. As I perceive the same circumstances, models of excellence exist, but variations on it are counted as intellectual inventions and artistic improvisations that encourage the development of human intellectual endeavor, problem solving, and thinking. Certainly, mimetic principles are supplanted by exploratory ones in this conception.

Jackson wonders whether there might not indeed be educational goals that are somehow ineffable and utterly indescribable in terms of the observable. The teacher does not know in advance what a student will say, do, or think in response to these goals, and this realization lies outside the framework of, and I quote, "any model that embraces the teacher and the student as interacting components in a functional unit." Jackson's way of handling this obviously important problem is to say that extant models have limits that are not acknowledged. I agree; there are many circumstances in which the teacher's goal is effecting changes in students which cannot be anticipated. I certainly agree with him, if he means that in many situations teachers do not have algorithms. But certainly, good teachers have heuristics. In most instructional situations, the teacher can apply didactic algorithms of reasonable precision. In other situations, however, they can use general rules of intelligent pedagogy and sensitive problem solving.

A combination of appropriate algorithms and general heuristics lies at the root of sound professional performance in many fields. When goals and means of reaching them can be specified in domains of knowledge, algorithms are strong methods. Where the requirements are more general and goals are unclear, as are means of attaining them, then heuristics are applied. It is this combination that Jackson's insights bring to my mind. Intelligent, proficient, and sensitive teachers, like others who are accomplished in other professions, require both algorithms and heuristics. Indeed, a hallmark of expertise in any profession is discrimination between situations that can, to best advantage, be handled by algorithms in contrast to less structured and less predictable situations where the use of heuristics is required. Perhaps the difference between the good teacher and the marvelous teacher lies in the ability to make this distinction quickly and smoothly. Jackson suggests as much, I believe, in his probing and thoughtful commentary.

To conclude, cognitive skills and affective understandings are profoundly influenced by the ways they are taught and used. We must take heed. For those of us interested in adaptive education, a central task of educational research is to produce a changed environment for learning—an environment that makes possible a genuine engagement with learning, where intellectual skills and knowledge of subject matter, and one's relationship to the environment become objects of interrogation and inquiry. With such an approach to education, as individuals acquire knowledge, they would also be empowered to think and to reason.

REFERENCES

Collins, Allan, and Stevens, Albert L. "Goals and Strategies of Inquiry Teachers." In *Advances in Instructional Psychology*, vol. 2, edited by Robert Glaser. Hillsdale, N.J.: Lawrence Erlbaum Associates, 1982.

Glaser, Robert. *Adaptive Education: Individual Diversity and Learning*. New York: Holt, Rinehart & Winston, 1977.

Glaser, Robert. "Education and Thinking: The Role of Knowledge." *American Psychologist* 39 (February 1984): 93-104.

B. The Knowledge Base for Adaptive Instruction: A Perspective from Classroom Research

Walter Doyle

Two tasks have traditionally dominated educational thought and research: (a) identifying effective teaching practices in classrooms, and (b) designing procedures for adapting instruction to differences among students. Preoccupation with these tasks is reasonable. Teachers differ and these differences must have significance in terms of effective teaching. Similarly, students differ and these differences should affect instructional design. In addition, strong moral sentiments surround the

During the preparation of this paper, the author was supported in part by a grant from the National Institute of Education for Research on Classroom Learning and Teaching. The opinions expressed here do not necessarily reflect the position or policy of the National Institute of Education and no official endorsement by that office should be inferred.

issues of effectiveness and adaptation. Every child has the right to be taught by an effective teacher and in a manner that suits his preferences, inclinations, learning style, and ability. To settle for less is to forsake the highest ideals of American education.

Despite these commonalities, the fields of teaching effectiveness and adaptive instruction have traditionally had separate constituencies and separate research traditions. Recently, however, this picture has changed. Classroom researchers are showing more interest in questions of design (Rosenshine 1983), and designers of adaptive programs are showing a greater sensitivity to the daily problems of using their designs in classrooms (see the chapters by Slavin and by Wang, Gennari, and Waxman in this volume).

In reacting to the chapters by Walberg; Grinder and Nelson; Gordon, DeStefano, and Shipman; and Jackson, I have concentrated on this convergence of interests between the fields of teaching effectiveness and adaptive instruction, and have examined ways in which the knowledge base of adaptive instruction might be further enriched by recent developments in classroom research. Five broad topics are considered: (a) the state of the existing knowledge base for adaptive instruction; (b) the effect of adaptive instruction on curriculum; (c) ways of accounting for the success of some adaptive programs; (d) possible perils of adaptation in institutionalized settings such as schools and classrooms; and (e) issues surrounding the role of the student in adaptive instruction.

WHAT WE KNOW ABOUT ADAPTIVE INSTRUCTION

The four chapters give a broad survey of the intellectual foundations of adaptive instruction, the large variety of programs that have been designed to translate ideas into practice, and, to a lesser extent, some of the intrinsic problems that lurk behind all of this effort. It is an impressive body of work. The idea, or perhaps the ideology, of adaptive instruction has clearly been with us for a long time and has stimulated a large amount of inquiry, program development, and, more recently, research on the nature of aptitude processes (see Snow, Federico, and Montague 1980). One is struck, however, by the fact that schooling for most students is not "adaptive," and adaptive programs so often fail to survive in any semblance of their original form for very long at the local school level. Indeed, the successful programs would seem to be those that depart the least from conventional patterns of classroom instruction. Are teachers and administrators unable or unwilling to appreciate the merits of adaptive instruction? Is the history of adaptive instruction simply another case of a folk culture resisting an advanced technology? Or are there serious flaws in both the philosophy and the technology of adaptive instruction? Is resistance a sign of folk wisdom rather than belligerence?

The authors of these chapters address the intrinsic problems of adaptive instruction in various ways. Two themes appear especially prominent. First, the knowledge base for conducting adaptive instruction—as defined, for instance, by research on attribute x treatment interactions (ATI)—is quite sparse. Gordon and his associates, in particular, attend to this literature, and their survey shows how little is actually known about the dynamic orchestration of student characteristics and instructional variables. Beyond some general suggestions for adapting to learning rate and a student's need for structure and prompts in instruction, there are few specific guidelines for designing instructional treatments to fit specific *learning* characteristics or dimensions of students. Although it may be polite or even morally necessary to attend to differences among students, it is not altogether clear what difference these differences make.

A similar conclusion was reached by Good and Stipek (1983) in a recent survey of research related to individual differences in the classroom. They concluded from their review that "we know of no dimension of individual differences that has unambiguous implications for instructional method" (p. 10). They further argue that any one construct related to differences among students contains only a limited amount of information relevant to instructional design. Thus, an overemphasis on a single dimension can be detrimental for some if not all students. They recommend, therefore, that teachers have a broad understanding of how students learn, continuously monitor students' progress, and adjust in a myriad of ways to evolving circumstances in the classroom. Unfortunately, neither the logic nor the empirical basis of these adjustments is very precise.

A second problem area for adaptive instruction concerns the workability of programs in classrooms. In these chapters, the classroom is only a shadow. Yet classroom studies (Emmer 1983; Good and Brophy 1984), as well as the experience of the developers of many of the programs represented in this volume, suggest that implementing adaptive instruction is difficult and expensive. In studies of mastery learning programs, Arlin (1982) and Arlin and Webster (1983) have recently provided compelling evidence that variations in the time students need to learn are quite problematic for teachers under classroom conditions. Students who finish early must wait while other students catch up, and such delays can lead to a breakdown of classroom order. Moreover, the differences among students who need remedial teaching are greater than an individual teacher can reasonably accommodate. As a result, remedial instruction is often not adapted to individual students despite the obvious need to do so.

The fact that many adaptive programs fade in practice may well be associated with difficulties of this kind. Clearly there is a need to incorporate information about classroom processes into the knowledge base of adaptive instruction.

ADAPTIVE INSTRUCTION AND CURRICULUM

A second prominent theme in the chapters centers on how adaptive instruction affects the curriculum. Jackson argues that the technology of adaptive instruction, with its need for explicit criteria of success and discrete modules of content, is applicable only to factual and algorithmic knowledge, that is, knowledge for which the form of both the finished performance and the steps leading to it are known in advance. He further maintains that this technology is inappropriate for "transformative" content, that is, content involving decisions, insight, and thought. If adaptive instruction is accepted as the ideal model for schooling, then transformative content is likely to be pushed out of the curriculum. Gordon and associates echo this concern for the restriction placed on content by adaptive instruction, but argue that we have simply not gone far enough, that adaptive programs are possible in principle in all areas of the curriculum if only we learn more about learners' characteristics and how these can be connected to instructional circumstances.

Part of the difference between Jackson's pessimism and Gordon's optimism is related to a fundamental difference in the conception of adaptive instruction. Jackson focuses on the common view of adaptive instruction in which the emphasis is on mastery and efficiency and the purpose is to maximize achievement across ability levels. In this approach, content must be shaped into an efficient and flexible delivery system. Gordon and his associates use an expanded notion of adaptive instruction in which the emphasis is primarily on interests and motivation and the purpose is to maximize personal development for each individual. In this latter approach, efficiency and technology are subordinated to richness and diversity.

Regardless of one's conception of adaptive instruction, however, more attention clearly needs to be given to the nature of academic work and to the intellectual processes that are involved in accomplishing this work (see Doyle 1983a), a topic that is for the most part neglected in these papers. I would underscore the suggestion by Gordon and his associates that the emerging knowledge in cognitive psychology concerning the nature and development of academic competence needs to be exploited more fully. In addition, greater emphasis needs to be placed on understanding the classroom processes associated with various types of academic work. In a project on academic work currently underway at the Research and Development Center for Teacher Education (see Doyle, Sanford, Clements, French, and Emmer 1983), we are finding that the demands of sustaining instructional events in a classroom often lead to a focus on only parts of the content of the curriculum. Some academic tasks, particularly those Jackson calls "transformative," are difficult to sustain under classroom conditions (see Carter and Doyle 1982).

ADAPTIVE INSTRUCTION AND ACHIEVEMENT

Walberg argues, on the basis of a summary of meta-analyses, that programs of adaptive instruction have, in general, a positive effect on various outcomes of schooling. Moreover, data on the classroom-based programs described in this volume suggest that they work—that students do learn content and acquire relevant social attitudes and a higher regard for themselves.

These positive results for adaptive programs stand in direct contrast to evidence concerning outcomes for adaptation initiated by individual teachers. In classrooms in which there is an emphasis on student choice and options for moving through the curriculum or a large amount of time spent with self-paced learning packets, achievement typically suffers (Rosenshine 1979). Part of this effect for classroom systems is probably accounted for by the difficulties a single teacher has in managing adaptations to individual students without a carefully designed and efficient program to guide the process. In most classrooms, the conditions that enhance achievement, such as task engagement and accountability, are easier to hold in place with group-paced instruction.

Aside from the issue of implementation, it is not clear how the successful adaptive programs get their effects. In many of the programs it would seem that adaptation is only broadly related to such student dimensions as ability and learning rate and that student "needs" are generally construed as academic needs, that is, the need at a particular moment for information about how to accomplish an academic task. Such programs are adaptive only in an opportunistic or administrative sense: They provide information or assistance to individual students at their request. (This type of adaptation would seem to be a central ingredient in Slavin's "team-assisted individualization" described later in this volume.) This feature may blunt some of the negative aspects of a mass processing system that is difficult for an individual student to stop when he or she is confused or needs help, but it hardly seems to embody the ideal of adapting to fundamental differences in development, culture, and learning style. At the same time, adaptive programs often make the tasks embedded in the curriculum very explicit. This explicitness increases the quality of instruction and thus allows more students to understand the work they are to accomplish. Explicitness also makes it more difficult to circumvent tasks or give approximate answers or solutions. Finally, explicitness foreshadows accountability by communicating to students the seriousness of the content: If someone has gone through this much trouble to define and order the work, it must be important to study. Finally, it would appear that the actual amount of time students spend with content in adaptive instruction is greater than in conventional instruction (see Arlin and Webster 1983). Both classroom and laboratory studies have indicated that time spent on content to be learned is associated with achievement (Rosenshine 1979).

From this perspective it would appear that adaptability is not the primary treatment dimension in adaptive instruction. What seems to be happening, rather, is that adaptive programs create *inclusionary* classrooms. That is, adaptive instruction is helpful in establishing conditions that include more students into the academic task system of a class, or, alternately, prevent more students from circumventing academic work. As a result, more students are given access to the main effects of instruction.

This analysis of how adaptive instruction gets its effects would seem to have an important message for teachers: Keep an eye on main effects. In other words, regardless of what procedures are used to arrange students for instruction, make sure they have access to information, time to practice with feedback, and are accountable for doing academic work.

There are two important areas, however, that seem to need concentrated attention by educational researchers and practitioners. First, some students do not learn from standard treatments. Such students, and I suspect not many fit this category, appear to need specialized instruction that is in some real sense adapted to their particular learning difficulties. Second, there are skills and concepts, such as domain-specific problem solving, that are difficult to teach, especially in classroom environments. It is precisely in these areas that the present knowledge base of adaptive instruction as well as the general data on the "success" of adaptive programs are of little help. More attention clearly needs to be given to these special design problems.

THE PERILS OF ADAPTATION

Few would argue against recognizing individual differences in instruction. Nevertheless, adaptive instruction in any form is not necessarily beneficial. Reference was made previously to Good and Stipek's (1983) argument that undue emphasis on a single dimension of individual differences, such as learning style, neglects other factors that need to be considered in designing instruction and can lead to harmful effects for at least some students in a class. In addition, the process of adapting instruction can have side effects, such as those noted by Jackson for curriculum, that need to be monitored.

Consistent with my general theme, I would argue that classrooms are a useful place to look for some of the perils of adaptive instruction. Recent studies (for example, Emmer 1983) show that teachers do respond to student differences in a variety of ways. The traditional division into three reading groups is a prominent example, suggesting that where there is a recognized technology and a culture to support its use, adaptation in instruction occurs. Teachers also appear to differentiate instruction primarily for drill in such areas as spelling, reading skills, and vocabulary. Classroom studies (see Doyle 1983b; Good 1983) also suggest that teachers interact with students frequently and often react differentially to students. Seatwork, for instance, is typically more interactive than the term itself often suggests. And during seatwork teachers often monitor progress and give corrective feedback. Finally, time is seldom "fixed" in classrooms. Teachers adjust the length of work segments to fit the completion rates of students and provide multiple opportunities to get work done. Classroom teaching, in other words, is often more adaptive than the stereotype of the "traditional" classroom or the usual control group condition in an instruction experiment.

What are the consequences of adaptation in classroom teaching? Here I think there are some instructive findings. First, differentiation can communicate differential expectations (Good 1981; Weinstein 1983). To adapt we often must classify, and teachers do this classifying in often crude but frequently accurate ways. But classifying can be tricky, particularly in institutional contexts. When an organization is required to "process" a large number of people, classification can easily become functional for bureaucratic rather than instructional purposes. Indeed, most of the knowledge we have about individual differences is typically used to place students in groups rather than to design instruction for them.

There is an additional consequence of adapting to student differences in classrooms that warrants attention. Differentiation often leads to fundamental differences in curriculum across ability levels, despite the best intentions to help lower-ability students catch up with their peers (see Borko 1983; Cazden 1981). These differences occur in both the amount that is covered and the fundamental character of what is covered. While high-ability students practice comprehension skills and read poetry, lower ability students do decoding exercises and vocabulary drills. Thus, adaptive instruction not only can restrict exposure for all students to a narrow band of the curriculum, as Jackson points out, but, given the contingencies of time and resources in schools, it can also restrict some students to only a small part of that narrow band.

I am not suggesting that classrooms are models of adaptive instruction. Nevertheless, they do provide useful illustrations of what can happen when adaptation occurs. The central point is that programs of adaptive instruction need to be monitored continuously to avoid some of the potentially negative consequences of such systems.

ADAPTIVE INSTRUCTION AND THE ADAPTIVE STUDENT

Judging from the chapters presented here, students are present in adaptive instruction in a curiously abstract, even mythical, way. In large measure they are carriers of aptitudes and abilities, but little attention seems to be paid to their perceptions of adaptive instruction, their behavior in adaptive programs, or the cognitive strategies and operations they use to navigate academic tasks in these settings. As Gordon and his associates observe, adaptive instruction has been more instruction conscious than learner conscious.

In contrast, students have recently become a major preoccupation in classroom research (Doyle 1977; Weinstein 1982), and this preoccupation is beginning to provide insights into how teaching works. In addition, this attention to students is providing a link between classroom research and advances in cognitive psychology (see Doyle 1983a). It would seem that a similar emphasis on students in adaptive instruction would yield important insights into the process of adaptation. In the following remarks I draw on classroom studies to provide a brief sketch of what benefits might accrue from placing students in a more central position in the knowledge base of adaptive instruction.

Recent work on information processing in classrooms suggests that the academic tasks students encounter in these environments provide the primary frameworks for thinking about subject matter (see Doyle 1983a). Tasks, in other words, organize students' processing and direct their attention selectively to resources that contribute to task accomplishment. Knowledge of tasks, therefore, provides insight into what students are required to think about in classrooms and the paths they are likely to use in doing academic work. The evidence also suggests that the task system overrides many stylistic features of a text or an instruction system (see Anderson, Reynolds, Schallert, and Goetz 1977; Pickert and Anderson 1976). Once students understand the task, they are able to ignore many stimuli that are not directly related to accomplishment. In other words, the instructional value of any one program dimension depends upon its place in the task system.

There are two important implications of this perspective. First, it is not likely that there will be differences in effects between instructional programs that contain the same task and provide equivalent information, in whatever form, that is useful for accomplishing the task. More generally, stylistic differences in instruction should not be expected to have consequences for achievement except insofar as they affect task clarity or resources. Second, knowledge about the nature of an academic task enables students to be adaptive. That is, once students know what the task is, they can use information from several sources as well as their accumulated knowledge of classroom task systems to accomplish the task. Indeed, considerable evidence is accumulating to suggest that students often invent rules and algorithms for doing academic work (Resnick and Ford 1981).

From a slightly different perspective, there is evidence that students can shape the nature and demands of academic work (see Davis and McKnight 1976; Doyle 1983a). Through a variety of maneuvers, students can adjust academic tasks at the public level by "negotiating" a more simple and explicit set of task requirements and at the private level by circumventing task requirements. Indeed, in one study students were found to transform assigned tasks by substituting their own tasks for the official ones (Laboratory of Comparative Human Cognition 1982).

The framework being advanced here suggests that the fit between instruction and outcomes is in practice often much looser than we are generally inclined to think. It also emphasizes the extent to which learners are able to adapt to a variety of academic tasks and instructional approaches as well as control the circumstances of instruction. In relation to this point, Good (1981) has underscored the curious fact that many lower ability students, who are likely to be least adaptable, are often required by "pull-out" programs and other remedial procedures to adapt to a greater number of learning tasks and task conditions than are their higher ability peers.

CONCLUSION

From the perspective of classroom research, and in particular an emphasis on the adaptive learner, the central question in adaptive instruction shifts from "How can instruction be made more adaptable?" to "When is adaptation necessary and what are its consequences?" This latter question would seem to be important for the development of knowledge about adapting instruction and for understanding what happens when programs of adaptive instruction are implemented in schools. In some instances it may well be that elaborate systems for adapting instruction are simply unnecessary. Main effects for instructional variables are robust, and the effectiveness of any instructional program is likely to be closely tied to these main effects. In addition, student adaptability, that is, the skills and executive routines necessary to cope with a variety of academic tasks and instructional systems, would seem to be an important outcome of schooling. In this light, adaptive instruction has value primarily as a temporary system that does some of the work of learning for students to enable them to get started on a set of learning tasks. Such adaptations must then be removed when they begin to interfere with learning to be adaptive.

REFERENCES

Anderson, Richard C.; Reynolds, Ralph E.; Schallert, Diane L.; and Goetz, Ernest T. "Frameworks for Comprehending Discourse." *American Educational Research Journal* 14 (Fall 1977): 367-81.
Arlin, Marshall. "Teacher Responses to Student Time Differences in Mastery Learning." *American Journal of Education* 90 (August 1982): 334-52.
Arlin, Marshall, and Webster, Janet. "Time Costs of Mastery Learning." *Journal of Educational Psychology* 75 (April 1983): 187-96.
Borko, Hilda. "Accommodating Student Diversity: Teachers' Preactive and Interactive Decisions." Paper presented at the annual meeting of the American Educational Research Association, Montreal, 1983.
Carter, Kathy, and Doyle, Walter. "Variations in Academic Tasks in High and Average Ability Classes." Paper presented at the annual meeting of the American Educational Research Association, New York, 1982.
Cazden, Courtney B. "Social Context of Learning to Read." In *Comprehension and Teaching: Research Reviews*, edited by John T. Guthrie. Newark, Del.: International Reading Association, 1981.
Davis, R.B., and McKnight, C. "Conceptual Heuristic, and S-algorithmic Approaches in Mathematics Teaching." *Journal of Children's Mathematical Behavior* 1, Supplement 1 (1976): 271-86.
Doyle, Walter. "Paradigms for Research on Teacher Effectiveness." In *Review of Research in Education*, vol. 5, edited by Lee S. Shulman. Itasca, Ill.: F. E. Peacock, 1977.
Doyle, Walter. "Academic Work." *Review of Educational Research* 53 (Summer 1983): 159-99. (a)

Doyle, Walter. *Managing Classroom Activities in Junior High English Classes: An Interim Report*, R and D Report, 6131. Austin: Research and Development Center for Teacher Education, The University of Texas at Austin, 1983. (b)

Doyle, Walter; Sanford, Julie P.; Clements, Barbara S.; French, B.; and Emmer, Edmund T. *Managing Academic Tasks: Interim Report of the Junior High School Study*, R and D Report, 6186. Austin: Research and Development Center for Teacher Education, The University of Texas at Austin, 1983.

Emmer, Edmund T. "An Investigation of Heterogeneous Elementary School Classrooms." Paper presented at the annual meeting of the American Educational Research Association, Montreal, 1983.

Good, Thomas L. "Teacher Expectations and Student Perceptions: A Decade of Research." *Educational Leadership* 38 (February 1981): 415-22.

Good, Thomas L. "Classroom Research: A Decade of Progress." Invited address presented at the annual meeting of the American Educational Research Association, Montreal, 1983.

Good, Thomas L., and Brophy, Jere E. *Looking in Classrooms*, 3rd ed. New York: Harper & Row, 1984.

Good, Thomas L., and Stipek, Deborah J. "Individual Differences in the Classroom: A Psychological Perspective." In *Individual Differences and the Common Curriculum*, Eighty-second Yearbook of the National Society for the Study of Education, Part 1, edited by Gary Fenstermecher and John I. Goodlad. Chicago, Ill.: University of Chicago Press, 1983.

Laboratory of Comparative Human Cognition. "A Model System for the Study of Learning Difficulties." *Quarterly Newsletter of the Laboratory of Comparative Human Cognition* 4 (1982): 39-66.

Pickert, J.W., and Anderson, Richard G. *Taking Different Perspectives on a Story*, Technical Report 14. Urbana: Center for the Study of Reading, University of Illinois at Urbana-Champaign, 1976.

Resnick, Lauren, and Ford, W.W. *The Psychology of Mathematics for Instruction*. Hillsdale, N.J.: Lawrence Erlbaum Associates, 1981.

Rosenshine, Barak. "Content, Time, and Direct Instruction." In *Research on Teaching*, edited by Penelope L. Peterson and Herbert J. Walberg. Berkeley, Calif.: McCutchan, 1979.

Rosenshine, Barak. "Teaching Functions in Instructional Programs." *Elementary School Journal* 83 (March 1983): 335-51.

Snow, Richard E.; Federico, Pat-Anthony; and Montague, William E. *Aptitude, Learning and Instruction*, 2 vols. Hillsdale, N.J.: Lawrence Erlbaum Associates, 1980.

Weinstein, Rhona S., editor. *Students in Classrooms: A Special Issue. Elementary School Journal* 82 (May 1982): 397-533.

Weinstein, Rhona S. "Student Perceptions of Schooling." *Elementary School Journal* 83 (March 1983): 237-312.

PART II

Educational Programs and Practices

CHAPTER

6

Cooperative Learning and Adaptive Education

David W. Johnson and Roger T. Johnson

INTRODUCTION: ADAPTIVE EDUCATION AND COOPERATIVE LEARNING

Adaptive instruction may be defined as the use of alternative instructional strategies and school resources to provide learning experiences that meet the different needs of individual students (Wang and Walberg 1983). The purpose of adaptive education is to increase students' achievement through increasing their time-on-task, reducing the amount of time needed for learning prescribed academic basics, and increasing the amount of school time available to teachers for instruction. The underlying assumption of adaptive instruction is that students learn in different ways and at different rates; effective instruction therefore requires both the inclusion of a variety of instructional procedures and learning experiences that match the needs of each student and the allocation of adequate amounts of time for all students to learn. Learning experiences and student characteristics need to be matched in order to maximize the efficiency of learning situations.

Instructional strategies that allow students to use different learning modes and have the flexibility for different students to study different material at different rates can be seen, therefore, as essential to adaptive education. One of the major factors involved in providing a variety of ways for students to learn is the way in which the learning goals and, consequently, interaction among students, are structured (Johnson and Johnson 1975, 1983). There are three ways in which learning goals may be structured—cooperatively, competitively, and individualistically. The basic assumptions in our work in this area have been:

1. How the teacher structures learning goals largely determines how students interact with one another, and the student-student interaction patterns exert considerable influence on the instructional outcomes.

2. There is an appropriate place for cooperative, competitive, and individualistic learning in any learning situation, and teachers need to utilize all three.

One of the advantages of cooperative learning is its high flexibility. Cooperative learning procedures may be used with any age student (from preschool through adult education), in any subject area, with a wide variety of curriculum materials and technological aids, and with any type of student. Heterogeneous as well as homogeneous groups may be used so that learning situations that involve gifted, medium-ability, and handicapped students can be created. In such a flexible situation the achievement of each student can be maximized, the appropriate learning tasks can be structured, and the important oral interaction and interpersonal support and encouragement can be given.

In this chapter we shall first define cooperative learning and examine our efforts to validate the theory and implement it within schools. We will then review the major school goals concerning achievement and note the research on cooperative learning that is applicable to those outcomes. The practical procedures for maximizing the adaptiveness of cooperative learning groups will be discussed, and the staff training and monitoring procedures that are useful in supporting program implementation will be covered. Finally, the cognitive and social development that result from the use of cooperative learning procedures will be noted.

COOPERATIVE LEARNING

There are five aspects of cooperative learning that need to be discussed in order to understand its nature, its inherent adaptiveness, and our research on and applications of cooperative learning strategies.

Goal Interdependence

Lewin's (1935) theory of motivation postulates that a state of tension within an individual motivates movement toward the accomplishment of desired goals, and that the drive for goal accomplishment motivates cooperative, competitive, and individualistic behavior. In formulating a theory of how the tension systems of different people may be interrelated, Deutsch (1949, 1962) conceptualized three types of goal structures that organize interpersonal behavior—cooperative, competitive, and individualistic. In a *cooperative* goal structure the goals of the separate individuals are so linked together that there is a positive correlation among their goal attainments. Under purely cooperative conditions, an individual can attain his or her goal if and only if the other participants can attain their goals. Thus a person seeks an outcome that is beneficial to all those with whom he or she is cooperatively linked. In a *competitive* social situation the goals of the separate participants are so linked that there is a negative correlation among their goal attainments. An individual can attain his or her goal if and only if the other participants cannot attain their goals. Thus a person seeks an outcome that is personally beneficial but is detrimental to the others with whom he or she is competitively linked. Finally, in an *individualistic* situation there is no correlation among the goal attainments of the participants. Whether an individual accomplishes his or her goal has no influence on whether other individuals achieve their goals. Thus a person seeks an outcome that is personally beneficial, ignoring as irrelevant the goal accomplishment efforts of other participants in the situation.

CRITICAL ELEMENTS OF COOPERATIVE LEARNING

In our conceptual application of cooperative learning procedures there is a set of basic elements that we recommend should always be included in any cooperatively structured learning activity:

1. Positive interdependence. This may be achieved through mutual goals (goal interdependence), divisions of labor (task interdependence), dividing materials, resources, or information among group members (resource interdependence), assigning students roles (role interdependence), and/or by giving joint rewards (reward interdependence). In order for a learning situation to be cooperative, students must perceive that they are positively interdependent with the other members of their learning group.

2. Face-to-face interaction among students. There is no magic in positive interdependence in and of itself; it is the interaction among students promoted by positive interdependence that promotes learning and social growth.

3. Individual accountability for mastering the assigned material. The purpose of a learning situation is to maximize the achievement of each individual student. Feedback mechanisms for determining the level of mastery of each student are necessary for students to provide appropriate support and assistance to each other.

4. Appropriate use of interpersonal and small-group skills. Placing socially unskilled students in a learning group and telling them to be cooperative will obviously not be successful. Students must be taught the social skills needed for high quality collaboration and be motivated to use them. These skills are detailed in D. Johnson (1981) and D. Johnson and F. Johnson (1982).

We additionally recommend that periodically students should be given time and a structure for analyzing how well their learning groups are functioning and that cooperatively structured lessons should be supplemented with appropriate competitive and individualistic ones. The specific components of the teacher's role are detailed in D. Johnson and Johnson (1975).

Adaptiveness to Learning Modes

One of the major advantages of cooperative learning is that it allows (a) different students to use different learning modes and (b) the same student to use different learning modes at different times. Students who are explaining how to solve a mathematics problem or how to complete a science experiment often find ingenious ways to represent solutions so that fellow group members can understand.

While discussing assignments and explaining to one another how to complete the work correctly, students have been observed to use preoperational, concrete operational, and formal operational explanations within the same discussion. Enactive activities and iconic and symbolic representations are often presented during a group study session. Besides visual learning, cooperative learning situations provide the alternatives of auditory learning and the use of oral explanations that may be essential for deeper level understanding, higher level reasoning, and long-term retention of the material being learned. Competitive and individualistic learning situations do not have the richness and adaptability of learning modes that are naturally present in cooperative learning situations.

Our Research Efforts and Procedures

For the past several years we have been conducting a program of research aimed at studying the relative impact of cooperative, competitive, and individualistic learning experiences. Basically we chose to conduct highly controlled field-experimental studies in actual classrooms and schools. Our typical study lasted three weeks, compared cooperative learning situations with individualistic and/or competitive learning situations, and involved students from different ethnic groups and ability levels. We typically obtained the help of three classroom teachers who agreed to assist us in conducting the study. In order to ensure that there were no differences among students in each condition, we randomly assigned students, making sure that there were an equal number of males and females; majority and minority; and high-, medium-, and low-ability students in each condition. To make sure that the high-quality teaching occurred in each condition, the teachers received a minimum of ninety hours of training on how to implement cooperative, competitive, and individualistic learning situations and were given a daily script to follow. In order to make sure that any differences among conditions we found were not due to differences in teaching ability, the teachers were rotated across conditions, so that each teacher taught each condition for one week. And to ensure that the study did in fact test our theory, we implemented cooperative, competitive, and individualistic learning in ways that were as unambiguous as possible. All the students studied the same curriculum. To verify that the teachers were in fact teaching the conditions appropriately, we observed them daily. Finally, we collected observations of how students interacted with each other. We were determined to conduct our research in as highly controlled and careful a way as possible so we could be confident about the results.

Our Training Efforts and Procedures

Based on the research on organization change within schools and the research on successful and unsuccessful educational innovation (D. Johnson 1970, 1979), we have initiated a large-scale application of the theory and research on goal structures and social interdependence (D. Johnson and R. Johnson 1975). Our initial assumptions are:

1. A conceptual application is more effective than a direct application. Based on the research conducted on the failures and successes of innovation in the 1950s and 1960s (Berman and McLaughlin 1978; Lawrence 1974; McLaughlin and Marsh 1980) it may be concluded that while teachers need to understand clearly what cooperative learning is and be given concrete strategies and specific skills on how to implement cooperative learning in their classrooms, effective training needs to allow teachers to adapt cooperative learning to their own subject areas, curriculum materials, circumstances, and students. Teachers need to do the work to "own" the strategies rather than to regard them as something they are asked to do. Prepackaged, direct applications are typically used for a while and then discontinued.

2. Effective training programs have to be "hands on," and "job embedded," with "on call" help and support for teachers when they need it (Berman and McLaughlin 1978; Lawrence 1974; McLaughlin and Marsh 1980). Effective training needs to emphasize demonstrations, "hands on" trying out of the strategies, and feedback about how well the teachers are implementing cooperative learning. Ongoing training over a period of years needs to be provided when individual teachers want and need it. Experts who can provide support and assistance have to be "on call" to demonstrate, co-teach, solve problems, and provide help when it is needed and wanted.

3. Teachers and other staff members must be structured into professional support groups aimed at teaching each other how to use cooperative learning strategies effectively and how to use all three goal structures in an integrated and coordinated way.

Over the past ten years we have followed these assumptions in training teachers in both in-service and preservice situations. Our conceptual models of cooperative learning and the integrated use of all three goal structures have been field tested in a wide variety of preschool, elementary, secondary, college, and adult education settings. A conservative estimate is that we and our colleagues have trained over 12,000 teachers. We have built an international network of school districts involved in long-term efforts to implement cooperative learning. Within the United States these school districts range from California to Maine, from Florida to the state of Washington, and from Texas to the Dakotas. We have worked with a number of school districts in Canada, from British Columbia to Quebec, and there are active school districts in Norway, Sweden, and Australia. Our implementation efforts are continuing. Field evaluations indicate that the appropriate use of cooperative learning procedures will promote the outcomes promised by the theory and the research.

Our basic model for working with these school districts is as follows. First, an awareness session of how cooperative learning may be structured is given to as many teachers within the district as will attend. We then recruit teams of teachers from the same school building, including the principal and special education teachers whenever possible. We then begin a dual process of (a) training the teachers in how to use cooperative learning procedures and in how to use all three goal structures in an integrated way, and (b) building a professional support group aimed at teaching each other how to use all three goal structures appropriately and competently. In our training program we present the teachers with a model of the teachers' role and guidelines for each step. Teachers then spend time translating our model into their own procedures, use them for a while, provide help and assistance in implementing cooperative learning to each other, and tailor the procedures for their specific needs, circumstances, students, and curriculums. We view the process of a teacher learning how to use routinely the three goal structures appropriately and competently as taking from two to three years.

ACHIEVEMENT PARADOX

There is an educational paradox directly related to the systematic and appropriate use of cooperative, competitive, and individualistic learning situations: *Our economic system is based on the quality of our work force, yet our schools are dominated by instructional procedures that the research indicates are less effective in promoting the achievement, the positive attitudes toward science and mathematics, and the technological literacy needed for a productive population.* Our society is in the midst of an achievement crisis. Our children and teenagers focus on the superficial learning of facts and avoid courses and careers based on scientific and technological literacy. This crisis calls into question the ability of our educational system to provide our society with psychologically well-adjusted and competent individuals who are motivated and able to pursue careers in scientific and technological fields. As a result of this crisis our society is faced with large numbers of individuals who are technologically ignorant, unversed in even the simplest principles of chemistry, physics, and biology, and unable to manage the high degree of technology needed in a modern economy and society. There is growing recognition, for example, that no country can build a high-quality economy with a low-quality work force, and that American productivity relies more on people than on machines. The achievement crisis in our schools is reflected in the following observations:

1. There has been a marked decline in scores on the Scholastic Aptitude Test (SAT). Although more students are staying in school longer and going on to college, all signs indicate that they are more poorly equipped in basic skills than their predecessors. The scores of our top students on the SAT have been falling along with the scores of our middle- and low-achieving students.

2. A number of economists have been stating that America must invest more in the quality of its work force or face a decline (Becker 1975; Schultz 1981). Science education is especially important, as increasing scientific and technological literacy has been far more important to the industrialization of the West than has been generally acknowledged (Schultz 1981).

3. Science education is generally disliked by teachers and students and relatively deemphasized in American schools (R. Johnson and Johnson 1982; Walberg 1982).

4. Functional illiteracy seems to be increasing among those who drop out of school as well as among those who finish (Lerner 1981). The result may be an ill-educated segment of the population that is unable to participate fully in our society.

In order to provide our society with a high-quality work force (and thereby a secure future) there are a number of outcomes that must be maximized by our educational system, including:

1. High achievement reflected in the mastery of the facts, information, and theories taught in school.

2. The development of critical thinking competencies and the use of higher level reasoning strategies.

3. The positive attitudes toward subject areas such as mathematics and science required to generate continuing motivation to study, take advanced training in, learn more about, and enter careers related to science and mathematics.

4. The ability to utilize one's knowledge and resources in collaborative activities with other people in career, family, community, and societal settings.

5. The psychological health and well-being required to participate effectively in our society.

Whether learning situations are structured competitively, individualistically, or cooperatively has some impact on these variables. The solution to our society's achievement crisis may be facilitated through the appropriate use of the three goal structures in instructional situations.

Social Interdependence and Achievement

In our studies we have found considerable evidence that cooperative learning experiences promote higher achievement than do competitive and individualistic learning experiences (see Table 6.1). Out of the twenty studies we have done that include achievement data, sixteen studies demonstrated that cooperative learning promoted higher achievement, two showed mixed results, and in two there were no differences among conditions. These studies have included college students and students from every grade but the eighth grade. They have used mathematics, English, language arts, geometry, social studies, science, physical science, and physical education curriculum. The studies have lasted from one day to nine months. They have included both males and females; upper-middle-, middle-, working-, and lower-class students; gifted, medium-ability, and low-ability students; students with mild to very severe handicapping conditions; and students from a number of minority groups. The length of the instructional sessions has varied from fifteen to ninety minutes.

The adaptability of cooperative learning is illustrated by the fact that in these studies students of high, medium, and low ability were mixed within the cooperative learning groups. Clearly the high-ability students did not suffer from working with medium- and low-ability students. In the four studies that measured the achievement of gifted students separately, three found they achieved higher when collaborating with medium- and low-ability students and one found no difference in achievement. Out of the twelve studies that measured the achievement of academically handicapped students, eleven studies revealed higher achievement when students cooperated and one study found no difference in achievement. It is evident, therefore, that cooperative learning procedures can provide appropriate instructional experiences for diverse students who work together.

Since the 1920s there has been a great deal of research on the relative effects of cooperative, competitive, and individualistic efforts on achievement and productivity. Our work is only a small part of this research effort. Despite the large number of studies conducted, however, social scientists have disagreed as to the conclusions that may be drawn from the literature. The traditional practice seemed to be to select a subset of studies that supported one's biases, declare that they are the only studies that are relevant to the question, place them in a review, and give one's summary impressions of their findings.

In order to resolve the controversies resulting from the various reviews on social interdependence and achievement we conducted a meta-analysis of all the studies that had been conducted in the area (D. Johnson, Maruyama, Johnson, Nelson, and Skon 1981). We reviewed 122 studies conducted between 1924 and 1981 that yielded 286 findings. Three methods of meta-analysis were used: voting method, effect-size method, and z-score method. The results indicate that cooperative learning experiences tend to promote higher achievement than do competitive and individualistic learning experiences. The average person working within a cooperative situation achieves at about the 80th percentile of the students working within a competitive or individualistic situation. These results hold for all age levels, for all subject areas, and for tasks involving concept attainment, verbal problem solving, categorizing, spatial problem solving, retention and memory, motor performance, and guessing-judging-predicting. For rote-decoding and correcting tasks, cooperation seems to be as effective as competitive and individualistic learning procedures.

INTERNAL DYNAMICS OF COOPERATIVE LEARNING GROUPS

Despite the large number of studies comparing the relative impact of cooperative, competitive, and individualistic learning situations on achievement, the processes that mediate or moderate the relationship between cooperation and productivity have been relatively ignored. Over the past several years we have examined a number of variables that may affect the achievement rate of cooperative learning groups. The potentially mediating or moderating variables we have studied are:

1. The type of learning task assigned.

2. The quality of learning strategy used to complete learning tasks.

3. The occurrence of controversy versus concurrence-seeking when students disagree with each other while completing learning tasks.

4. The time-on-task engaged in while completing the learning tasks.

5. The cognitive processing engaged in while interacting about the learning tasks.

6. The peer regulation and feedback engaged in while interacting about the learning tasks.

7. The active involvement in learning occurring while completing the learning tasks.

8. The ability levels of group members.

9. Group cohesion.

The specific references to support the statements made below may be found in D. Johnson and Johnson 1983.

Type of Task

In our original review of the literature (D. Johnson and Johnson 1974, 1975) the evidence indicated that for simple, mechanical, previously mastered tasks that require no help from other students, competition promoted greater quantity of output than did cooperative or individualistic efforts. Believing that the type of task might be an important variable, we and our students conducted a series of studies examining the relative effects of cooperative, competitive, and individualistic goal structures on achievement on a variety of school-related tasks. The studies focused on white first- and fifth-grade students from both urban and suburban settings and black high school students from an urban setting. The results are surprisingly consistent. On mathematical and verbal drill-review tasks, spatial-reasoning and verbal problem-solving tasks, pictorial and verbal sequencing tasks, tasks involving the comparison of the attributes of shape, size, and pattern, and a knowledge-retention task, cooperation promoted higher achievement than did either competitive or individualistic efforts. On a specific knowledge acquisition task both cooperation and competition promoted higher achievement than did individualistic efforts. These findings are all the more important as care was taken to optimize the effectiveness of competitive and individualistic instruction.

Currently there is no type of task for which cooperative efforts are *less* effective than competitive or individualistic efforts. For most tasks (and especially the more important learning tasks such as concept attainment, verbal problem solving, categorization, spatial problem solving, retention and memory, motor, guessing-judging-predicting) cooperative efforts are more effective in promoting achievement. We therefore left this area of study and moved to an examination of the quality of the strategies being used in learning situations.

Quality of Learning Strategy

The next potentially explanatory variable we studied was the quality of the reasoning strategy students used to complete their assignments. In a pair of studies (D. Johnson, Skon, and Johnson 1980; Skon, Johnson, and Johnson 1981) we found that students working cooperatively used strategies superior to those used by students working either competitively or individualistically. These strategies included category search and retrieval, intersectional classification, formulating equations from story problems, and formulating strategies for avoiding repetitions and errors in a spatial reasoning task. From these findings we can conclude that the discussion process in cooperative groups promotes the discovery and development of higher quality cognitive strategies for learning better than does the individual reasoning found in competitive and individualistic learning situations. In a later study (D. Johnson and Johnson 1981) we found that students working cooperatively reported using higher thought processes more often than did students working individualistically.

Controversy Versus Concurrence-Seeking

Involved participation in cooperative learning groups will inevitably produce conflicts of ideas, opinions, conclusions, theories, and information among members. When such controversies arise, they may be dealt with constructively or destructively, depending on the teacher's response and the students' level of social skills. We have conducted a series of studies (Lowry and Johnson 1981; Smith, Johnson, and Johnson 1981) and reviewed the research literature (D. Johnson 1980; D. Johnson and Johnson 1979) on controversy. When managed constructively, controversy promotes epistemic curiosity or uncertainty about the correctness of one's views, an active search for more information, and consequently higher achievement and retention of the material being learned. Individuals working alone in competitive and individualistic situations do not have the opportunity for such a process, and therefore achieve less.

Time-on-Task

Another possible explanation for the superiority of cooperation over competitive or individualistic efforts in promoting higher achievement is that students in cooperative learning groups spend more time-on-task. In a number of studies we observed the amount of on-task time in the three types of learning situations. Our results indicate that in two of the studies more on-task behavior was found in the cooperative condition, while in four of the studies no significant difference in on-task behavior was found. From these results it may be concluded that cooperative learning situations may promote more on-task behavior than the other two goal structures, but probably there is little difference in observed actual on-task behavior among the three goal structures.

Cognitive Processing

One of the most promising mediating variables identified in our meta-analysis (D. Johnson et al. 1981) as explaining part of the relationship between cooperation and achievement was the oral rehearsal that has been found necessary for storing information into memory, promoting long-term retention of information, and increasing achievement. Two of our students, Lyons (1982) and Roy (1982), developed an observational instrument that measured the amount of lower-level (repetition of information), intermediate-level (stating of new information), and high-level (explanations, rationales, integration) rehearsal within learning situations. The results of our studies indicate that cooperative efforts contain more low-, intermediate-, and high-level oral rehearsal of information by low-, medium-, and high-ability students than do individualistic efforts. The results also indicate that within the cooperative condition, intermediate-level oral rehearsal was related to achievement.

Peer Support, Regulation, and Feedback

A number of studies have found more peer regulation, feedback, support, and encouragement of task-related efforts in cooperative than in individualistic learning situations (Johnson 1980). Such peer interaction is viewed as important for task engagement and for the motivation of less "mature" learners, who may need an external agent to provide more guidance and monitoring of their progress through the steps required to complete a task. For the past two years we have been working on an observational measure of peer academic support, encouragement, regulation, and feedback. We found more peer encouragement, feedback, and regulation in the cooperative than in the individualistic condition. Within the cooperative condition, peer academic encouragement and regulation were significantly related to achievement.

Active Mutual Involvement in Learning

Within a cooperative learning situation, students are required to discuss the material being learned with one another and we directly observed the active oral involvement of students in completing assigned learning tasks. There is considerably more active oral involvement in cooperative than in individualistic learning situations. This active engagement of providing task-related information was found to be significantly correlated with achievement in the cooperative condition.

There is evidence that the more cooperative students' attitudes are, the more they express their ideas and feelings in large and small classes and the more they listen to the teacher, whereas competitive and individualistic attitudes are unrelated to indices of active involvement in instructional activities (D. Johnson and Ahlgren 1976; D. Johnson, Johnson, and Anderson 1978). Cooperative learning experiences, compared with competitive and individualistic ones, seem to result in a greater desire to express one's ideas to the class (D. Johnson, Johnson, Johnson, and Anderson 1976; Wheeler and Ryan 1973). Cooperative learning experiences, compared with competitive and individualistic ones, promote greater willingness to present one's answers and thus create more positive feelings toward the instructional experience (Garibaldi 1979; Gunderson and Johnson 1980).

Ability Levels of Group Members

Another potentially mediating variable within cooperative learning groups is the interaction among students from diverse ability levels. There may be an important advantage to having high-, medium-, and low-ability students work together on completing assignments and learning material. A number of our studies have compared the achievement of high-, medium-, and low-ability students involved in cooperative learning activities with the achievement of their counterparts working alone individualistically or competitively. There can be little doubt that the low- and medium-ability students especially benefit from working collaboratively with peers from the full range of ability differences. There is also evidence that high-ability students are better off academically when they collaborate with medium- and low-ability peers than when they work alone; at the worst, it may be argued that high-ability students are not hurt by interacting collaboratively with their medium- and low-ability classmates. One of the important internal dynamics of cooperative learning groups, therefore, may be the opportunity for students with different achievement histories to interact with one another to complete assigned learning tasks.

Group Cohesion

Within cooperative learning groups, members typically develop considerable liking for each other and attachment to being a member of the group (D. Johnson, Johnson, and Maruyama 1983). These positive feelings toward the group and the other members may have a number of important influences on motivation to achieve and actual achievement.

OTHER ACHIEVEMENT-RELATED OUTCOMES

In addition to performance in achievement-oriented situations, there are a number of other achievement-related outcomes that are important, as has already been pointed out. We discuss here two of those outcomes—critical thinking and attitudes toward subject areas.

Critical Thinking

In many subject areas related to science and technology the teaching of facts and theories is considered to be secondary to the teaching of critical thinking and the use of higher level reasoning strategies. The aim of science education, for example, has been to develop individuals "who can sort sense from nonsense," or who have the critical thinking ability to grasp information, examine it, evaluate it for soundness, and apply it appropriately. The superiority of cooperation over competitive and individualistic efforts in promoting achievement on problem-solving and reasoning tasks (D. Johnson, Maruyama, Johnson, Nelson, and Skon 1981) indicates that cooperation may promote more critical thinking. As noted previously, we have found in our own studies that students in cooperative learning situations use higher-level reasoning strategies than do students in competitive and individualistic learning situations.

Attitudes Toward Subject Areas

If we are to provide a high-quality labor force for our society, graduates from our educational system must have a high degree of scientific and technological literacy, and a high percentage of our top students must enter science-related careers. Yet there is considerable evidence that most students in the United States dislike science, fail to take advanced science courses in high school, and are not majoring in science and related careers in college (Walberg 1982). There is a critical need, therefore, to develop instructional strategies that will promote more positive attitudes toward science and increase students' continuing motivation to study, take further courses in, enter careers in, and learn more about that subject area. Our colleagues and ourselves have conducted a series of studies that indicate that cooperative learning experiences, compared with competitive and individualistic ones, promote more positive attitudes toward the subject area and the instruction experience. There is also evidence that cooperative learning experiences promote more continuing motivation to learn than do individualistic learning experiences (Lowry and Johnson 1981; Smith, Johnson, and Johnson 1981).

Fairness of grading is often a factor influencing attitudes toward a subject. Within many schools teachers are concerned that when students work cooperatively, and receive the same grade or a joint reward for their efforts, they will believe that the grading system is unfair. Having students work together on a joint product is often seen as being less fair to each student than having each student work alone to produce an individual product for which he or she receives an individual grade. While students who "lose" in a competitive learning situation commonly perceive the grading system as being unjust and consequently dislike the class or teacher (D. Johnson and Johnson 1975), it is of considerable importance that students within cooperative learning situations perceive the distribution of grades and other rewards as being fair. Otherwise they may withdraw from the group's efforts to achieve and maintain effective working relationships among members. Deutsch (1979) presents data from a number of experiments indicating that before a task is performed, there is a general perception that a competitive grading system is fairest, but after a task is completed, a cooperative grading system where all group members receive the same grade or reward is viewed as the fairest. In a large-scale study of three urban and suburban school districts (D. Johnson and Johnson 1983), we found that the more students experienced long-term cooperative learning experiences, and the more cooperation they perceived in their classes, the more they believed that everyone who tries has an equal chance to succeed in class, that students get the grades they deserve, and that the grading system is fair. In an earlier study Wheeler and Ryan (1973) found that students prefer group grades over individual ones. Related to these results are our findings that the vast majority of students tend to prefer cooperative over competitive or individualistic learning experiences. In the real world of the classroom, joint grades and rewards seem to be perceived as fairer by students than traditional competitive and individualistic grading systems.

STRUCTURING ADAPTIVENESS INTO COOPERATIVE LEARNING GROUPS

As can be seen from the research, cooperative learning provides considerable adaptiveness in which gifted, medium-ability, and academically handicapped students can work together in a way that benefits all. The students learn to adapt material by finding the most effective learning mode for each group member, allowing members to work at different rates, encouraging and supporting efforts to achieve, giving explanations cast in concrete operational and formal operational reasoning processes, presenting iconic as well as symbolic representations, and so forth. When a group is stuck and unable to explain to one of its members how to solve a problem or complete an assignment, the teacher becomes a consultant to the group and helps them derive a strategy for doing so. Far from slowing the achievement of group members, such activity seems to create greater depth of understanding, the discovery of higher level reasoning strategies, and greater retention of the material being studied.

There are ways that teachers can structure adaptiveness into a learning group. Different students, for example, may be given material at different levels of difficulty. In a spelling group, for instance, different students can receive a different number of words and different words to memorize. The group is then evaluated on the percentage correct each member achieves. The same procedure can be used in other subject areas such as mathematics, where different numbers of problems or different types of problems could be given to different group members. Another procedure is for different roles to be assigned to group members so that one member reads the assignment, another student ensures that everyone participates, and so forth, so that each student can perform a useful function that is commensurate with his or her ability and achievement history. Divisions of labor within the group can be structured so that in a science lesson one student collects swampwater, another learns how to make a slide, another learns how to use the microscope, and another prepares a group report. Students with different achievement histories can be given assignments within the division of labor that take their abilities into account. The only limit on the adaptiveness that may be structured into a cooperative group is the creativity of the teacher.

SOCIALIZATION PARADOX

There is a paradox within our society that is directly related to the systematic use of cooperative, competitive, and individualistic learning situations: *Our society is filled with alienated children, teenagers, and young adults, yet within schools competitive and individualistic efforts are emphasized, where students are isolated from and pitted against each other in large, bureaucratic, and impersonal schools.* Many children, teenagers, and young adults are deprived of and may never experience the caring and committed relationships needed for effective socialization and healthy cognitive and social development. More specifically, our society is faced with many children, adolescents, and young adults who:

1. may never be able to build and maintain productive careers or families.

2. feel fragmented and disconnected from their associates and society.

3. may be unable to interact competently with others who are from different cultural, ethnic, or social class backgrounds, or who are from the opposite sex, or who are handicapped.

4. may be demoralized and view attempts to solve our national and world problems as hopeless and beyond our capabilities.

5. may be a permanent underclass cut off from the opportunity structures of our society.

One of the major advantages of cooperative learning is that it is possible to promote simultaneously high achievement and constructive socialization and development. There is considerable research that indicates cooperative learning experiences promote more constructive and caring facilitative peer relationships, greater perspective-taking ability, higher self-esteem, and more constructive and facilitative relationships with teachers, greater interpersonal and small-group skills, and greater psychological health (D. Johnson and Johnson 1983).

The importance of cooperative learning procedures goes beyond achievement, positive attitudes toward subject areas such as science and mathematics, and ability to think critically. The ability of all students to learn to work cooperatively with others is the keystone to building and maintaining stable marriages, families, careers, and friendships. Being able to perform technical skills such as reading, speaking, listening, writing, computing, and problem solving are valuable but of little use if the person cannot apply those skills in cooperative interaction with other people in career, family, and

community settings. Schools have long been places that have promoted unrealistic expectations of what career, family, and community
life may be like. Most careers do not expect people to sit in rows and
compete with colleagues without interacting with them. Team work,
communication, effective coordination, and divisions of labor characterize most real life settings. It may be time for schools to more
realistically reflect the reality of adult life. The success we have had in
training teachers to use cooperative learning procedures is evidence
that schools can in fact become realistic socializing and training
organizations for our society.

CONCLUSIONS

We are in a period of educational history where there is a discrepancy between the instructional methods being used in the schools
and the instructional methods verified by research to be most effective. Despite the considerable amount of research indicating that
cooperative learning has many advantages, current instruction in
America is dominated by inappropriate interpersonal competitive and
individualistic learning. School is perceived to be basically competitive (D. Johnson and Johnson 1976; R. Johnson 1976; R. Johnson,
Johnson, and Bryant 1974), and current evidence indicates that only 3
to 5 percent of instructional time may be spent in cooperative learning
(Wang and Walberg 1983).

*The research indicates that achievement will be higher when learning situa-
tions are structured cooperatively rather than competitively or individualistically.
There are a number of factors, however, that may mediate the relationship
between cooperation and achievement.* While the type of task may not
matter a great deal, the internal processes that promote higher
achievement in cooperative learning groups may include the promotion of high-quality reasoning strategies, the constructive management of conflict over ideas and conclusions, increased time-on-task,
more elaborative information processing, greater peer support and
regulation, more active mutual involvement in learning, beneficial
interaction between students of different achievement levels, and
increased liking by group members for each other and the learning
situation. In addition, the implications of these results for teachers
interested in using cooperative learning procedures are as follows:

1. Cooperative procedures may be used successfully with any type of academic task, although the greater the conceptual learning required the greater the efficacy of cooperation will tend to be.

2. Whenever possible, cooperative groups should be structured so that controversy among group members is possible and managed constructively.

3. Students should be encouraged to keep each other on task and discuss the assigned material in ways that ensure elaborative rehearsal and the use of higher level learning strategies.

4. Students should be encouraged to support each other's efforts to achieve, regulate each other's task-related efforts, provide each other with feedback, and ensure that all group members are verbally involved in the learning process.

5. As a rule, cooperative groups should contain low-, medium-, and high-ability students.

6. Positive relationships among group members should be encouraged.

In addition, our research indicates that cooperative learning experiences, compared with competitive and individualistic ones, promote greater competencies in critical thinking, more positive attitudes toward the subject areas being studied, and greater perceptions of the grading system being fair. The key to solving our "quality of labor force" crisis may be to substantially increase the amount of time students learn cooperatively while they are in school.

We have enriched our theorizing and research by simultaneously training teachers throughout the United States and in several other countries to use cooperative learning procedures effectively. The fact that the procedures necessary for teachers to use the three goal structures appropriately have been specified and field-tested in a variety of settings makes this kind of training possible. Our inquiry highlights the current discrepancy between what educators commonly do and what our current level of knowledge about effective instruction recommends. We need to reconcile school practice with current research, and encourage a healthy portion of learning to be cooperative.

Table 6.1
Summaries of Characteristics of Studies

Characteristics	Johnson, Johnson, Anderson 1976[1]	Johnson, Johnson, Scott 1978[2]	Johnson, Johnson 1979[3]	Garibaldi 1979[4]	Johnson, Johnson, Skon 1979[5]	Johnson, Johnson, Tauer 1979[6]
				Studies		
Length of study	17 days	50 days	3 days	1 day	6 days	5 days
Grade level	5	5, 6	5	10, 11, 12	1	4, 5, 6
Subject area	Basic skills; language	Mathematics	Drill-review; problem solving; knowledge acquisition; knowledge retention	Mathematics; English	Mathematics; reading	Geometry
Group size	4	4	4, 5	2	3	4, 5
Type of heterogeneity	Sex; ability (high, medium, low)	Sex; ability (high, average, low)	Sex	Sample all black; public/private schools; social class (lower, working, middle)	Sex; mathematics and reading ability (high, average, low)	Sex; ability (high, medium, low)
Length of instructional session	45-60 minutes	60 minutes	60 minutes	60 minutes	40 minutes	60 minutes
Sample size	30	30	66	92	64	69
Conditions	Cooperative; individualistic	Cooperative; individualistic	Cooperative; competitive; individualistic	Cooperative; inter-group competition; individualistic; interpersonal competition	Cooperative; competitive; individualistic	Cooperative; competitive; individualistic
Achievement results*	Mixed	Mixed	Coop. > Ind. & Comp.	Coop. > Ind. & Comp.	Coop. > Ind. & Comp.	Coop. > Comp. > Ind.
Handicap Type	—	—	—	—	—	—
Achievement	—	—	—	—	—	—
Gifted achievement	—	—	—	—	—	—
Time-on-task	—	—	—	—	—	—
References						

*+ means cooperation significantly higher; 0 means no difference; — means no data on this variable.

References

1. David W. Johnson, Roger T. Johnson, Jeanette Johnson, and Douglas Anderson, "The Effects of Cooperative vs. Individualized Instruction on Student Prosocial Behavior, Attitudes toward Learning, and Achievement," *Journal of Educational Psychology* 68 (August 1976): 446-52.
2. David W. Johnson, Roger T. Johnson and Linda Scott, "The Effects of Cooperative and Individualized Instruction on Student Attitudes and Achievement," *Journal of Social Psychology* 104 (April 1978): 207-216.
3. David W. Johnson and Roger T. Johnson, "Conflict in the Classroom: Controversy and Learning," *Review of Educational Research* 49 (Winter 1979): 51-70.
4. Antoine Garibaldi, "The Affective Contributions of Cooperative and Group Goal Structures," *Journal of Educational Psychology* 71 (December 1979): 788-95.
5. David W. Johnson, Roger T. Johnson, and Linda Skon, "Student Achievement on Different Types of Tasks under Cooperative, Competitive, and Individualistic Conditions," *Contemporary Educational Psychology* 4 (April 1979): 99-106.
6. David W. Johnson, Roger T. Johnson, and Maureen Tauer, "Effects of Cooperative, Competitive, and Individualistic Goal Structures on Students' Achievement and Attitudes," *Journal of Psychology* 102 (July 1979): 191-98.

Characteristics	Martino, Johnson, 1979 [7]	Johnson, Skon, Johnson 1980 [8]	Armstrong, Johnson, Balow 1981 [9]	Lowry, Johnson 1981 [10]	Smith, Johnson, Johnson 1981 [11]	Skon, Johnson, Johnson 1981 [12]
				Studies		
Length of study	9 days	6 days	17 days	10 days	10 days	3 days
Grade level	2, 3	1	4, 5	5, 6	6	1
Subject area	Swimming	Mathematics, spatial reasoning; categorization and retrieval	Reading; vocabulary development	Social Studies; science	Social Studies; science	Categorization and retrieval; language acquisition; mathematical reasoning
Group size	2	3	3, 4	4	4	3
Type of heterogeneity	Sex; ability (normal progress, learning disabled)	Sex; ability (high, medium, low)	Sex; ability (learning disabled, nonhandicapped)	Class membership; sex; ability (high, and low reading)	Sex; ability (high, medium, low)	Sex; ability (high, medium, low)
Length of instructional session	60 minutes	60 minutes	90 minutes	60 minutes	65 minutes	45 minutes
Sample size	12	45	40	80	84	86
Conditions	Cooperative; individualistic; nonhandicapped vs. handicapped	Cooperative; competitive; individualistic; gifted	Cooperative; individualistic; learning disabled vs. normal progress	Controversy; concurrence seeking	1. Controversy, concurrence, individual; 2. High, medium, low ability	1. Cooperative, competitive, individualistic; 2. High, medium, low ability; 3. Homogeneous vs. heterogeneous groups

Table 6.1
Summaries of Characteristics of Studies (continued)

Characteristics	Martino, Johnson, 1979[7]	Johnson, Skon, Johnson 1980[8]	Armstrong, Johnson, Balow 1981[9]	Lowry, Johnson 1981[10]	Smith, Johnson, Johnson 1981[11]	Skon, Johnson, Johnson 1981[12]
				Studies		
Achievement results	Coop. > Ind.	Coop. > Comp. & Ind.	Coop. > Ind.	Contro. > Concurrence seeking	Contro. > Concurrence seeking & Ind.	Coop. > Comp. & Ind.
Handicap						
Type	Learning disabled	—	Learning disabled	—	Learning disabled	Learning disabled
Achievement	+	—	+	—	+	+
Gifted achievement	—	+	—	—	+	+
Time-on-task	—	—	—	—	—	—

References

7. Linda Martino and David W. Johnson, "Cooperative and Individualistic Experiences among Disabled and Normal Children," *Journal of Social Psychology* 107 (April 1979): 177-83.

8. David W. Johnson, Linda Skon, and Roger T. Johnson, "The Effects of Cooperative, Competitive, and Individualistic Conditions on Children's Problem-solving Performance," *American Educational Research Journal* 17 (Spring 1980): 83-93.

9. Barbara Armstrong, David W. Johnson, and Bruce Balow, "Effects of Cooperative versus Individualistic Learning Experiences on Interpersonal Attraction between Learning-disabled and Normal-progress Elementary School Students," *Contemporary Educational Psychology* 6 (April 1981): 102-9.

10. Nancy Lowry and David W. Johnson, "The Effects of Controversy on Students' Epistemic Curiosity, Achievement, and Attitudes," *Journal of Social Psychology* 115 (October 1981): 31-43.

11. Karl Smith, David W. Johnson, and Roger T. Johnson, "Can Conflict Be Constructive? Controversy versus Concurrence Seeking in Learning Groups," *Journal of Educational Psychology* 73 (October 1981): 651-63.

12. Linda Skon, David W. Johnson, and Roger T. Johnson, "Cooperative Peer Interaction versus Individual Competition and Individualistic Efforts: Effects on the Acquisition of Cognitive Reasoning Strategies," *Journal of Educational Psychology* 73 (February 1981): 83-92

		Studies				
Characteristics	Humphreys, Johnson Johnson 1982[13]	Nevins, Johnson, Johnson 1982[14]				Johnson, Johnson 1982[15]
		Study 1	Study 2	Study 3	Study 4	
Length of study	30 days	30 days	20 days	17 days	9 months	16 days
Grade level	9	1	7	9	1	11
Subject area	Physical Science	Reading	Mathematics	Mathematics	Social Studies	Mathematics
Group size	4	3	3	3	3	4
Type of heterogeneity	Sex	Sex; ability (high, medium, low)	Sex	Sex; handicapped vs. nonhandicapped	Sex; ability (high, medium, low)	Sex; handicap: severe learning and behavior problems, EMR; ability (high, medium, low)
Length of instructional session	60 minutes	30 minutes	15 minutes	44 minutes	50 minutes	55 minutes
Sample size	44	23	11	16	22	31
Conditions	Cooperative; competitive; individualistic	Cooperative; individualistic	Cooperative; individualistic	Cooperative; individualistic	Cooperative; individualistic	1. Cooperative; individualistic 2. Nonhandicapped, handicapped
Achievement results	Coop. > Ind. > Comp.	Coop. > Ind.	Coop. > Ind.	Coop. > Ind.	Coop. > Ind.	Coop. > Ind.
Handicap Type	—	Learning disabled	Learning disabled	Learning disabled	Learning disabled	EMR: severe learning and behavior problems
Achievement	—	+	+	+	+	+
Gifted achievement	—	—	—	—	—	—
Time-on-task	—	—	—	—	—	+

References

13. Barbara Humphreys, Roger T. Johnson, and David W. Johnson, "Effects of Cooperative, Competitive, and Individualistic Learning on Students' Achievement in Science Class," *Journal of Research in Science Teaching* 19 (May 1982): 351-56.

14. Ann Nevin, David W. Johnson, and Roger T. Johnson, "Effects of Group and Individual Contingencies on Academic Performance and Social Relations of Special Needs Students," *Journal of Social Psychology* 116 (February 1982): 41-59.

15. David W. Johnson and Roger Johnson, "The Effects of Cooperative and Individualistic Instruction on Handicapped and Nonhandicapped Students," *The Journal of Social Psychology* 118 (1982): 257-258.

Table 6.1

Summaries of Characteristics of Studies (continued)

Characteristics	Johnson, Johnson, DeWeerdt, Lyons, Zaidman 1983 [16]	Johnson, Johnson, Roy, Zaidman 1985 [17]	Johnson, Bjorkland, Krotee 1984 [18]	Johnson, Johnson 1984 [19]	Johnson, Johnson 1985 [20]
Length of study	10 days	15 days	6 days	15 days	15 days
Grade level	7	4	University students	4	3
Subject area	Science	Social studies	Golf skill of putting	Social Studies, Science	Mathematics
Group size	4	4	4	4	3
Type of heterogeneity	Handicap: severely functionally handicapped, autistic; sex; ability (high, medium, low)	Sex; ability (high, medium, low); handicapped, class ethnic membership	Physical ability (high, medium low)	Learning disabled; social class; ability (high, medium, low)	Hearing-deaf
Length of instructional session	40 minutes	55 minutes	45 minutes	55 minutes	55 minutes
Sample size	48	48	115	48	30
Conditions	Cooperative; individualistic	1. Cooperative; individualistic 2. High, medium, low ability	Cooperative; competitive; individualistic	1. Cooperative; individualistic 2. Handicapped vs. nonhandicapped	Cooperative; individualistic

Achievement	N.S.	Coop. > Ind.	Coop. > Comp. > Ind.	Coop. > Ind.	N.S.
Handicap Type	Severely adaptively handicapped, autistic	Learning disabled		Emotionally disturbed, learning disabled	Hearing impaired
Achievement	—	+	—	+	0
Gifted achievement	—	0	—	—	—
Time-on-task	—	0	—	0	—

+ means cooperation significantly higher; 0 means no difference

16. Roger T. Johnson, David W. Johnson, Nancy DeWeerdt, Virginia Lyons, and Brian Zaidman, "Integrating Severely Adaptively Handicapped Seventh-grade Students into Constructive Relationships with Nonhandicapped Peers in Science Class," *American Journal of Mental Deficiency* 87, no. 6 (1983): 611-18.

17. David W. Johnson, Roger T. Johnson, Patricia Roy, and Brian Zaidman, "Oral Interaction in Cooperative Learning Groups: Speaking, Listening, and the Nature of Statements Made by High-, Medium-, and Low-achieving Students," unpublished manuscript, University of Minnesota, 1983.

18. Roger T. Johnson, Robert Bjorkland, and March Krotee, "The Effects of Cooperative, Competitive, and Individualistic Students Interaction Patterns on Achievement and Attitudes on the Golf Skill of Putting," *Research Quarterly for Exercise and Sport*, in press.

19. David W. Johnson and Roger Johnson, "Building Acceptance of Differences between Handicapped and Nonhandicapped Students: The Effects of Cooperative and Individualistic Instruction," *Journal of Social Psychology* 122 (April 1984): 257–267.

20. David W. Johnson and Roger T. Johnson, "Mainstreaming Hearing-impaired Students: The Effect of Effort in Communicating on Cooperation and Interpersonal Attraction," unpublished manuscript, University of Minnesota, 1983.

REFERENCES

Becker, Gary. *Human Capital*. Chicago: University of Chicago Press, 1975.
Berman, Paul, and McLaughlin, Milbrey. *Federal Programs Supporting Educational Change, vol. 8: Implementing and Sustaining Innovations*. Santa Monica, Calif.: Rand Corporation, 1978.
Deutsch, Morton. "A Theory of Cooperation and Competition." *Human Relations* 2 (1949): 129-52.
Deutsch, Morton. "Cooperation and Trust: Some Theoretical Notes." In *Nebraska Symposium on Motivation*, edited by Marshall R. Jones. Lincoln, Neb.: University of Nebraska Press, 1962, pp. 275-320.
Deutsch, Morton. "A Critical Review of Equity Theory: An Alternative Perspective on the Social Psychology of Justice." *International Journal of Group Tensions* 9 (1979): 20-49.
Garibaldi, Antoine. "The Affective Contributions of Cooperative and Group Goal Structures." *Journal of Educational Psychology* 71 (December 1979): 788-95.
Gunderson, Barbara, and Johnson, David W. "Building Positive Attitudes by Using Cooperative Learning Groups." *Foreign Language Annals* 13 (1980): 39-46.
Johnson, David W. *The Social Psychology of Education*. New York: Holt, Rinehart & Winston, 1970.
Johnson, David W. *Educational Psychology*. Englewood Cliffs, N. J.: Prentice-Hall, 1979.
Johnson, David W. "Group Processes: Influences of Student-Student Interactions on School Outcomes." In *Social Psychology of School Learning*, edited by James McMillan. New York: Academic Press, 1980.
Johnson, David W. "Student-Student Interaction: The Neglected Variable in Education." *Educational Researcher* 10 (January 1981): 5-10.
Johnson, David W., and Ahlgren, Andrew. "Relationship between Students' Attitudes about Cooperative Learning and Competition and Attitudes toward Schooling." *Journal of Educational Psychology* 68 (February 1976): 92-102.
Johnson, David W., and Johnson, Frank P. *Joining Together: Group Theory and Group Skills*, 2d ed. Englewood Cliffs, N.J.: Prentice-Hall, 1982.
Johnson, David W., and Johnson, Roger T. "Instructional Structure: Cooperative, Competitive, or Individualistic." *Review of Educational Research* 44 (Spring 1974): 213-40.
Johnson, David W., and Johnson, Roger T. *Learning Together and Alone: Cooperation, Competition, and Individualization*. Englewood Cliffs, N.J.: Prentice-Hall, 1975.
Johnson, David W., and Johnson, Roger T. "Students' Perceptions of and Preferences for Cooperative and Competitive Learning Experiences." *Perceptual and Motor Skills* 42 (June 1976): 989-90.
Johnson, David W., and Johnson, Roger T. "Conflict in the Classroom: Controversy and Learning." *Review of Educational Research* 49 (Winter 1979): 51-70.
Johnson, David W., and Johnson, Roger T. "Effects of Cooperative and Individualistic Learning Experiences on Interethnic Interaction." *Journal of Educational Psychology* 73 (June 1981): 444-49.
Johnson, David W., and Johnson, Roger T. "The Socialization and Achievement

Crises: Are Cooperative Learning Experiences the Solution?" In *Applied Social Psychology Annual 4*, edited by Leonard Bickman. Beverly Hills, Calif.: Sage Publications, 1983.

Johnson, David W.; Johnson, Roger T.; and Anderson, Douglas. "Student Cooperative, Competitive, and Individualistic Attitudes and Attitudes toward Schooling." *Journal of Psychology* 100 (November 1978): 183-99.

Johnson, David W.; Johnson, Roger T.; Johnson, Jeanette; and Anderson, Douglas. "The Effects of Cooperative vs. Individualized Instruction on Student Prosocial Behavior, Attitudes toward Learning, and Achievement." *Journal of Educational Psychology* 68 (August 1976): 446-52.

Johnson, David W.; Johnson, Roger T.; and Maruyama, Geoffrey. "Interdependence and Interpersonal Attraction among Heterogeneous and Homogeneous Individuals: A Theoretical Formulation and a Meta-analysis of the Research." *Review of Educational Research* 53 (Spring 1983): 5-54.

Johnson, David W.; Maruyama, Geoffrey; Johnson, Roger T.; Nelson, Deborah; and Skon, Linda. "Effects of Cooperative, Competitive, and Individualistic Goal Structures on Achievement: A Meta-analysis." *Psychological Bulletin* 89 (January 1981): 47-62.

Johnson, David W.; Skon, Linda; and Johnson, Roger T. "The Effects of Cooperative, Competitive, and Individualistic Conditions on Children's Problem-Solving Performance." *American Educational Research Journal* 17 (Spring 1980): 83-93.

Johnson, Roger T. "The Relationship between Cooperation and Inquiry in Science Classrooms." *Journal of Research in Science Teaching* 13 (January 1976): 55-63.

Johnson, Roger T., and Johnson, David W. "What Research Says about Student-Student Interaction in Science Classrooms." In *Education in the 80's: Science*, edited by Mary B. Rowe. Washington, D.C.: National Education Association, 1982, pp. 25-37.

Johnson, Roger T.; Johnson, David W.; and Bryant, Brenda. "Cooperation and Competition in the Classroom." *Elementary School Journal* 74 (December 1974): 172-81.

Lawrence, Gordon. *Patterns of Effective Inservice Education: A State of the Art Summary of Research on Materials and Procedures for Changing Teacher Behaviors in Inservice Education.* Tallahassee, Florida: Florida State Department of Education, 1974.

Lerner, Barbara. "The Minimum Competence Testing Movement: Social, Scientific, and Legal Implications." *American Psychologists* 36 (October 1981): 1057-66.

Lewin, Kurt. *A Dynamic Theory of Personality*. New York: McGraw-Hill, 1935.

Lowry, Nancy, and Johnson, David W. "The Effects of Controversy on Epistemic Curiosity, Achievement, and Attitudes." *Journal of Social Psychology* 115 (October 1981): 31-43.

Lyons, Virginia. "A Study of Elaborative Cognitive Processing as a Variable Mediating Achievement in Cooperative Learning Groups." Doct. dissertation, University of Minnesota, 1982.

McLaughlin, Milbrey, and Marsh, David D. "Staff Development and School Change." *Teachers College Record* 80 (September 1980): 69-94.

Roy, Patricia. "Analysis of Student Conversation in Cooperative Learning Groups." Master's thesis, University of Minnesota, 1982.

Schultz, Theodore. *Investing in People*. Berkeley, Calif.: University of California Press, 1981.

Skon, Linda; Johnson, David W.; and Johnson, Roger T. "Cooperative Peer Interaction versus Individual Competition and Individualistic Efforts: Effects on the Acquisition of Cognitive Reasoning Strategies." *Journal of Educational Psychology* 73 (February 1981): 83-92.

Smith, Karl; Johnson, David W.; and Johnson, Roger T. "Can Conflict Be Constructive: Controversy versus Concurrence Seeking in Learning Groups." *Journal of Educational Psychology* 73 (October 1981): 651-63.

Walberg, Herbert J. "Educational and Scientific Literacy." Mimeographed report, University of Illinois, 1982.

Wang, Margaret C., and Walberg, Herbert J. "Adaptive Instruction and Classroom Time." *American Educational Research Journal* 20 (Winter 1983): 601-26.

Wheeler, Ronald, and Ryan, Frank. "Effects of Cooperative and Competitive Environments on the Attitudes and Achievement of Elementary School Students Engaged in Social Studies Inquiry Activities." *Journal of Educational Psychology* 65 (December 1973): 402-7.

CHAPTER

7

Computer-Assisted Instruction

Sigmund Tobias

It is altogether fitting that computer-assisted instruction (CAI) is considered in a book devoted to adaptive education. The computational power of computers, their speed, flexibility, and ability to retrieve vast amounts of information rapidly have led to the expectation that the computer will be the ideal tool to implement adaptive instructional practices. The purpose of this chapter is to assess how close this promise has come to realization.

CAI has received an enormous impetus from the microcomputer boom. These machines are cheap, versatile, and attractive to students, teachers, and members of the educational establishment. In a brief history of microcomputers, Kinne (1982) notes that the birth of the microcomputer boom can be traced to January 1975 when the first advertisement for a microcomputer kit appeared. During the first months in which this kit was advertised firm orders were received for

Preparation of this paper was facilitated by a grant from the Basic Research Program of the Army Research Institute for the Behavioral and Social Sciences. The views and opinions expressed are those of the author and should not be construed as official, or as reflecting the views of the Department of the Army or the U.S. government.

what the manufacturer estimated were the first three years of production! The first computer store opened in July 1975 and by 1976 there were fifty-six such stores, and nearly five hundred by 1977. Fully assembled microcomputers were offered through a growing network of retail stores by 1977.

The total factory value of microcomputers in 1981 was $1.6 million, and by 1983 this figure had risen to an incredible $5.4 billion (Pollack 1983). Similarly impressive was the breakdown regarding potential buyers of microcomputers: 43 percent of these were bought by small business and government organizations, 25 percent by home users, 22 percent by major corporations, and 10 percent by educational institutions. Becker (1983a) surveyed a nationally representative sample of U.S. schools, and reported that 53 percent of all schools had at least one microcomputer. A greater percentage of secondary schools (grade six and up) were likely to have a microcomputer than were elementary schools, with 91 percent of the secondary schools with more than 1200 students having at least one microcomputer.

We are, then, at a critical juncture in the development of CAI. The microcomputer boom exerts a powerful pressure for utilization of this equipment for instruction. Unlike prior technological innovations in education, this pressure does not come solely from the top (that is, the educational and research establishment), but also from the consumers of educational services: students and their parents. In an open society such as ours it is very unlikely that such pressures can be resisted for very long.

A review such as the present one faces substantial problems caused by the activity in the field. Anything written about CAI becomes outdated very rapidly. The inevitable interval between the time this chaper was written and when it will be read suggests that some of the material will be obsolete, and that some new material will not have been reported here. The reader, therefore, is referred to contemporary CAI journals for newer developments.

CAI USE IN THE SCHOOLS

Surveys have indicated a substantial increase in the use of computers for instruction. Generally, however, these studies say little about how microcomputers are actually used in the schools. There are some preliminary investigations addressed to this question. Shavelson,

Winkler, Stasz, and Robyn (1983) examined the relationship among teachers' attitudes, their knowledge of computers, and subject matter, and the uses of microcomputers for instruction. In a survey of forty-three computer-using school districts, Shavelson et al. sought to interview a total of sixty teachers expert in the use of computers for instruction. Computer literacy was so low that ten to fifteen districts would have to be visited in order to find sixty expert teachers in CAI. "The burden of meeting national goals of computer literacy in CAI is placed squarely on the shoulders of a very small, overworked cadre of teachers" (Shavelson et al. 1983, p. 2). Preliminary results indicated that most computer applications consisted of drill and practice, with few examples of more sophisticated uses. Many teachers who successfully used CAI tended to be removed from classes and assigned to administrative responsibilities.

Becker (1983b) surveyed a representative sample of schools about their computer use. He found that elementary schools reported use of computers for one or more of the following purposes: 64 percent introduction to computers, 59 percent drill and practice, 47 percent programming, 41 percent tutoring, 27 percent problem solving, 24 percent recreational games, 20 percent demonstrations, laboratories, and simulations, and only 3 percent for student text editing. Secondary schools reported the following usage: 85 percent for introduction to computers, 76 percent for programming, 31 percent drill and practice, 29 percent business and vocational education, 29 percent problem solving, 22 percent demonstrations and laboratory simulations, 20 percent tutoring, 19 percent recreational games, 15 percent record keeping, and 7 percent student text editing.

Becker (1983b) also surveyed schools regarding whether microcomputers were used more or less than anticipated for instruction in programming; among the elementary schools, 26 percent reported less and 25 percent more use than anticipated. With respect to drill and practice, 35 percent of the elementary schools reported less and 21 percent more use than anticipated. Similarly, in secondary schools programming use was reported by 11 percent of the schools as being less and by 15 percent as more than expected: drill and practice was reported to be less than expected by 34 percent of the schools, with 13 percent reporting it to be more than expected. Becker also found that in the first three years of acquiring microcomputers both elementary and secondary schools increased their use of the machines for programming. In secondary schools, CAI drill and practice decreased over the first three years; such use remained relatively stable in the elementary schools.

Kull and Archambault (1983) surveyed 559 Schools of Education regarding instruction in computer literacy. Courses stressing CAI development and software evaluation were reported by 19 percent, and 15 percent reported teaching only CAI developments. The Schools of Education reported teaching the following computer languages: BASIC (43 percent), BASIC and LOGO (25 percent), BASIC, LOGO, and PILOT (12 percent), and only LOGO (4 percent). In analyzing differences between the bulk of the respondents and 100 schools that answered the survey later, Kull and Archambault found a 40 percent increase in institutions reporting summer institutes in computer literacy. The microcomputer boom has evidently resulted in a secondary boom in computer literacy courses, institutes, and workshops.

The studies reported above suggest that more rigorous investigations of the uses to which computers are actually put in the schools are needed. The surveys document a major need for instructing teachers in more effective uses of computers. Bork (1983) reports his impression that "courses for teachers are generally very poor, except in a very few selected areas of the country, and print materials available to help teachers are weak. . . . I have looked at a variety of these courses. I can report that in many ways the almost blind lead the blind. Regional and national conferences for teachers are almost as bad in terms of the quality of assistance available" (p. 18). Bork goes on to suggest that it may be necessary to implement computer literacy programs for teachers on microcomputers to assure quality control.

These studies suggest a different criterion for the effectiveness of teacher literacy courses. Rather than merely offering the usual post-test and attitude measures, surveys of computer use could be conducted before and after such courses. One would hope that effective courses will lead to increases in the variety, flexibility, and imaginativeness with which computers are used and a decrease in using them merely as electronic page turners.

DRILL AND PRACTICE

In drill and practice CAI basic instruction is received off the machine, and computers are used only to monitor student practice. As indicated above this is the predominant CAI mode in contemporary education. Drill and practice programs are available from a variety of vendors, including the manufacturers of most microcomputers, and from many organizations that develop courseware. In addition, numerous drill and practice programs are prepared locally by individual teachers or by curriculum development groups.

Representative examples of drill and practice materials include programs to monitor students' arithmetic computation, multiple-choice vocabulary building exercises, drills to help students recall important historical dates and events, and practice in finding geographical locations. In some cases these programs adapt to students by adjusting the difficulty of the drill provided to the students' prior work. That is, students who have been doing well receive more difficult materials, and those with lower performance get easier exercises. Content adaptations may also include giving students extra practice with material on which they experience special difficulties. In other cases drill and practice programs may consist of little more than conventional multiple-choice questions presented by computer.

Shavelson et al. (1983), Bork (1982), and others report widespread dissatisfaction with the quality of existing drill and practice software. This dissatisfaction can probably be attributed to the fact that school administrators who purchased computers for CAI are under some pressure to demonstrate rapid instructional uses for them. Since drill and practice materials are easy to program and widely available, they are an expedient solution to the problem of demonstrating instructional use of recently acquired equipment.

The most widely publicized use of CAI in the 1960s and 1970s consisted of time-shared drill and practice materials in different parts of the United States supplied from a large computer at Stanford University (Suppes and Morningstar 1972). A commercial offshoot of that project still supplies such materials from a locally housed mini-computer system connected to a variable number of terminals. These materials have recently been evaluated by Ragosta, Holland, and Jamison (1982). It is probably safe to estimate that a great majority of the drill and practice programs used in schools are either locally generated or supplied by commercial vendors. Typically, these materials are unaccompanied by evaluative data of any kind. This should be a source of concern to both educators and CAI professionals.

TUTORIAL SYSTEMS

An important influence in present-day CAI is the development of intelligent tutoring systems. In general, such systems "abandoned one of CAI's early objectives, namely that of providing total courses, and have concentrated on building systems which provide supportive environments for more limited topics" (Sleeman and Brown 1982, p. 8). The degree to which tutorial systems adapt to students varies with the particular implementation. Tutorial systems in general can adapt instruction to students by determining from the data accumulated in students' prior performance the type of material to be presented, its difficulty, and the rate of presentation. Intelligent tutoring systems perform some of the following functions: (a) problem-solving monitors, (b) laboratory instructors, and (c) consultants. They have been implemented in areas such as electronic troubleshooting (Brown, Burton, and de Kleer 1982), medical diagnosis (Clancey 1982), program debugging (Miller 1982; Soloway, Rubin, Woolf, Bonar, and Johnson 1982) as well as in a number of mathematical fields. Some of these systems will be briefly reviewed here. The interested reader is referred to Sleeman and Brown (1982) for more detailed descriptions.

Burton's DEBUGGY

In some tutorial systems, instructional adaptations depend on accurate diagnosis of students' misconceptions. Brown and Burton (1978) proposed that student errors in mathematics may not be random, but rather a systematic application of a misconception or "bug." Such bugs may occur when students delete part of the correct procedure, add incorrect procedures, or replace correct procedures with incorrect ones. A similar conception guided the work of Stevens, Collins, and Goldin (1982), who demonstrated that sixteen bugs accounted for 58 to 72 percent of student errors in their responses to a human tutor's questions. Matz (1982) suggested that in algebra errors were the result of unsuccessful but reasonable attempts to adapt previously acquired knowledge to a new situation. Burton (1982) developed a computer-based system to detect subtraction errors, called DEBUGGY in an off-line version and IDEBUGGY in an interactive form.

The system is based on a set of hypotheses that include 110 primitive and about 20 compound bugs. When the 130 bugs are compared with students' answers an initial set of hypotheses is generated containing any bug that explains at least one wrong answer to an arithmetic test. Each bug is then classified, and when successfully identified, a student's incorrect answers can be reproduced perfectly. In the off-line version, the results of the diagnostic process are printed out. The interactive version, IDEBUGGY, has not been used as extensively as the off-line version. It presents the opportunity to examine hypotheses regarding a bug by presenting arithmetic problems specifically designed to test for that particular bug. Difficulties in generating a correct diagnosis can thus be overcome to some extent by generating problems to test hypotheses until the incorrect ones can be discarded.

In an evaluation and extension of the DEBUGGY programs, Vanlehn (1981) found that experts differed more from one another's diagnosis of bugs than they differed from that made by DEBUGGY. Vanlehn reported that 34 percent of the errors made by students in several samples could *not* be diagnosed by DEBUGGY. It was also found that the pattern of bugs was generally not stable over time. In two reliability studies, only 12 percent of the students had similar bugs on two tests given a few days apart. Long-term reliability data were similarly unstable. Efforts to improve the consistency of diagnoses are continuing.

PLATO and TICCIT Systems

Two of the better known tutorial CAI systems are Project PLATO (Program Logic for Automatic Teaching Operations) and the TICCIT (Time Shared, Interactive Computer-Control Information Television) system. PLATO, initially developed at the University of Illinois (Bitzer and Skaperdas 1971), is in wide use at various universities, and through the Control Data Corporation also offers a wide variety of courses for training in business and industry. PLATO operates in time-shared modes from a main frame computer that may be located some distance from the site at which instruction is offered. TICCIT (Stetten 1971) operates from two locally housed minicomputers to which up to 128 terminals can be connected.

A large variety of courseware is available on PLATO. In some cases this courseware was prepared by instructors interested in using the system, and in others it was prepared centrally. In general, PLATO courseware is not based on one coherent instructional model, and may consist of a whole course or of segments to be used in a variety of courses. TICCIT courseware, on the other hand, is composed of complete courses and follows a consistent design with a heavy emphasis on both learner control of instruction and a concept-learning paradigm offering rules, examples, and practice. TICCIT courses are offered at community colleges for credit in areas such as algebra and English.

A later section of this chapter will be concerned with the evaluations of CAI in general. Since PLATO and TICCIT have already been described it is probably most effective to summarize evaluative data concerning these projects here. An evaluation of both projects at community colleges (Alderman, Appel, and Murphy 1978) indicated few significant differences in achievement between PLATO and control classes taught by the same instructor without PLATO. There was substantial variation in the number of hours students spent on the PLATO system, ranging from less than one to more than twenty hours. Instructors were given the freedom to decide the time their students would have on PLATO leading to the variable use. Finally, student attrition was slightly lower in PLATO classes than in controls.

A similar evaluation of TICCIT (Alderman, Appel, and Murphy 1978) indicated that in mathematics there was a significant difference of approximately 10 percent favoring TICCIT classes compared to controls. While the results for English classes were not as dramatic, TICCIT courses also appeared to yield higher achievement there. Student reactions to TICCIT were generally positive, although when compared to classroom instruction, attitudes to TICCIT were generally somewhat lower and student attrition was significantly higher than in control classes. Specifically, the average rate of completion for mathematics courses was only 16 percent for TICCIT classes compared to 50 percent for lecture sections. In English, 55 percent of the students completed TICCIT classes, compared to 66 percent for lecture-discussion sections. Analysis of the data indicated that these results were not attributable to student dropout; instead, "students stayed with the TICCIT program but simply failed to complete all the lessons required in order to earn college credit" (p. 43).

The results of these evaluations suggest that when students spent the time on these tutorial systems considered necessary by the instructional designers, achievement results were quite positive. Provisions to monitor student work on these tutorial systems were clearly required to improve the rate with which students completed their work.

DIALOGUE SYSTEMS

In dialogue systems students can interact with computers in a natural language format relatively free of constraints in vocabulary or symbols. The development of such systems poses an important challenge to CAI. Dialogue systems, of course, are interactive; at present they are generally *not* capable of planning ahead for student-system exchanges involving more than one or two steps. Further developments depend on advances in artificial intelligence research so that computers can recognize the "meaning" of student communications, and respond in equally meaningful units. When fully implemented, dialogue systems will be capable of adaptive instruction in the sense that the instructional content will depend largely on system-student interaction, which is, of course, likely to vary from student to student. Some representative dialogue systems will be described here to give a sense of present developments in this area. Other systems are described in the *Proceedings of the National Conference on Artificial Intelligence* (American Association for Artificial Intelligence 1982).

ARGOT is a long-term research project with the ultimate objective of describing a mechanism that can participate in an extended English dialogue on a reasonably well-specified range of topics (Allen, Frisch, and Litman 1982). The aim of the project was to create a dialogue system that would serve as a computer operator. ARGOT is divided into many subsystems that run concurrently. One subsystem, the "task-goal" reasoner, recognizes goals, such as mounting tapes, reading files, and so forth. Another subsystem, the "communicative goal" reasoner, recognizes goals such as introducing a topic, clarifying or elaborating on previous utterances, and modifying the current topic. The third subsystem, the "linguistic reasoner," provides input that reflects the content of the utterances to the other subsystems. Each of the subsystems is intended to perform both recognition of communications and generation of actions responding to them, although the generative side of the system is not currently implemented. At present the system is capable of playing the role of computer operator in fairly extended dialogues.

The UNIX Consultant (Wilensky 1982) is an intelligent natural language system that allows naive computer users to communicate with the UNIX operating system. UNIX is a flexible time-sharing system operating on a variety of large machines (Kernighan and Morgan 1982), which users address with a prespecified vocabulary set. The UNIX Consultant attempts to allow users to communicate with UNIX in ordinary English; it is currently capable of handling simple dialogues. Two major components of the program include PHRAN (PHRasal ANalyzer), the routine designed to understand natural language, and PHRED (PHRasal English Diction), which handles natural language production. One of the primary design goals of PHRAN was that it could easily be extended to new linguistic forms and domains. Applying PHRAN to UNIX was, then, a test of PHRAN's versatility in addition to being a useful application. Once the representation of a new form has been agreed upon, it takes only a few minutes to extend PHRAN to a new area. PHRAN currently understands requests regarding twenty-five substantially different topics, each in a different linguistic format.

The development of KAMP (short for Knowledge and Modalities Planner) is a first step in planning natural-language utterances that allow the satisfaction of multiple goals in a single utterance (Appelt 1982). The system also plans utterances tailored to the knowledge of the hearer as well as to the context of the discourse, and provides for the integration of physical and linguistic actions. KAMP is organized to plan a hierarchy of linguistic actions. Locutionary acts (such as informing, requesting, promising, and thanking) are at the highest level. Surface speech acts (command, ask, and declare) are one level below. Concept activation (propositional acts) forms the next level, and utterances form the lowest level. KAMP is based on the logic that before a speaker can make a request, it must be determined whether the hearer has enough knowledge to carry the request out, or whether the hearer can form a plan for acquiring the knowledge. If the hearer can do neither of these, the speaker must furnish the knowledge to enable the hearer to carry out the requested action. Currently, KAMP is capable only of simple dialogue consisting of one or two steps.

Dialogue systems depend upon a number of subsidiary systems in order to engage in effective two-way communication. These subsystems fall into two major categories: (a) generation systems and (b) translation systems.

Generation Systems

Luria (1982) developed a program that answers questions about stories. The program looks down a causal chain (furnished by another program designed to understand stories) and figures out in what part of the chain the answer to the question may be found. An answer expresser uses general rules of expression to determine how to make an answer understandable, informative, and interesting. Presently the program is not connected to a language parser or to a language generator. The questions and answers are translated from conceptual form by hand.

McDonald and Conklin (1982) developed a simple technique for planning the generation of natural language texts that describe photographs of natural scenes. Input to the system consists of a simulation of the output from a visual computer recognition system. A planner determines the order in which objects will be mentioned in the text and what will be said about them by judging their "salience" or relative importance. The decision about which objects to leave out is handled by defining a cut-off salience rating below which objects are ignored. This information is then fed to a generator. At present, the salience-based planner has been implemented and its connection to the text generator simulated by hand. The program was developed to produce short paragraphs describing photographs of houses. Representations of house scenes are presently hand-simulated, and the planner works from a data base of objects in the scene and the spatial relations between them.

Translation Systems

These systems act as subsidiary routines in dialogue systems for the purpose of translating utterances into communications understood by the computer system. Grover (1982) has developed a model for dealing with temporal phenomena in English. The processing scheme is based on the information and operations shown to exist in a communication by linguistic analysis. The model is presently incomplete, but key portions of it have been implemented in a PASCAL program.

Hirst and Charniak (1982) described two cooperating mechanisms that are intended to disambiguate word senses and search for connections between concepts in order to define satisfying meanings. The system has two components: a "marker passer" finds connections between concepts in a system of frames, and another subsystem provides a protocol for negotiation between ambiguous words and cases. These cooperating mechanisms allow linguistic and word knowledge to be unified, frequently eliminating the need to use inference in word disambiguation. At present, both subsystems exist only in prototype form.

EVALUATIONS OF CAI

There are a number of research reviews of the effects of CAI. Vinsonhaler and Bass (1972) reviewed the results of ten independent studies using drill and practice CAI and found that elementary school children generally had performance gains of one to eight months compared to controls. Jamison, Suppes, and Wells (1974) reviewed the effects of a variety of instructional media. They concluded that there was evidence for increased achievement when CAI was used to augment regular instruction at the elementary school level; this effect was particularly marked for disadvantaged students. These reviewers also concluded that CAI resulted in substantial savings of student time at secondary and college levels, and was at least as effective as alternative instructional modes.

A number of investigators applied meta-analysis in their reviews of CAI effects. Hartley (1978) reviewed the effects of CAI on mathematics in elementary and secondary schools. She reported that CAI raised student achievement by .41 standard deviation, which is equivalent to raising the achievement of these students from the 50th to the 60th percentile. CAI was found to be less effective than peer tutoring, and more effective than either individual learning packets or programmed instruction.

Edwards, Norton, Taylor, Weiss, and Dusseldorp (1975) reviewed the literature on CAI effectiveness and concluded that when CAI supplemented instruction it was more effective than normal instruction alone. On the other hand, when CAI was substituted for traditional instruction 45 percent of the studies showed greater achievement gains by CAI students, 40 percent found little or no difference, while 15 percent showed mixed results. Edwards et al. suggested that the available evidence prevented the conclusion that one CAI mode was more effective than others. They also concluded that, in general, CAI was more effective than other nontraditional instructional methods. All the studies reviewed indicated that students took less time to learn via CAI than from other instructional methods. Finally, it was noted that there was some evidence that retention was not as high for CAI students compared to control groups.

Burns and Bozeman (1981) also conducted a meta-analysis of studies comparing the effectiveness of CAI and control instruction in mathematics in elementary and secondary schools. They found that when instruction was supplemented with either drill and practice or tutorial CAI, achievement was significantly increased. Elementary school students gained somewhat more from drill and practice than secondary students, and the opposite pattern existed for tutorial CAI. Burns and Bozeman also reported that the tutorial had a somewhat stronger effect than did drill and practice. Drill and practice was effective for students at all ability levels, except for those in the average range. Tutorial CAI was found to be more effective for all ability levels than control conditions.

Kulik, Kulik, and Cohen (1980) used meta-analysis to review the effectiveness of CAI for college teaching. They concluded that CAI increased the achievement scores of college students by approximately .25 standard deviation. Kulik, Bangert, and Williams (1983) also conducted a meta-analysis of the effects of CAI on secondary school students. They found CAI to be generally more effective than comparison modes. An interesting aspect of this analysis was that students exposed to drill and practice apparently gained less than those using the tutorial materials, and that simulation had stronger effects than the tutorial mode. These reviewers also reported that CAI apparently had its strongest effects with low-ability students, followed in order by those with middle and high ability. In eight of ten studies reporting attitudinal data, reactions to CAI were more positive than to control classes, although the effect sizes were small. In two of the studies reporting data on the amount of time taken, CAI was found to be much more efficient.

In general, these reviews indicate that all modes of CAI are effective in raising the achievement of students compared to controls. Where available, results indicated that simulations had the biggest effect, followed by tutorial applications and by drill and practice. CAI generally took less time than comparable modes. It was also suggested that CAI was somewhat more effective at secondary and elementary levels than at college levels. The data with respect to student ability were inconsistent, although several reviews and meta-analyses found an inverse relationship between effect size and ability level.

Some CAI systems have interesting attributes deserving a longer description. In addition to their intrinsic interest these systems incorporate state of the art CAI attributes and serve as milestones for future CAI developments. Two systems to be described are the WEST Coach and Project STEAMER.

The WEST Coach

Computer-assisted coaches have many of the features of other tutorial systems. In view of the implementation of these programs in informal learning environments, the term "coach," originated by Goldstein (1982), appeared more congenial than "tutor" (Burton and Brown 1982). The WEST program was developed by Burton and Brown to help students play a game on the PLATO system. The game, developed by Bonnie Anderson in Robert Davis's Elementary Mathematics Project (Dugdale and Kibbey 1977), was intended to give students monitored practice with a variety of mathematical operations in a game-like atmosphere. A coaching program was needed since most students using the game utilized elementary operations such as addition and subtraction rather than gaining experience with more complex operations.

The PLATO version of WEST simulated a board game requiring players to travel in a series of moves. The number of spaces for each move were determined by digits on three "spinners" supplied from a random numbers generator. Players could combine these three digits by using any legitimate mathematical operation including exponentiation, or by using negative numbers, parentheses, and so forth. The game also has such features as short cuts to the goal; opportunities to "bump" opponents, forcing them to return to the beginning; and spaces "safe" from bumping. Typically students play against the machine, although two students can play against each other.

The domain for coaching is determined by differences between the moves actually made by a student and what an expert would regard as more optimal moves, a segment of the WEST program. The coaching system was developed around a set of "issues" composed of the skills and concepts students were expected to master. An "issue recognizer" monitors students' behavior for evidence that particular concepts or skills are used correctly and to construct a model of students' behavior. An "issue evaluator" knows how to use various parts of the model to determine if the student is weak in that issue. Issues are arranged in three levels, the lowest consisting of the basic mathematical operations. The second level consists of skills needed to play the game, such as bumping an opponent, the direction of a move, since both forward and backward moves are legal, and so forth. The third level deals with general game-playing skills, such as monitoring opponent's moves.

At the start of the game the program determines the areas in which players could profit from coaching. A "speaker" component of the program produces explanations attached to each issue for presentation to the student when they occur during the game. Another question addressed by the program is, When should students playing the game be interrupted so that they are most likely to profit from coaching? There are some self-evident occasions, such as when students ask for help. Others are less clear cut, since it is important to minimize guidance so that students can enjoy the fun of playing the game. A pedagogical subprogram addresses these questions.

The pedagogical component is based on a number of underlying principles, the most basic of which is that "it is best for the student to discover for himself as much of the structure of a situation as possible. . . . Many human tutors interrupt far too often, generally because of a lack of time or patience" (p. 89). Some of the principles embodied in the program include: the coach will offer an alternative move only when its outcome is dramatically superior to the students' move; the student is allowed to repeat a turn if a better move is offered; tutoring is not suggested on two consecutive moves; and if students make an exceptionally good move they are congratulated. If a student is losing consistently, the level of play will be adjusted by providing the computer with poorer spinner numbers than students receive to equate the quality of play. These pedagogical principles were based on practical experiences with a variety of tutoring environments.

A comparison between coached and uncoached students indicated that the coached group used more elaborate combinations of mathematical operations than controls, and that they also employed a greater percentage of special moves. Some students also commented that the "coach" manifested a good understanding of their weaknesses. Students in the coached group also commented that they "enjoyed playing the game considerably more than the uncoached group" (p. 98).

An interesting innovation in this program is the incorporation of the expert-novice distinction—the subject of much contemporary research in instructional psychology. Adaptation to student differences occurs by ascertaining students' present status and expert performance. The objective for different students, then, becomes advancing them to become expert in playing the game.

Project STEAMER

In this project the propulsion system of a ship is simulated so that trainees can get lifelike experience operating various system components (Stevens et al. 1981). The effects of these operations on changes in plant parameters, including pressures, temperature, and fluid flows, are shown. System components are displayed in animated colored diagrams that can be manipulated by the student, for example, observing the effect of opening a valve on the flow of fluid in that part of the subsystem. The animation unambiguously shows how the components responsible for a change in the system relate to other components or to prior changes. The simulation includes all elements of the propulsion system, including fuel, combustion, water resistance, drag factors, speed, and so forth. All the important valves and pipes required by the propulsion system are included. Students can view each of the major system components on one of two displays and can also obtain a cross-section view.

The system includes an explanation generator to describe how components work, a set of explanations for basic principles in physics, as well as other descriptions providing guidance on operations procedures. New devices can be added to the system by specifying their connections to existing components, and by supplying text and graphics for the new equipment. The advantage of systems such as STEAMER is that they provide learning environments ordinarily inaccessible to students.

The mathematical model for STEAMER is so powerful that students can symbolically rearrange equipment, such as valves and pipes, in a manner different from that existing within the system, or aboard any ship. Rather than merely simulating the existing system the mathematical model can be extrapolated to determine outcomes of combinations of equipment that do not exist in the system. Such usage permits designing a new system, and testing whether it will actually operate.

Project STEAMER suggests an advanced use of computers combining design, simulation, and extrapolation of the model that has very powerful significance for CAI. At advanced levels students can, by the use of such a model, not only master simulations of the existing systems but innovate and create new systems at the terminal after having mastered the fundamentals of the particular areas of knowledge. In this way, computers provide students with a tool with which they can actually conduct investigations at the frontiers of knowledge without requiring the enormous development expense and resources such an effort would ordinarily require. Use of computers in such a mode can result in learning that has an element of excitement that is missing in more traditional instructional modes.

DISCUSSION

The microcomputer boom has intensified interest in CAI. While computer professionals and some educators have advocated CAI for over twenty years, the present differs from the past in important ways. Formerly CAI was hardly visible in most schools. A number of demonstration projects received publicity in the technical and popular media, but equipment for CAI was unavailable in the overwhelming majority of schools. This situation has changed dramatically. Most school systems are purchasing microcomputers, and developments are proceeding so rapidly that many systems cannot supply accurate data on the number of computers presently utilized for CAI. In addition, some parents, some students, and some teachers have developed a good deal of interest in CAI. Finally, most individuals in contemporary society have some first-hand contact with computers at work, at play, and in ever-increasing numbers in the home. These factors combine to create a situation in which computers will be an increasing presence in the schools and will be used for both instruction and other tasks whether schools are ready for them or not.

The ways in which computers are presently used raises some concern. Surveys indicate that the predominant use of CAI is for drill and practice, for instruction in programming, and to give a general introduction to computers. Tutorial CAI is rare and there is little use of the equipment for text processing, which would surely be a useful application in composition courses at all levels. Becker (1983a) reported that many schools report less use of drill and practice CAI than originally anticipated. Whether this reduction is due to student boredom, teacher disenchantment, or use of the equipment for other purposes is unclear.

Other than use for instruction in programming, the surveys of CAI use suggest that the equipment is used for the type of instruction that could have been implemented just as well without computers (Montague 1982). Such CAI use raises the possibility that students may become bored with the equipment once the Hawthorne effect wears off. Since computers are assuming such a dominant role in society, ultimately more imaginative and flexible CAI applications will become more widely available in the schools. At that time students who have become disenchanted with lock-step CAI modes may have to be induced back to CAI, which they initially turned to with such excitement.

It should be noted that a multiyear evaluation of drill-and-practice CAI conducted by Ragosta, Holland, and Jamison (1982) produced little evidence of the Hawthorne effect. It may not be accidental that the CAI programs used in that evaluation adapt the difficulty of the problems presented to the students' achievement on the materials. Such adaptation, rare in programs sold by vendors or those generated by teachers and local school systems, may make drill and practice programs more challenging and interesting to students and reduce potential Hawthorne effects.

Instructional adaptations in various CAI modes occur mainly in terms of the instructional content, and its rate. In most modes in which adaptive instruction occurs the program determines what should be taught to the student by reviewing the outcomes of prior trials, or by examining the other aspects of the interaction with students. There is little adaptation of the method of instruction; once the content is identified, all students learn the material pretty much in the same way. Scientifically based adaptations of the method of instruction require a body of knowledge composed of replicated interactions between characteristics on which students differ, and various instructional methods. This area of research, called aptitude-treatment interaction (ATI), has unfortunately not advanced sufficiently to permit such research-based adaptations. Consideration of the problems in ATI research is beyond the scope of the present chapter. For a thorough discussion of the content and methodological problems in this area, interested readers may refer to Cronbach and Snow (1977) and to Tobias (1976, 1981, 1982).

The infrequent use of tutorial CAI is probably attributable to a number of factors. Imaginative programs such as the WEST tutor require more complex systems and more core storage than is available in most microcomputers in schools. The WEST coach program, for example, presently requires about 1,000,000 bytes of core storage. It seems certain that programs such as these will become more accessible to schools as the cost of core storage keeps decreasing and progress in programming languages makes it possible to execute such routines more efficiently.

It is also of concern that there are frequent reports of little integration of CAI into the total school curriculum. Even imaginative CAI programs can have little impact on the attainment of the school's objectives unless they are a part of the total instructional system. School personnel are complaining, apparently with some justice, about the poor quality of CAI software. Failure to integrate existing software into the overall instructional system raises questions regarding whether better software will do much to advance student attainment of the school's objectives.

The somewhat chaotic state of CAI in today's schools is attributable in part to the microcomputer boom and the speed with which such equipment is being introduced into schools. If schools are not ready to employ computers effectively, they will have to learn to do so rapidly, since there is no sign of a letup in the microcomputer boom. A national clearinghouse that would evaluate existing CAI courseware, much the way commercially available tests are evaluated (Buros 1978), appears urgently needed to assist schools in the selection of useful CAI programs.

Several other major developments are required in order to hasten the advent of effective educational CAI. First, and perhaps most important, is raising computer literacy among teachers. Computer literacy courses for teachers are increasing dramatically, although their quality is apparently variable. Computer literacy often takes the form of instructing teachers in a programming language, frequently BASIC. It is questionable whether this is the most effective way of promoting CAI. Even if some teachers become relatively proficient programmers they are likely to prepare drill and practice courseware, since a very high level of programming skill is required for the preparation of tutorial programs such as those described above. However, there is little need for more drill and practice materials, especially since it is unlikely that the average teacher will turn out material that is markedly superior to that presently available.

This discussion suggests that alternative goals for computer literacy programs in schools are urgently needed. It seems important to educate teachers and other school personnel so that available equipment will be used more imaginatively. Ideally, such courses should suggest that CAI is most effectively used to deliver the kind of instruction that cannot be done as well by other means, specifically using simulations and more sophisticated tutorial systems. The results of the Kulik et al. (1983) meta-analyses indicated that increases in student achievement were greater for tutorial and simulation CAI than for drill and practice. It can be hypothesized that, unlike drill and practice, simulations can be done more effectively with CAI than by other instructional strategies. In simulations the computational power of the computer can be combined with its ability both to display and react adaptively to students' prior responses. While most simulations will not be as powerful as those of STEAMER, they nonetheless are an ideal use of CAI. A further objective of computer literacy courses could be to educate school people in the principles of instructional systems design. Such instruction may enable them to determine the suitability of courseware for specific curricular objectives and make educators more capable of integrating CAI into the overall instructional system.

The flexibility and power of tutorial and coaching programs such as WEST, BUGGY, and STEAMER obviously have exciting potentials for CAI. Such programs are innovative in conception and implementation, and they provide hope for more imaginative CAI. WEST contains a representation of the knowledge and type of responses an expert would make. When expert knowledge is represented in the program, the domain in which instruction is to occur can easily be defined by the gap between students' knowledge and that of the expert. Instruction can be skipped in areas in which the student's knowledge is similar to that of the expert and can be focused on those segments where the gap between students and experts is large. Representation of expert knowledge also permits instructional designers to concentrate on the strategies used by the expert, as distinguished from knowledge alone, and those employed by students. Instruction in both strategic tactics and knowledge is obviously more useful than either alone. Representing experts in tutorial programs, therefore, enables instruction more nearly to approximate the interaction between an expert tutor and a novice student than was heretofore possible. This conception should have an important impact in improving tutorial CAI.

It should be noted, however, that the most innovative tutorial CAI implementations have been in areas where the content domain is relatively tightly circumscribed, or as Burton and Brown (1982) indicate, constitute closed systems. When the content domain can be precisely defined, it becomes possible to prepare flexible CAI systems. The precise domain definition limits the content of student machine exchanges and hence makes such interactions more manageable. In the last ten years we have seen many exciting examples of such developments, and we can hope for other implementations where the domain in which the instruction is to occur can be specifically defined.

Substantial progress has also occurred in the artificial intelligence area and in the development of dialogue systems. In these systems the content domain is not precisely specified, and much work remains to be done to enable computers to engage in effective two-way dialogue with students. The various dialogue systems described above indicate that hopes in these areas are high, but most present implementations are far from satisfactory to developers and users alike. Plans for effective dialogue systems abound, but in most cases are imperfectly or partially implemented at present. Since there is considerable research activity in artificial intelligence, developments in this field are likely to be rapid, and important breakthroughs can be expected in the next few years.

If tutorial systems such as those described above become rapidly and widely available in the near future, and dialogue systems begin to make their appearance, the problems of integrating these modes into the school curriculum remain. Few people would suggest that computers will replace teachers, hence the equipment will have to be accommodated into the existing school system. Such accommodation requires an informed and receptive environment so that the machines can be effectively used. Thus, making progress on technical problems in developing tutorial and dialogue systems should, hopefully, be accompanied by similar progress in improving the effectiveness with which computers are used in schools. Such a joint effort is required to make it possible for CAI to attain its promise of providing effective adaptive instruction in the schools.

REFERENCES

Alderman, Donald L.; Appel, Lola Rhea; and Murphy, Richard T. "PLATO and TICCIT: An Evaluation of CAI in the Community College." *Educational Technology* 18 (April 1978): 4-45.

Allen, James F.; Frisch, Alan M.; and Litman, Diane J. "ARGOT: The Rochester Dialogue System." In *Proceedings of the National Conference on Artificial Intelligence,* Pittsburgh, August 1982. Pittsburgh, Pa.: American Association for Artificial Intelligence, 1982.

American Association for Artificial Intelligence. *Proceedings of the National Conference on Artificial Intelligence,* Pittsburgh, Pa., 1982.

Appelt, Douglas E. "Planning Natural-Language Utterances." In *Proceedings of the National Conference on Artificial Intelligence,* Pittsburgh, August 1982. Pittsburgh, Pa.: American Association for Artificial Intelligence, 1982.

Becker, Henry J. "How Are Schools Using Microcomputers? First Report from a National Survey." Paper presented at the Annual Meeting of the American Educational Research Association, Montreal, April, 1983. (a)

Becker, Henry J. *School Uses of Microcomputers,* Issue No. 3. Baltimore, Md.: Center for Social Organization of Schools, Johns Hopkins University, October 1983. (b)

Bitzer, Donald L., and Skaperdas, D. "The Design of Economically Viable Large-scale Computer-based Education." In *Computers in Institutions: Their Future for Higher Education,* edited by Roger E. Levien. Santa Monica, Calif.: Rand Corporation, 1971.

Bork, Alfred. "The Fourth Revolution: Computers and Learning." In *The Computer: Extension of the Human Mind, Conference Proceedings,* July 1982. Eugene, Ore.: College of Education, University of Oregon, 1982. Pp. 12-29.

Bork, Alfred. "Computer-based Learning in the Schools: The Two Major Problems." *Educational Computer Magazine* 18, no. 1 (1983): 18.

Brown, John S., and Burton, Richard R. "Dignostic Models for Procedural Bugs in Basic Mathematical Skills." *Cognitive Science* 2 (April-June 1978): 155-92.

Brown, John S.; Burton, Richard R.; and deKleer, Johan. "Pedagogical, Natural Language, and Knowledge Engineering Techniques in SOPHIE I, II, III." In *Intelligent Tutoring Systems,* edited by D.H. Sleeman and John S. Brown. New York: Academic Press, 1982.

Burns, Patricia K., and Bozeman, W.C. "Computer-Assisted Instruction and Mathematics Achievement: Is There a Relationship?" *Educational Technology* 21 (October 1981): 32-39.

Buros, Oscar, editor. *Eighth Mental Measurements Yearbook.* Highland Park, N.J.: Gryphon Press, 1978.

Burton, Richard R. "Diagnosing Bugs in a Simple Procedural Skill." In *Intelligent*

Tutoring Systems, edited by D. H. Sleeman and John S. Brown. New York: Academic Press, 1982.

Burton, Richard R., and Brown, John S. "An Investigation of Computer Coaching for Informal Learning Activities." In *Intelligent Tutoring Systems*, edited by D. H. Sleeman and John S. Brown. New York: Academic Press, 1982.

Clancey, William J. "Tutoring Rules for Guiding a Case Method Dialogue." In *Intelligent Tutoring Systems*, edited by D. H. Sleeman and John S. Brown. New York: Academic Press, 1982.

Cronbach, Lee J., and Snow, Richard E. *Aptitudes and Instructional Methods: A Handbook for Research on Interactions*. New York: Irvington, 1977.

Dugdale, Sharon, and Kibbey, David. *Elementary Mathematics with PLATO*. Urbana, Ill.: Computer-Based Education Research Laboratory, University of Illinois, July 1977.

Edwards, Judith; Norton, Shirley; Taylor, Sandra; Weiss, Martha; and Van Dusseldorp, Ralph. "How Effective is CAI? A Review of the Research." *Educational Leadership* 33 (November 1975): 147-53.

Goldstein, Ira. "The Genetic Graph: A Representation for the Evolution of Procedural Knowledge." In *Intelligent Tutoring Systems*, edited by D. H. Sleeman and John S. Brown. New York: Academic Press, 1982.

Grover, Mark D. "A Synthetic Approach to Temporal Information Processing." In *Proceedings of the National Conference on Artificial Intelligence*, Pittsburgh, August 1982. Pittsburgh, Pa.: American Association for Artificial Intelligence, 1982.

Hartley, Susan S. "Meta-analysis of the Effects of Individually Paced Instruction in Mathematics." Doct. dissertation, University of Colorado, 1977. *Dissertation Abstracts International* 38 (1978): 4003.

Hirst, Graeme, and Charniak, Eugene. "Word Sense and Case Slot Disambiguation." In *Proceedings of the National Conference on Artificial Intelligence*, Pittsburgh, August 1982. Pittsburgh, Pa.: American Association for Artificial Intelligence, 1982.

Jamison, Dean; Suppes, Patrick; and Wells, Stuart. "The Effectiveness of Alternative Instructional Media: A Survey." *Review of Educational Research* 44 (Winter 1974): 1-67.

Kernighan, Brian W., and Morgan, Samuel P. "The UNIX Operating System: A Model for Software Design," *Science* 215 (February 12, 1982): 799-83.

Kinne, Harold C. "The Microcomputer Revolution." In *The Computer: Extension of the Human Mind, Conference Proceedings*, July 1982. Eugene, Ore.: College of Education, University of Oregon, 1982. Pp. 86-90.

Kulik, James A.; Bangert, Robert L.; and Williams, George W. "Effects of Computer-based Teaching on Secondary School Students." *Journal of Educational Psychology* 75 (February 1983): 19-26.

Kulik, James A.; Kulik, Chen-Lin C.; and Cohen, Peter A. "Effectiveness of Computer-based College Teaching: A Meta-analysis of Findings." *Review of Educational Research* 50 (Winter 1980): 525-44.

Kull, Judith A., and Archambault, Francis K., Jr. "A Survey of Teacher Preparation in Computer Education." Paper presented at the annual meeting of the American Educational Research Association, Montreal, April 1983.

Luria, Marc. "Dividing Up the Question Answering Process." In *Proceedings of the National Conference on Artificial Intelligence*, Pittsburgh, August 1982. Pittsburgh, Pa.: American Association for Artificial Intelligence, 1982.

McDonald, David D., and Conklin, E. Jeffery. "Salience as a Simplifying Metaphor for Natural Language Generation." In *Proceedings of the National Conference on Artificial Intelligence*, Pittsburgh, August 1982. Pittsburgh, Pa.: American Association for Artificial Intelligence, 1982.

Matz, M. "Towards a Process Model for High School Algebra Errors." In *Intelligent Tutoring Systems*, edited by D. H. Sleeman and John S. Brown. New York: Academic Press, 1982.

Miller, Mark L. "A Structural Planning and Debugging Environment for Elementary Programming." In *Intelligent Tutoring Systems*, edited by D. H. Sleeman and John S. Brown. New York: Academic Press, 1982.

Montague, William E. "Analysis of Cognitive Processes in the Specification of Interactive Instructional Presentations for Computer-based Instruction." Paper presented at the annual meeting of the American Educational Research Association, New York, 1982.

Pollack, A. "Big IBM Has Done It Again," *New York Times*, 27 March 1983, pp. 1, 28.

Ragosta, Marjorie; Holland, P.W.; and Jamison, D. T. *Computer-Assisted Instruction and Compensatory Education: The ETS/LAUSD Study. Executive Summary and Policy Implications*. Report no. 20. Princeton, N.J.: Educational Testing Service, 1982.

Shavelson, Richard; Winkler John D.; Stasz, Cathleen; and Robyn, Abbey. *Teachers' Instructional Uses of Microcomputers*. Progress Report. Santa Monica, Calif.: Rand Corporation, 1983.

Sleeman, D. H., and Brown, John S., editors. *Intelligent Tutoring Systems*. New York: Academic Press, 1982.

Soloway, Elliot M.; Rubin, Eric; Woolf, Beverly; Bonar, Jeffrey; and Johnson, Lewis W. *MENO-II: An AI-based Programming Tutor*. Report no. 258. New Haven, Ct.: Department of Computer Science, Yale University, 1982.

Stetten, Kenneth J. "The Technology of Small, Local Facilities for Instructional Use." In *Computers in Instruction: Their Future for Higher Education*, edited by Roger E. Levien. Santa Monica, Calif.: Rand Corporation, 1971.

Stevens, Albert; Collins, Allan; and Goldin, Sara E. "Misconceptions in Students' Understanding." In *Intelligent Tutoring Systems*, edited by D.H. Sleeman and John S. Brown. New York: Academic Press, 1982.

Stevens, Albert; Roberts, Bruce; Stead, Larry; Forbus, Kenneth; Steinberg, Cindy; and Smith, Brian. *STEAMER: Advanced Computer-aided Instruction in Propulsion Engineering*. Report no. 4702. Cambridge, Mass.: Bolt, Beranek and Newman, 1981.

Suppes, Patrick, and Morningstar, Mona. *Computer-assisted Instruction at Stanford, 1966-68: Data, Models, and Evaluation of the Arithmetic Programs*. New York: Academic Press, 1972.

Tobias, Sigmund. "Achievement Treatment Interactions." *Review of Educational Research* 46 (Winter 1976): 61-74.

Tobias, Sigmund. "Adaptation to Individual Differences." In *Psychology and Education: The State of the Union*, edited by Frank Farley and Neal Gordon. Berkeley, Calif.: McCutchan Publishing Corp., 1981.

Tobias, Sigmund. "When Do Instructional Methods Make a Difference?" *Educational Researcher* 11 (April 1982): 4-9.

Vanlehn, Kurt. *Bugs Are Not Enough: Empirical Studies of Bugs, Impasses, and Repairs in Procedural Skills.* Palo Alto, Calif.: Palo Alto Research Center, March 1981.

Visonhaler, John F., and Bass, Ronald K. "A Summary of Ten Major Studies on CAI Drill and Practice." *Educational Technology* 12 (July 1972): 29-32.

Wilensky, Robert. "Talking to UNIX in English: An Overview of UC." In *Proceedings of the National Conference on Artificial Intelligence*, Pittsburgh, August 1982. Pittsburgh, Pa.: American Association for Artificial Intelligence, 1982.

A Design for Improving Secondary Education

Herbert J. Klausmeier

The central aim of compulsory secondary education is to meet the educational needs of every student of school age and also to meet societal needs. In general, secondary schools have not made as much progress in achieving this aim as the public desires (National Commission on Excellence in Education 1983). This lack of progress is due to the fact that local schools have not developed their own improvement capability, that is, they have not developed means for systematically identifying areas of needed improvement and then planning and implementing related improvement programs from year to year.

The inability of local schools to improve their own educative processes has many causes. One difficulty is that the district office has no improvement capability and accordingly cannot provide leadership to the schools. Another obstacle is that local school staff members typically perceive their roles only as teachers, counselors, or administrators, not as members of a professional team working together to improve education in their school. Other deterrents are the lack of research-based knowledge regarding improvement processes and the continuation of ineffective organizational structures that resist change of any kind. At the same time, changes in the family, the school community, and society at large are making demands on education that are increasingly difficult to meet. In satisfying these increasing demands, a school must do more for individual students and in different ways than it did in the past.

To address the problem of improving secondary schooling, Klausmeier and Lipham planned and carried out a project during the period 1976-1983 that included research and the dissemination of materials. Lipham's research goal was to extend knowledge regarding the implementation of educational change, including the impact of educational leadership and the involvement of staff in educational decision making. He and his graduate students in educational administration conducted thirteen studies in over one hundred secondary schools across the nation. The findings from this research are included in chapters of a book (Klausmeier, Lipham, and Daresh 1983) and are also summarized in an article (Lipham 1983).

Klausmeier and his staff conducted improvement-oriented research with five schools. Prior to starting the research, Klausmeier formulated a design for the renewal and improvement of secondary education. The design was based on a synthesis of input from many practitioners and scholars associated with the Wisconsin Center for Education Research; research and theory regarding the improvement of secondary schooling; and research on learning, development, and instructional design, including that of Klausmeier (1980), Klausmeier and Allen (1978), and Klausmeier and Associates (1979). The design incorporates three improvement strategies and eight school structures and processes that facilitate implementation of the strategies. As a school becomes able to achieve desired student outcomes by implementing the strategies, it develops its own improvement capability.

The first draft of the design was reviewed by scholars and practitioners to secure their judgments regarding the extent to which it indicates desirable means and directions for improving secondary education. This draft was revised and then used in two studies in 1977-78. T. Klausmeier (1978) developed a questionnaire and a structured interview based directly on the design. The questionnaire was administered to the staffs of six middle schools and junior high schools across the nation, and a sample of each staff was interviewed. The schools, with enrollments ranging from 400 to 1400, were located in large cities, medium-size cities, or suburbs. Maier (1978) conducted a similar study with the staffs of four high schools of four states. Both Klausmeier and Maier found that the staff members believed that the processes described would result in markedly improved secondary education. Based on the results of these studies, minor revisions were made in the design. This revision provided the substantive framework for subsequently developing instructional materials that explain the design and how to implement it. The usability of the revised design and its effectiveness in the improvement of education were tested operationally through research conducted cooperatively with five schools.

The research was conducted as five intensive case studies over a period of four years. Steuben Middle School in Milwaukee, Wisconsin; Webster Transitional School in Cedarburg, Wisconsin; Carl Sandburg Junior High School in Mundelein, Illinois; Cedarburg High School in Cedarburg, Wisconsin; and Hood River Valley High School in Hood River Valley, Oregon, participated in the study. These schools are located in small-town, suburban, and large-city environments. The student enrollment of the schools ranged from 300 to 1400. It is assumed that findings that are common to the five schools are generalizable to other schools with these characteristics.

No two schools implemented the improvement strategies in an identical manner, made operational identical organizational structures, or used identical data-gathering instruments and procedures. Accordingly, the detailed results for each school are presented in a separate chapter of a monograph (Klausmeier, Serlin, and Zindler 1983). This chapter provides a concise summary for two schools to show what the research entailed. Less information is given for the other three schools. Before proceeding to the research procedures and results, we shall examine the main features of the design.

FEATURES OF THE DESIGN

The design is organized according to ten components of an effectively functioning secondary school. For each component there is a comprehensive objective that corresponds to a broad program objective. The enabling objectives for each comprehensive objective specify the means for achieving the comprehensive objective. Two sets of objectives are concerned with improvement strategies, and the other eight incorporate the school structures and processes that facilitate implementation of the strategies.

The three improvement strategies are called individual educational programming, individual instructional programming, and goal setting. Each strategy may be clarified by examining the kinds of improvement activities that were planned and carried out by the schools in implementing the strategy.

The *individual educational programming strategy* involves arranging an educational program of course work and other activities for each student each semester that satisfies the student's educational needs and learning characteristics and that also meets district and state requirements. The student and the student's advisor consider the student's needs and the requirements when planning the student's educational program, monitoring the student's progress, and evaluating the student's program at the end of the semester. To arrange an appropriate educational program in the academic subjects *for students achieving below expectancy*, the advisors took actions such as the following:

— Advising the student to take more academic courses.

— Advising the student to take more units of academic courses.

— Advising the student to take advanced rather than elementary academic courses.

— Advising the student to take advanced rather than elementary units of academic courses.

— Advising the student to spend more time at school and/or out of school on course-related activities.

— Encouraging the student to attend classes more regularly.

— Advising the student to spend less time on an out-of-school job and/or extracurricular activities and to take more courses and/or units of courses in the academic subjects.

Notice that the preceding activities were for *students achieving below expectancy in the academic subjects*. Other activities were carried out with other students. For example, changes were made as necessary in the curriculum, evaluation, and other school structures and processes to provide better educational programs for individual students.

The *individual instructional programming strategy* involves arranging an instructional program for each student in each course that takes into account the student's aptitudes, interests, motivation, learning styles, career goals, and other personal and social characteristics. This requires the teacher to plan and then carry out an appropriate instructional program for each of his or her students enrolled in each course. Normally, the student's programs are planned during the first two class meetings. This strategy does not imply only one-to-one instruction or only individual assignments. Rather, whole-class instruction, small-group activities, and individual activities are used by the teacher to take into account the individual student's characteristics, the nature of the subject matter, and the teacher's preferred use of methods and materials.

In providing effective instructional programs for individual students in the academic subjects, some teachers in all five schools carried out activities such as the following:

— Encouraging students to use the entire class period in active learning.

— Adapting the content and instructional materials to the student's capability for learning the particular course objectives.

— Using individual assignments, small-group work, and whole-class instruction to take into account each student's learning styles and interests and also the nature of the subject matter.

— Providing for out-of-class, course-related activities, including homework.

— Modeling enthusiasm for the subject matter and the students.

— Securing greater effort on the part of the students achieving below expectancy.

— Getting students of low motivation to take more initiative to learn.

— Providing encouragement and other social reinforcements, especially to the lower-achieving students.

The *goal-setting strategy* may be employed with individual students or with groups of students, such as those of one grade. The strategy involves evaluating the student's instructional program in each course, the student's educational program, and the school's total educational program and then using the results of the evaluation in setting improvement goals and planning and implementing related improvement activities. The goal-setting strategy for groups of students may be applied to any outcome of the school's educational program, including student achievement, attitudes, self-concepts, attendance, and discipline. Based on the evaluation results for the current year, the school staff sets goals for the following year and plans and carries out improvement activities to achieve the goals. To improve student achievement in a curricular area, the relevant staff sets a goal for a group of students, such as that of a grade, to attain the following year. The staff then plans and carries out improvement activities to attain the goal.

Setting a goal to maintain a satisfactory level of achievement or to raise an unsatisfactory level is a very powerful improvement strategy. After setting a goal to raise the mean achievement of the students of a grade, the school staffs of the present project carried out activities such as the following:

— Applying the individual instructional programming strategy in the existing courses.

— Applying the individual educational programming strategy to aid students in making better selections of existing courses.

— Increasing the amount of time allocated for instruction for all the students of the grade in the course or curricular area where achievement was low.

— Changing the content and objectives of the course or curricular area for all the students of the group where achievement was low.

— Requiring another course and/or a unit of an existing course to be taken by all the students in the subject field where achievement was low.

— Arranging for out-of-class instruction, for example, computer-assisted instruction during the school day, after-school study, and/or summer classes, mainly for students experiencing specific difficulties.

The preceding are only some of the activities directed toward *raising the mean achievement of the students of a grade;* other activities were also implemented. Furthermore, different activities were required to attain goals such as increasing attendance, developing more favorable attitudes toward learning, or building more positive self-concepts.

In addition to the preceding strategies, the design for the renewal and improvement of secondary education incorporates school structures and processes that facilitate the implementation of the strategies. These structures and processes were either already operational in the research schools or were started after the project began. A brief outline of the ten components, the strategies, and the organizational structures and processes follows.

The individual educational programming strategy and the individual instructional programming strategy are incorporated in Component 1 of the design because of their close relationship to one another.

Component 1: Educational Programming for the Individual Student

a. An *individual educational program* of course work and other activities is arranged for each student each semester that satisfies the student's developmental needs and characteristics and that also meets district and state requirements.

b. An *individual instructional program* that takes into account the student's aptitudes, interests, motivation, learning styles, career goals, and other personal and social characteristics is arranged for the student in each course and any other activity that is part of the student's total educational program.

Component 2: Curricular Arrangements

The curriculum is structured to meet state and district requirements, but it can be adapted by the school and individual teachers to take into account the differing educational needs of students.

Component 3: Experiential Learning and Career Education

Career education is arranged for all students; experiential-learning activities and work experience in the community are arranged for each student who can profit from them.

Component 4: Student Decision-Making Arrangements

Students progressively assume more responsibility for planning, implementing, and evaluating their programs and activities with a lesser amount of adult direction and control.

Component 5: Evaluation and Goal-setting Strategy

The individual student's progress toward attaining his or her course objectives, the student's instructional program in each course, the student's total educational program, and the school's total educational program are evaluated systematically, and the results of the evaluation are used in improving the educative processes of the school. (The goal-setting strategy is outlined in the enabling objectives.)

Component 6: Administrative Arrangements and Processes

The school's administrative arrangements provide for cooperative planning and shared decision making by the persons responsible for implementing the plans and decisions, mainly administrators, counselors, teachers, and students.

Component 7: Organization for Instruction and Student Advising

The faculty and students are organized into small groups that permit personalized instruction and advising.

Component 8: Home-School-Community Relations

Effective communication and cooperative educational efforts between the school and the community are carried out as part of a program of home-school-community relations.

Component 9: Internal and External Support Arrangements

The environment for learning and instruction in the school and for work and other educative experiences in the community is enriched through the intellectual, technical, and material support provided by school and school district groups, and by external agencies, such as the state education agency, intermediate education agencies, teacher-education institutions, and professional associations.

Component 10: Continuing Research and Development

Knowledge is extended regarding learning, instruction, school structures and processes, and other factors related to schooling through research and development conducted by school personnel and cooperating individuals and agencies.

OPERATIONAL VALIDATION OF THE DESIGN

The validation of the design required both development and research. The objective of the development was for each participating school to start or refine the three improvement strategies and to develop school structures and processes that would enable the school to implement the strategies. The research had four purposes. One was for each school to maintain a satisfactory level of student achievement from year to year or to raise an unsatisfactory level through implementation of the three improvement strategies. Maintaining or raising achievement in English, mathematics, and reading was a common concern of the five schools. A second purpose of the research was to determine the extent to which each school could carry out its own data collection and analysis and then plan and carry out improvement activities based on the results. A third objective was to relate the changes that occurred in student achievement from year to year to the implementation of the improvement strategies and to unanticipated events that occurred and that influenced student achievement. The fourth objective was to relate the organizational structures and processes of each school to its implementation of the strategies.

RESEARCH PROCEDURES

Each school gathered and analyzed data annually regarding student outcomes, including achievement in English, mathematics, and reading; student attitudes toward various aspects of schooling; and attendance. Some schools also collected other data that they desired, for example, other areas of student achievement, student self-concepts, and discipline referrals. The schools analyzed their information on achievement and mental ability for the students of each grade and in some cases for the students of each teaching team. An achievement profile, as well as a record of daily attendance, was available for each student. After the first year of data collection, the schools used the information to evaluate the effectiveness of their initial improvement activities and to plan and carry out other improvement activities the ensuing year. Project personnel provided consultation to the schools regarding the analysis and the interpretation of the data on student outcomes and, to a lesser extent, regarding their improvement activities.

Each school provided the project with information that was used in describing the school as it was functioning in 1977-78. The ten components of the design that were explained earlier were used in preparing the description. Each year thereafter each school provided the project information regarding its annual planned improvements that were designed to maintain or to raise student achievement or to improve any other student outcomes desired by the school. Two other kinds of information were provided to the project. One was the planned improvements that were not related to the selected student outcomes. The other was unanticipated events that occurred and that may have influenced achievement of the desired student outcomes.

After the last data collection, the achievement and mental ability information that each school collected on each student was analyzed by the project on both a cross-sectional and a longitudinal basis. Cedarburg High School was an exception to this pattern for reasons that are clarified in the discussion of the results for that school. In the cross-sectional analysis, the mean achievements of the students of the same grade in school across the four years were compared, for example, the means of the students of grade ten of 1977-78, 1978-79, 1979-80, and 1980-81. Analysis of covariance, with mental ability the covariate, made it possible to take into account differences in mental ability among the successive grades and between the males and females. Where differences among the means of the students of the successive grades were found to be significant at or beyond the .05 level, comparisons were made of the means of every pair of grades.

A longitudinal cohort consisted of a group of students who entered the first grade of a school, took all the tests, and remained through the last grade. For each cohort, repeated measures analysis of variance was used to identify three main effects: gain between times of testing, quarters in mental ability, and sex. Where a difference significant at or beyond the .05 level was found, comparisons were made of the mean gains between each time of testing. This analysis was performed for each cohort.

During the four years each school had two or three longitudinal cohorts whose achievement and gains in achievement were compared. Analysis of covariance, with mental ability the covariate, was performed to determine three main effects: cohort, gain, and sex. Analysis of covariance was used in order to take into account differences between the cohorts in mental ability and between the males and females in mental ability. Accordingly, the mean achievements of the quarters in mental ability of the different cohorts could not be compared. Although extensive analyses of the longitudinal data were made, the many findings regarding the gains in achievement made by each cohort, by the quarters in mental ability, and by the males and females are only summarized later in this chapter. The detailed findings for each school are reported in Klausmeier, Serlin, and Zindler (1983). Data regarding student attitudes and attendance were also analyzed, using descriptive statistics. Tests of statistical significance were not performed.

The last phase of the research method employed by the project director was to relate the changes in student outcomes that occurred from year to year to the planned improvements that were made and the unanticipated events that occurred. The schools' organizational structures and processes also were related to their implementation of the improvement strategies.

Effects of Implementing the Improvement Strategies on Student Achievement

The mean achievements of the students of each later grade were compared with those of each earlier grade in order to relate the changes in student achievement from year to year to the implementation of the improvement strategies and to the unanticipated events that occurred in each school. A significantly higher mean achievement by a later grade is interpreted as a positive effect of implementing the strategies, and a significantly lower achievement is regarded as a negative effect unless there was some unanticipated event that might have offset a positive effect. Similarly, a nonsignificant difference is regarded as neutral unless there was some unanticipated event that might have offset the positive results of implementing the improvement strategies.

Steuben Middle School (SMS)

SMS is an integrated urban school located in Milwaukee, Wisconsin. The racial composition of the student body from year to year is about 48 percent black, 10 percent Hispanic, 3 percent native American, and 39 percent white. The socioeconomic level of the student population qualifies SMS for ESEA Title I programs and services. The staff, administrators, and parents of SMS students have worked together since 1973 to effect the transition of the school from a traditional junior high school to a middle school.

The total enrollment in grades seven and eight was 751 in 1977-78, 830 in 1978-79, 851 in 1979-1980, and 874 in 1980-81. The grade six enrollment dropped from 92 to 36 during the four years as grade six was being phased out. For this reason the data for grade six were not analyzed.

In 1977-78, all of the SMS teachers of language, reading, mathematics, science, and social studies and the students were organized into Instructional and Advisory Units (I & A units) consisting of four academic teachers and about 120 students. Each team of four academic teachers had its 120 students for a block of time each day and provided the students instruction in language, mathematics, reading, science, and social studies.

The administrative arrangement employed at SMS to plan, monitor, and implement its research and improvement activities was an Instructional Improvement Committee that was formed in 1977-78. This committee consisted of the principal, the learning coordinator, and at least one teacher from each of its I & A units.

During the four years of the project, some changes were made in the administrative arrangements of the school. In 1978-79, a school research committee was formed from the membership of the Instructional Improvement Committee to review and interpret the annual test results. The department chair positions were eliminated in 1980-81 and their duties were assumed by the school's learning coordinator. Some of the I & A units were reorganized from year to year to take into account changes in enrollments in grades six, seven, and eight. The major staff change was the loss of six aides in 1980-81.

The individual instructional programming strategy was being implemented in the academic subjects in 1977-78, and it was refined each year thereafter. Individual educational programming was being implemented only informally in 1977-78 inasmuch as the same academic subjects were required of all students, and in these subjects individual instructional programming was being implemented. Starting in 1978-79 and continuing thereafter, the educational programs of only a few of the students were monitored and evaluated each semester. Goal setting, planning, and carrying out related improvement activities were started on a trial basis by three of the I & A unit teams in the second semester of 1978-79 and were made operational by all of the I & A teams in 1979-80 and 1980-81. Accordingly, individual instructional programming and goal setting were implemented quite fully for the first time in 1979-80, while individual educational programming was implemented to a much lesser extent and informally.

Mental ability scores were available for most of the students, based on administration of the Otis-Lennon Mental Ability Test when the students were in grade five. The Metropolitan Achievements Tests were administered in May of each year, starting in 1977-78. The results of this 1977-78 testing were not summarized and interpreted by the school staff until the first semester of the 1978-79 school year. Hence, only minor refinements were made in implementing the instructional programming strategy in the second semester of 1978-79. Accordingly, the grade seven and grade eight classes of 1978-79 did not experience any major planned improvement. However, a strong effort was made by the staff to raise the achievement in grades seven and eight in 1979-80, the year in which the goal-setting strategy was implemented for the first time in all of the I & A units.

Table 8.1 gives the comparison of the earlier and later grade seven and grade eight classes. To facilitate the interpretation of the results, the table shows whether the mean achievements of each grade of each later year were significantly higher at or beyond the .05 level (S+), significantly lower (S−), or not significantly different from the means of the same grade of each earlier year. Table 8.1 also gives the percentile that is equivalent to each mean. The size or amount of the difference between any two means that was found significant is indicated by the difference between the two respective percentiles. The voluminous tables giving the means, standard deviations, and tests of significance for each total grade, each sex, and each quarter in mental ability are reported in Klausmeier, Serlin, and Zindler (1982).

The means of the grade seven and grade eight classes in 1978-79 were significantly higher than those of the 1977-78 classes in two instances, significantly lower in one instance, and not significantly different in five instances. On the other hand, the means of the last two grade seven and grade eight classes were significantly higher than the means of one or both of the first two classes in seventeen instances and not significantly different in fifteen instances. For the mean differences that were significant, the equivalent percentile differences ranged from 5 to 14 for grade seven and from 5 to 10 for grade eight. These differences are regarded as of high practical significance with respect to the improvement of student achievement.

Table 8.1
Adjusted Means (ANCOVA) and Equivalent National Percentile Ranks for Successive Grade 7 and Grade 8 Classes: Steuben Middle School

	Comparisons of Successive Groups					
	1978-79 vs 1977-78	1979-80 vs 1977-78	1980-81 vs 1977-78	1979-80 vs 1978-79	1980-81 vs 1978-79	1980-81 vs 1979-80
Grade 7						
Reading Total	S−	NS	NS	S+	S+	NS
Language	S+	S+	S+	NS	S+	S+
Spelling	NS	NS	S+	NS	NS	NS
Math Total	NS	S+	S+	NS	S+	NS
Grade 8						
Reading Total	NS	NS	S+	NS	NS	S+
Language	NS	NS	S+	NS	S+	NS
Spelling	S+	S+	S+	NS	NS	NS
Math Total	NS	S+	S+	NS	S+	NS

	Adjusted Means and Equivalent Percentile Ranks							
	1977-78		1978-79		1979-80		1980-81	
	$\bar{X}$	%ile	$\bar{X}$	%ile	$\bar{X}$	%ile	$\bar{X}$	%ile
Grade 7								
Reading Total	43.44	34	39.92	29	42.66	34	43.11	34
Language	38.21	30	41.17	32	42.09	36	45.27	42
Spelling	26.17	40	27.31	44	26.74	44	27.69	48
Math Total	50.75	30	54.95	36	60.14	44	60.06	44
Average Student N	223		323		289		304	
Grade 8								
Reading Total	48.98	30	50.03	32	48.28	28	52.46	35
Language	44.66	30	45.37	30	46.77	32	48.08	34
Spelling	27.64	32	29.25	36	29.74	38	30.57	39
Math Total	60.45	32	62.53	34	65.43	36	68.38	42
Average Student N	228		237		267		224	

S+ The mean of the group of the later year was significantly higher than the mean of the group of the earlier year.
S− The mean of the group of the later year was significantly lower than the mean of the group of the earlier year.

Table 8.2
Adjusted Means and Differences Between Means
for Two PACE and Two Longitudinal Cohorts: CHS

	Cohort 1				Cohort 2		
	Gr. 9 77-78	Gr. 10 78-79	Gr. 11 79-80	Gr. 12 80-81	Gr. 9 78-79	Gr. 10 79-80	Gr. 11 80-81
Reading							
PACE	15.62	17.49	18.61	19.79	14.15	16.03	18.67
TRAD	13.37	15.39	15.70	16.93	14.11	15.82	17.75
Diff.	2.25	2.10	2.91	2.86	0.04	0.21	0.92
Language							
PACE	15.82	17.72	18.21	19.41	15.85	17.60	19.59
TRAD	13.19	15.18	15.54	16.01	14.95	16.48	18.45
Diff.	2.63	2.54	2.67	3.40	0.90	1.12	1.14
Math							
PACE	13.85	17.34	18.66	19.16	14.03	16.56	18.99
TRAD	12.76	14.98	15.11	16.24	12.93	14.96	16.61
Diff.	1.09	2.36	3.55	2.92	1.10	1.60	2.38
Student N			PACE	61		PACE	87
			TRAD	122		TRAD	130

These consistently positive results, starting in 1979-80, are attributable to the concurrent implementation of the goal-setting strategy and to providing better instructional programs for individual students. Based on these achievement test results and the information regarding the implementation of the improvement strategies and the school structures and processes, we conclude that the improvement capability of SMS was quite well established by the third year. It became even more effective in the fourth year.

Webster Transitional School (WTS)

WTS is the only middle school of the Cedarburg School District, Cedarburg, Wisconsin, a Milwaukee suburb. It enrolls students in grades six, seven, and eight. The students are Caucasian. The socio-economic level of the community is middle- and upper-middle class. The student enrollment was 761 in 1977-78, 711 in 1978-79, 686 in 1979-80, and 712 in 1980-81.

The organization for instruction and advising, the block-teaching arrangement, the required subject fields, the administrative arrangements for educational improvement, and the timing of the improvement strategies at WTS were similar to those of SMS. However, WTS formally implemented individual educational programming, and its testing program was different from SMS.

A locally constructed language arts test and a locally constructed mathematics test were administered to all the students each year in the fall, the spring, or both. Four scores from these tests were analyzed: parts of speech, sentences, language, and mathematics. The Gates-MacGinitie Tests of Reading, yielding a comprehension score and a vocabulary score, were administered only in the spring of each year. The Short Test of Educational Ability was administered in grade seven. The test scores of individual students were available for final analysis for grade six starting in 1977-78, grade seven in 1978-79, and grade eight in 1979-80. Accordingly, data were available for three grade six, three grade seven, and two grade eight classes as well as for two grade six, seven, and eight longitudinal cohorts.

The mean achievement of the grade six class in the spring of 1978-79 was significantly higher than that of the 1977-78 class in one comparison and not significantly different in the other. The mean achievements of the grade six and grade seven classes of 1979-80, the first year in which the goal-setting strategy was implemented, were significantly higher than the means of the prior classes in four instances and not significantly different in the other nine. The means of the grade seven and the grade eight classes of 1980-81 were significantly higher than the means of the prior classes in nineteen comparisons, significantly lower in three comparisons, all involving reading vocabulary, and not significantly different in the other two. The negative finding regarding reading vocabulary is related to a fundamental deficiency in the school district's language arts curriculum that extends from the primary school into the high school. Insufficient attention is given to reading vocabulary at all of the school levels; however, the middle school staff could not make the changes in the curriculum that were necessary to overcome the deficiency.

The consistently higher achievements by the later grade six and grade seven classes of 1979-80 and the later grade seven and grade eight classes of 1980-81 are attributable to the concurrent implementation of all three improvement strategies. Inasmuch as WTS was able to implement the strategies to achieve these desired student outcomes, we conclude that it has established a functional improvement capability.

Carl Sandburg Junior High School (CSJHS)

CSJHS enrolls students in grades seven and eight. It is the only junior high school in the Mundelein Elementary (K-8) School District, Mundelein, Illinois, a suburban district northwest of Chicago. The community consists mainly of white collar, middle-class Caucasians. The student enrollment of CSJHS was 380 in 1977-78, 346 in 1978-79, and 322 in 1979-80. The school changed its test battery in 1980-81 in accordance with a plan worked out by a district committee in 1977-78; therefore, data were not analyzed for 1980-81.

The organization for instruction and advising, the block-teaching arrangement, the required subject fields, the timing of the improvement strategies, and the pattern of IQ and standardized achievement testing of CSJHS were similar to those of SMS. However, there was no educational improvement committee at CSJHS. Instead, the principal and the teachers functioned as a principal-faculty committee.

The data were analyzed in the same manner as at SMS. The mean achievements of the 1978-79 grade seven and grade eight classes in reading total, language, spelling, mathematics computation, mathematics concepts, mathematics problem solving, and mathematics total were not significantly different from the means of the earlier 1977-78 classes in thirteen comparisons, and one later mean was significantly lower. On the other hand, the means of the 1979-80 classes were significantly higher than those of the two earlier years in fifteen comparisons and not significantly different in the other thirteen.

Six of the thirteen nonsignificant comparisons of the 1979-80 classes with the earlier classes involved grade eight language arts. The two grade eight English teachers were new to CSJHS and, therefore, new to the implementation of the improvement strategies. This probably contributed to the lack of significantly higher achievement.

The positive results for 1979-80 are attributed to more effective implementation of the individual instructional programming strategy and the concurrent implementation of the goal-setting strategy. Based on these positive effects of implementing the strategies and the information regarding the school structures and processes, we conclude that CSJHS had established an improvement capability that was functioning effectively in the third year.

Hood River Valley High School (HRVHS)

HRVHS enrolls students in grades ten, eleven, and twelve. It is the only high school in Hood River County, Oregon. The area is small town and rural. The economy is based on agriculture and forestry. The community is mainly middle-class, Caucasian, with a few families of Asian background. There is a considerable amount of transient labor. Student enrollment was 785 in 1977-78, 736 in 1978-79, 700 in 1979-80, and 607 in 1980-81.

The teachers of HRVHS were organized into broad fields. There were no departmental chairpersons. However, each broad field had a coordinator. Broad fields that had more than five teachers had at least one team leader in addition to the coordinator.

The administrative arrangement used to plan, monitor, and implement the improvement activities included two standing committees that were already functioning in 1977-78—a curriculum committee and a school cabinet. The curriculum committee consisted of the principal and seven elected teachers. The school cabinet consisted of the administrative team, five teachers, each of whom served as a coordinator of a broad curriculum field, and the IMC coordinator.

The administrative arrangement for the improvement activities did not change from year to year, nor did the broad fields arrangement. The loss in student enrollment was accompanied by a substantial reduction in the teaching staff in 1980–81.

In 1977–78 each teacher, administrator, and counselor served as an educational advisor, or guide, to approximately fifteen students. In implementing the individual educational programming strategy, these guides consulted with their advisees weekly or more often regarding which courses and units of courses to enroll in, but they did not evaluate the effectiveness of their advisees' educational programs at the end of the semester or year. To arrange more effective educational programs for students, the following changes were made:

— Starting a grade ten mathematics placement program in 1978-79.

— Requiring a semester course in English for all grade ten students instead of permitting English to be elective starting 1979-80.

— Increasing the attention given to reading in all the content subject fields starting in 1979-80.

— Advising all students regarding mathematics and English courses by mathematics and English teachers starting in 1980-81; requiring students to complete three successive units of a course with a grade of C or higher rather than only one starting in 1980-81; and increasing the requirements in the academic subjects for high school graduation and decreasing the electives and the "survival skills" requirements in 1980-81.

The preceding changes in the requirements for high school graduation did not apply to the grade twelve class of 1980-81.

Throughout the project the teachers arranged individual instructional programs for each student enrolled in their courses. Goal setting and planning and carrying out related improvement activities were started in 1979-80 and continued in 1980-81. Thus, all three strategies were implemented concurrently in the last two years.

The General Aptitude Test Battery was administered to the students when they were in grade 9 of junior high school. The Stanford Test of Academic Skills was administered annually in the spring to all students. The spring test results of 1977-78 were not summarized and interpreted until the first semester of the second school year, 1978-79. Accordingly, only minor improvements were made in the spring of 1978-79. Therefore, the changes in student achievement from the first to the second year do not reflect changes or refinements in the implementation of the improvement strategies.

The means of the 1978-79 grade ten, eleven, and twelve classes were not significantly different from the means of the 1977-78 classes in any of the three tested areas—English, mathematics, or reading. However, the means of the last two grade ten classes were significantly higher than the means of the first two classes in nine of twelve comparisons and not significantly different in the other three. The mean achievements of the last two grade eleven classes were significantly higher than those of the first two classes in five comparisons and not significantly different in the other seven. The means of the two later grade twelve classes were not significantly different from the means of the two prior grade twelve classes.

The higher achievements by grades ten and eleven are accounted for by the prior planned changes made for grade ten that were also made for grade eleven. The fact that the grade ten group achieved significantly higher in 1979-80 than in 1977-78 in all three subjects, while the grade eleven group did not until 1980-81, is accounted for in terms of which classes experienced the planned changes. For example, the grade eleven class of 1979-80 did not take the required English class when in grade ten but the 1980-81 grade eleven class did. On the other hand, the grade twelve class of 1980-81 did not experience the planned changes made in the curriculum, advising, and instruction when in grades ten and eleven that the grade ten and grade eleven classes of 1980-81 did.

The positive results for the grade ten and grade eleven classes are judged to have resulted from the planned changes made in connection with the concurrent implementation of the three improvement strategies, starting in 1979-80. Lack of significantly higher achievement by the last two grade twelve classes is presumed to have resulted because these grade twelve students did not experience the planned changes when in grades ten and eleven. Based on these findings and taking into account the information regarding the school structures and processes, we conclude that HRVHS had established an improvement capability in 1979-80 and continued it in 1980-81.

Cedarburg High School (CHS)

CHS enrolls students in grades nine through twelve. It is the only high school in the Cedarburg, Wisconsin, school district. Many Cedarburg residents work in Milwaukee, which is about 20 miles distant. There is some industry and farming in the district. The community is mainly white collar, middle- and upper-middle class, and Caucasian. The total enrollment of the school was 1376 in 1977-78, 1313 in 1978-79, 1279 in 1979-80, and 1214 in 1980-81.

As part of a district plan that started with the grade nine class of 1977-78, the teachers and students of Cedarburg High School were organized into one of three programs: a program for potential dropouts, a program called Progress in Alternative Continuous Education (PACE), or a traditional program that was continued from the prior year. The PACE alternative was the experimental one in which two of the improvement strategies were implemented. In 1977-78, there were 30 entering grade nine students in the program for potential dropouts,

99 in PACE, and 211 in the traditional program. All of the students in grades ten through twelve were already in the traditional program in 1977-78, and they continued in it.

The plan of the school district was to extend the PACE alternative upward by one grade each year as the first grade nine PACE group moved ahead, and to have a new grade nine PACE group start each year. However, the assistant principal, who was the coordinator of the PACE program, resigned at the end of the 1978-79 school year. After his resignation, the PACE program continued in grades nine and ten, but it was only partially extended into grade eleven in 1979-80 and even less into grade twelve in 1980-81. A district committee administered the PACE program during the last two years. A teacher employed on a half-time basis served as the coordinator.

Individual educational programming was implemented effectively with the first grade nine and grade ten PACE students during 1977-78 and 1978-79, and to a lesser extent with the grade eleven students in 1979-80 and 1980-81. Individual instructional programming was implemented for these grade nine and grade ten PACE students quite effectively, but for only some of the grade eleven PACE students in the last two years. The goal-setting strategy was not implemented with any PACE classes.

Since the grade ten, eleven, and twelve students of 1977-78 continued in the traditional program, there were no baseline classes for these grades. However, there were two PACE and two traditional longitudinal cohorts. Students of the first pair of cohorts, consisting of the grade nine students who entered the PACE and traditional programs in 1977-78 and remained in these programs thereafter, were tested each year in grades nine through twelve. Students of the second pair of cohorts, who entered grade nine in 1978-79, were tested in grades nine through eleven. The Short Test of Educational Ability was administered in grade nine annually. The Iowa Tests of Educational Development were administered in October to all the grade nine students in 1977-78, the grade nine and ten students in 1978-79, the grade nine, ten, and eleven students in 1979-80, and the grade nine, ten, eleven, and twelve students in 1980-81.

The data for the two pairs of PACE and traditional cohorts were analyzed separately using analyses of covariance. Table 8.2 presents the adjusted means and the differences between the means of the

PACE and the traditional cohorts. The differences between the PACE and the traditional cohorts in grade nine reflect the results of their education prior to grade nine. The differences each year thereafter reflect the results of the prior year at CHS. These differences were not tested for statistical significance because the PACE students voluntarily chose to enter the grade nine program and had a higher mean mental ability and a higher mean entering achievement level than the traditional students. However, the size and consistency of the differences are regarded as sufficient to be of practical importance.

The differences between the means of the first PACE cohort and the traditional cohort when in grade twelve were consistently larger than in grade nine in reading, language, and mathematics, favoring the PACE cohort. The same pattern held for PACE Cohort 2 and traditional Cohort 2 from grade nine to grade eleven. These differences consistently favoring the PACE cohorts suggest that the individual educational programming and the individual instructional programming carried out with the two PACE cohorts during grades nine and ten had positive effects. The positive effects may be due in part to the higher ability of the PACE students. However, the traditional cohorts had a greater opportunity to raise their achievement since their mean achievements when starting in grade nine were consistently lower than the grade nine PACE means. Moreover, the possibility of topping out on the tests in the fall of grades eleven and twelve was greater for the PACE students.

Although the PACE cohorts gained more than the traditional cohorts, CHS did not establish an improvement capability because of the instability of the school's administrative arrangements. The district office maintained the program during the last two years.

Notes Regarding Attendance, Attitudes, and Differences Between Sexes and Among Quarters in Mental Ability

1. Attendance and student attitudes toward various aspects of schooling were relatively stable from year to year except when a school made a systematic attempt to better either of these areas. When this was done, incidences of betterment occurred but not as frequently as for student achievement. At the same time, activities carried out to raise student achievement did not appear to have any effect on attitudes.

2.   The longitudinal cohorts of SMS and CSJHS gained significantly in each area tested from grade seven to grade eight. The
cohorts of WTS, HRVHS, and CHS gained in some subjects between
each time of testing and in all subjects between all except two different
times of testing.

3.   The mean achievement of the girls was consistently higher
than that of the boys in language and spelling in grades seven and
eight of SMS and CSJHS, in reading total and language total in
grades nine, ten, and eleven of CHS, and in English in grades ten,
eleven, and twelve of HRVHS. No consistent pattern of sex differences
was found in mathematics. The boys' achievement was significantly
higher than that of the girls in mathematics problem solving in grades
seven and eight at SMS; however, the mean of the girls was higher at
CSJHS in mathematics computation, mathematics concepts, and
mathematics total in grade seven. The mean of the boys was significantly higher than that of the girls in mathematics in grades nine, ten,
eleven, and twelve of CHS; however, the difference was not significant
in grades ten, eleven, or twelve of HRVHS.

Neither sex gained more than the other in mathematics from one
time of testing to the next in any school, grades seven through twelve.
The girls of at least one cohort, but not all cohorts, gained more than
the boys in spelling and reading from grade seven to grade eight and
in English during one or more of the high school years. (The previous
findings are based only on standardized test scores. WTS was not
included in this analysis because it used locally constructed tests.)

4.   The most surprising finding pertained to the gains made from
year to year by the four quarters in mental ability of each of the
several longitudinal cohorts. Only 26 of 684 comparisons showed
significant differences among the four quarters in the amount gained.
There were no significant gains at CHS. Moreover, in a number of the
26 instances the lowest quarter of a cohort gained more than one or
both of the two highest quarters of the same cohort.

It cannot be established that implementation of the improvement
strategies was definitely associated with the lack of significant differences in the gains made by the girls and the boys or among the four
quarters in mental ability. However, in all of the schools the improvement strategies were implemented in the same manner for boys and
girls and for the four quarters in mental ability. Thus, it is possible
that the equal attention to individual students, regardless of sex or
mental ability, contributed to the lack of differences in the gains.

SUMMATIVE EVALUATION OF THE MATERIALS

Instructional materials based on the design for the renewal and improvement of secondary education were developed duing 1978-1980 under the supervision of Klausmeier and Lipham. The improvement strategies and facilitative organizational structures of the design are explained in Klausmeier, Lipham, and Daresh (1983). Ten filmstrips depict practices of secondary schools across the nation that are in accord with the design. In nine audiocassettes describing school experiences, a teacher and another person from schools depicted in the filmstrips explain their practices and indicate how they got started. A manual provides suggestions for implementing each strategy and making operational each facilitative structure (Klausmeier and Daresh 1983).

An evaluation of the materials was conducted in 1980-81 in school settings and in universities (Klausmeier 1982). The evaluation showed the materials to be usable and effective in in-service programs conducted by the participating schools. They were also evaluated as readily usable and effective in university courses in secondary education, secondary curriculum, educational administration, educational leadership, and educational supervision. In these courses, they were more often used as supplementary material rather than as the basic text.

With support from the Faye McBeath Foundation, the book and the manual were revised in 1983 to take into account the results of the preceding evaluation, the improvement-oriented cooperative research reported in this chapter, other research on planned change, leadership, and decision making, and recent research and scholarly reports regarding secondary education.

CONCLUSIONS AND DISCUSSION

The cross-sectional analyses performed on students' test scores showed that the mean achievements of the later grades of 1978-79 at Steuben Middle School, Webster Transitional School, Carl Sandburg Junior High School, and Hood River Valley High School were not significantly different from the means of the earlier grades of 1977-78. But, as noted earlier, they were not expected to be higher since these schools made only minor improvements in their practices in the second semester of the second school year, 1978-79.

The means of the later 1979-80 and 1980-81 grades of these four schools were significantly higher than the means of the earlier grades of 1977-78 and 1978-79 in 67 instances, not significantly different in 69, and significantly lower in three (all in reading vocabulary in one school). The higher achievements of these later grades are due mainly to implementing the goal-setting strategy and to a lesser extent to the refinement of the instructional programming strategy and the educational programming strategy. Thus, implementation of the goal-setting strategy appeared to be the determining factor in bringing about consistently higher student achievement, while implementing the other strategies maintained the same level of achievement from year to year.

Cedarburg High School implemented only the individual instructional programming strategy and the individual educational programming strategy in grades nine and ten and to a lesser extent in grade eleven. The implementation of these strategies also yielded positive results.

The preceding positive results must be interpreted in the context of four schools that had a reduction in teachers or aides in one or both of the last two years. Also, the loss of both experienced language arts teachers in 1979-80 at Carl Sandburg Junior High School probably accounts for six grade eight language arts comparisons being nonsignificant. Nine nonsignificant differences at Hood River Valley High School might have been significant had the later grade eleven students of 1979-80 and the later grade twelve students of 1979-80 and 1980-81 experienced the planned improvements that were made in grade ten after they had already completed that grade.

Two other points should be borne in mind regarding the changes from year to year. First, the achievements of students of ages thirteen and seventeen in the academic subjects tended to go down during the 1970s, as shown by the National Assessment of Educational Progress (1978 a, b; 1979 a, b; 1980). Accordingly, maintaining the same level of achievement rather than experiencing a loss from year to year might be interpreted as a positive rather than a neutral effect. Second, some of the nonsignificant differences occurred after the means of the students of the third year were already significantly higher than those of an earlier grade. Maintaining this higher level of achievement also might be considered positive rather than neutral.

Based upon the consistently positive results, it is concluded that the design provides relevant guidelines for the renewal and improvement of secondary education. In this context, the design is considered to be validated as both usable and effective. Even though the number of schools was small, the uniformity of the results across these schools of greatly different characteristics in different locales is noteworthy.

The results of implementing the improvement strategies were more consistent across the two middle schools and the junior high school than the two high schools. Moreover, the strategies, structures, and processes of the design appeared to be more readily adapted and implemented by the middle schools and the junior high school. Although this is the case, the improvement strategies and the organizational structures and processes were found to be effective at the high school level in each grade in which they were implemented appropriately.

The schools set goals in terms of student achievement, and they used norm-referenced and criterion-referenced achievement tests to assess the attainment of the goals. They used the results of their mental ability tests to estimate the expected level of achievement of the students. The schools might have set goals in terms of other student outcomes in the cognitive domain, such as creativity or writing skills. Similarly, they might have employed other means of measuring student outcomes and might not have used the students' mental ability scores. The design is not prescriptive in this regard; rather, each school makes the decisions regarding desired outcomes and measurement tools.

The schools did not set goals to improve their advising, administrative, evaluation, or other school processes. However, this might have been done. The goal-setting strategy incorporated in the design and the related planning and monitoring processes are intended to be as applicable to school structures and processes as they are to improving student achievement.

The difference between implementing this design for the renewal and improvement of secondary education and acting on the findings from school effectiveness research warrants a brief discussion. The design focuses on how a school can bring about educational improvement, including how it establishes a permanent improvement capability. School effectiveness research has identified many characteristics of effective schools, including effective instructional leadership, expectations for high student achievement, an orderly, safe learning environment, clear goals, and careful monitoring and evaluation of student progress (Edmonds 1982; Purkey and Smith 1982). However, the descriptors of effective schools do not indicate the structures or processes that a school can use to become effective. For example, how a school with unclear goals, lack of order, and low student achievement is to become goal-directed, orderly, and high achieving is not made clear. This design does not directly answer these questions either. Rather, it specifies what a school does to maintain a continuing improvement capability:

1. establish an administrative arrangement consisting of the principal, a counselor, representative teachers, and possibly students and parents, to coordinate the school's improvement program;

2. review and update the school's educational philosophy, aims, and educational program annually;

3. identify areas of improvement annually, using the results of its own evaluation and needs assessment;

4. set measurable goals that specify maintaining a desired level of student outcomes or raising unsatisfactory levels;

5. develop a plan to attain the goals, including the implementation of individual educational programming and individual instructional programming;

6. acquire the knowledge and develop the skills that are needed to implement the planned activities by conducting its own preparation/in-service activities or by securing external assistance;

7. work out the managerial-operational procedures, for example, work schedules of staff, procurement of instructional materials and evaluation tools, that are needed to implement the planned activities;

8. implement the goal-directed improvement activities;

9. monitor progress to assure attainment of the goals; and

10. evaluate the effectiveness of the activities annually and use the evaluation results for further improvement.

A school that has developed an improvement capability is able to address any characteristic of effective schools that it may select for improvement, as well as other areas.

POSTSCRIPT

When the last data on student outcomes were collected in the schools in 1980-81, it appeared that four schools had developed a permanent improvement capability. There was some uncertainty regarding Cedarburg High School. During the next two years economic conditions worsened nationally and this was reflected in program reductions, staff reductions, or both in all five schools. Accordingly, it might have been expected that the four schools would not maintain their improvement capability into 1982-83. This was not the case.

Steuben Middle School was continuing all of its organizational arrangements in 1982-83 and was implementing the instructional programming and goal-setting strategies. It was one of five Wisconsin middle schools nominated by the chief state school officer of Wisconsin to be recognized as a school of excellence by the Secondary School Recognition Program initiated by Secretary Bell. Moreover, the remaining junior high schools of Milwaukee had become middle schools; and each one was developing an improvement capability similar to that of Steuben Middle School as part of a district project on school effectiveness.

Carl Sandburg Junior High School was continuing in much the same pattern as in 1980-81. Enrollment had stabilized at about the 1980-81 level. Individual instructional programming and goal setting were being implemented. Students of each grade were being grouped for instruction according to their entering achievement levels in language arts and mathematics. This reduced the teacher's task in providing suitable instructional programs for each student. The facilitative organizational structures were continuing in the same pattern as earlier.

Webster Transitional School was continuing its improvement strategies and school organizational structures and processes much as in 1980-81. In the interim, a district committee had worked toward improving the district curriculum in reading vocabulary. A standardized test administered to the grade seven students in May of 1983

showed the mean achievement of the students to be above the anticipated mean, based on aptitude, in all areas tested—reading total,
spelling, language total, mathematics total, reference skills, science,
and social studies. The means for both subtests—reading vocabulary
and reading comprehension—were above expectancy. (The tests were
not administered in grades six and eight.) Webster was one of 144
secondary schools selected as a school of excellence by the Secondary
Recognition Program initiated by Secretary Bell.

Hood River Valley High School was continuing its organizational
arrangements and its implementation of the three improvement strategies. Both individual instructional programming and individual
educational programming had been refined, the teacher-advisor program was continuing, and parental participation had markedly increased. A more structured program of education was being
implemented.

The PACE and traditional alternatives of Cedarburg High School
had been discontinued by 1982-83. However, many aspects of the
earlier PACE program had been extended throughout the school.
These included objective-based instruction in all academic subjects,
and teachers serving as advisors to students, planning and monitoring
the students' educational programs and reporting progress to the
students and their parents in individual conferences. Also, an academic improvement committee had been formed and was functioning
effectively. Implementation of the goal-setting strategy had begun.
Standardized test results for April, 1983, indicated that the mean
achievement of both the grade nine and the grade eleven students was
above the anticipated mean, based on aptitude, in all areas tested:
reading, spelling, language, mathematics, reference skills, science,
and social studies. Moreover, the achievements for grade eleven were
relatively higher than for grade nine. (The tests were not administered
in grades ten and twelve.) Thus, Cedarburg High School, like the
other schools, had established an effective improvement capability.

This chapter reports the research that validated the design for the
renewal and improvement of secondary education as effective and
usable. In August of 1982 the Superintendent of Public Instruction of
Wisconsin endorsed the design and committed the Department of
Public Instruction to assist in diffusing it in Wisconsin. Although
there was no mechanism for nationwide implementation at the time
this chapter was written, I expect at least 25 percent of the Wisconsin

middle schools and 10 percent of the high schools to be utilizing the design in part or in totality in 1985.

REFERENCES

Edmonds, Ronald R. "Programs of School Improvement: An Overview." *Educational Leadership* 40 (December 1982): 4-11.

Klausmeier, Herbert J. *Learning and Teaching Process Concepts: A Strategy for Testing Applications of Theory.* New York: Academic Press, 1980.

Klausmeier, Herbert J. *Usability and Effectiveness of a Program for the Renewal and Improvement of Secondary Education in Local School and University Settings: A Summative Evaluation.* Arlington, Va.: ERIC Document Reproduction Service, 1982.

Klausmeier, Herbert J., and Allen, Patricia S. *Cognitive Development of Children and Youth: A Longitudinal Study.* New York: Academic Press, 1978.

Klausmeier, Herbert J., and Associates. *Cognitive Learning and Development: Information Processing and Piagetian Perspectives.* Cambridge, Mass.: Ballinger Publishing Co., 1979.

Klausmeier, Herbert J., and Daresh, John C. *Secondary School Improvement Manual for the Wisconsin Program for the Renewal and Improvement of Secondary Education.* Madison, Wis.: Wisconsin Center for Education Research, 1983.

Klausmeier, Herbert J.; Lipham, James M.; and Daresh, John C. *The Renewal and Improvement of Secondary Education: Concepts and Practices.* Wanham, Md.: University Press of America, 1983.

Klausmeier, Herbert J.; Serlin, Ronald C.; and Zindler, M.C. *Supplementary Tabular Information to Accompany the Research Monograph,* Improvement of Secondary Education through Research: Five Longitudinal Case Studies. Program Report 83-8. Madison, Wis.: Wisconsin Center for Education Research, 1982.

Klausmeier, Herbert J.; Serlin, Ronald C.; and Zindler, M.C. *Improvement of Secondary Education through Research: Five Longitudinal Case Studies.* Madison, Wis.: Wisconsin Center for Education Research, 1983.

Klausmeier, T.W. *Desirability of IGE/Secondary Objectives and Their Implementation in IGE Junior High Schools.* Technical Report No. 461. Madison, Wis.: Wisconsin Center for Education Research, 1978.

Lipham, James M. "Leadership and Decision Making for Effective Educational Change." *Executive Review* 3, no. 8 (1983): 1-6.

Maier, M.J. *Desirability and Feasibility of IGE/Secondary Objectives in Selected Senior High Schools.* Technical Report No. 493. Madison, Wis.: Wisconsin Center for Education Research, 1978.

National Assessment of Educational Progress. *Results of Two National Reading Assessments: Some Performance Up; Some Down.* Denver, Colo.: National Assessment of Educational Progress, 1978 (a).

National Assessment of Educational Progress. *Three National Assessments of Science: Changes in Achievement, 1969-77.* Denver, Colo.: National Assessment of Educational Progress, 1978 (b).

National Assessment of Educational Progress. *Mathematical Achievement: Knowledge, Skills, Understanding, Applications.* Denver, Colo.: National Assessment of Educational Progress, 1979 (a).

National Assessment of Educational Progress. *National Assessment Results in Social-Studies/Citizenship.* Denver, Colo.: National Assessment of Educational Progress, 1979 (b).

National Assessment of Educational Progress. *Writing Achievement 1969-79: Results from the Third National Writing Assessment.* Denver, Colo.: National Assessment of Educational Progress, 1980.

National Commission on Excellence in Education. *A Nation at Risk: The Imperative for Educational Reform.* Washington, D.C.: National Commission on Excellence in Education, 1983.

Purkey, Stewart C., and Smith, Marshall S. "Too Soon to Cheer? Synthesis of Research on Effective Schools." *Educational Leadership* 40 (December 1982): 64-69.

CHAPTER
9

The Adaptive Learning Environments Model: Design, Implementation, and Effects

Margaret C. Wang, Patricia Gennari, and Hersholt C. Waxman

The overall goal of the Adaptive Learning Environments Model (ALEM) is to establish and maintain school environments that ensure optimal opportunities for learning success for most, if not all, students through the provision of adaptive instruction. The design of the program is based on the premises that students learn in different ways

The research reported here was supported by the Learning Research and Development Center of the University of Pittsburgh, supported in part as a research and development center by funds from the National Institute of Education. The opinions expressed do not necessarily reflect the positions or policies of this agency, and no official endorsement should be inferred.

The authors extend their sincere appreciation to Rita Catalano for her editorial assistance and to Patte Kelly for her assistance in preparing the tables and figures.

and at different rates and that one alternative for maximizing learning is to provide instruction which adapts to those differences. Furthermore, the accommodation of student differences requires a variety of instructional methods and learning experiences that are matched to the learning characteristics and needs of individual students, as well as explicit interventions that increase each student's capability to profit from available instructional and learning alternatives. Thus, modification of the environment to accommodate student differences (for example, use of alternative instructional strategies, provision of different amounts of instruction, allowance for individual differences in rates of learning, provision of a variety of learning options) has been an important design consideration in the development of the ALEM. In addition to necessary adjustments in the learning environment, however, the design incorporates the use of interventions, when needed, to modify each student's capability to function under, and profit from, such school learning environments (Wang 1980a).

DESIGN OF THE PROGRAM

Essentially, the ALEM curriculum combines prescriptive, or "direct," instruction that has been shown to be effective in ensuring mastery of basic academic skills (Bloom 1976; Glaser 1977; Rosenshine 1979) with aspects of informal, or open, education that are considered to be conducive to generating attitudes and processes of inquiry, self-management and responsibility for learning, and social cooperation (Johnson, Maruyama, Johnson, Nelson, and Skon 1981; Marshall 1981; Peterson 1979; Wang 1983a; Wang and Stiles 1976). Among the expected program outcomes for students are increased competence and confidence in their own abilities to acquire skills in academic learning and in management of their behaviors and the classroom environment. At the same time, a high degree of program implementation is expected to result in increased amounts of time spent by teachers providing instruction rather than managing students.

Figure 9.1 shows the conceptual model of program design and evaluation research that has provided the basis for the program of research leading to development and validation of the ALEM. As shown in Figure 9.1, the model consists of three major components.

The first is the program design component (shown by the rectangular boxes on the left-hand side of Figure 9.1). The second component is related to program implementation in school settings (represented by the circle); and the third component focuses on evaluation of related process and product outcomes.

Program design begins with the identification of instructional goals and student characteristics. This information constitutes basic input into the design of those program dimensions that are critical for the ongoing provision of adaptive instruction in classroom settings, as well as those dimensions related to classroom-level support for program implementation. The arrows in Figure 9.1 suggest that outcomes are evaluated in relation to (a) the actual presence or absence of critical program dimensions; (b) the extent to which implementation of the dimensions leads to specific classroom processes that are hypothesized to be characteristic of adaptive instruction; and (c) the extent to which the classroom processes lead to students' social and academic competence.

Two categories of critical program dimensions have been identified as classroom-level requirements for effective implementation of adaptive instruction (see the two large rectangular boxes on the left-hand side of Figure 9.1). These dimensions are related to the process of providing adaptive instruction, and to the classroom management and resource supports required for effective implementation of adaptive instruction. The dimensions associated with effective provision of adaptive instruction are Creating and Maintaining Instructional Materials, Developing Student Self-Responsibility, Diagnostic Testing, Instructing, Interactive Teaching, Monitoring and Diagnosing, Motivating, Prescribing, and Record Keeping. Dimensions identified as critical for supporting classroom implementation of adaptive instruction are Arranging Space and Facilities, Establishing and Communicating Rules and Procedures, and Managing Aides. It is important to note here that, insofar as they represent program design features and classroom practices that have been found to be effective by many researchers and practitioners (Brophy 1979; National School Public Relations Association 1981; Walberg 1984), the individual program dimensions are not unique to the ALEM. The uniqueness lies in the complementary functions served by the planned clustering and systematic integration of the dimensions into a comprehensive program. In fact, the contention is that any single dimension is

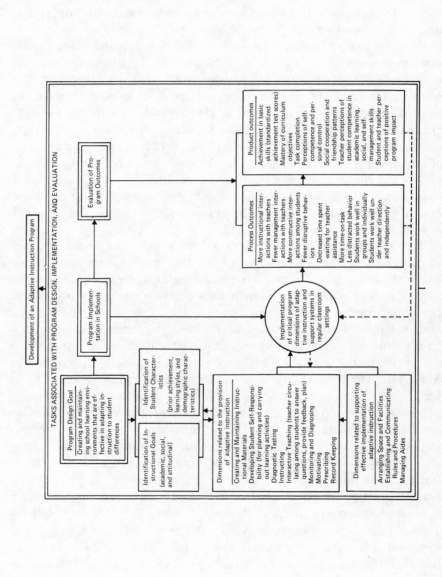

Development of an Adaptive Instruction Program

TASKS ASSOCIATED WITH PROGRAM DESIGN, IMPLEMENTATION, AND EVALUATION

Program Design Goal
Creating and maintaining school learning environments that are effective in adapting instruction to student differences

Identification of Instructional Goals
(academic, social, and attitudinal)

Identification of Student Characteristics
(prior achievement, learning styles, and demographic characteristics)

Dimensions related to the provision of adaptive instruction
Creating and Maintaining Instructional Materials
Developing Student Self-Responsibility (for planning and carrying out learning activities)
Diagnostic Testing
Instructing
Interactive Teaching (teacher circulating among students to answer questions, provide feedback, plan)
Monitoring and Diagnosing
Motivating
Prescribing
Record Keeping

Dimensions related to supporting effective implementation of adaptive instruction
Arranging Space and Facilities
Establishing and Communicating Rules and Procedures
Managing Aides

Implementation of critical program dimensions of adaptive instruction and support systems in regular classroom settings

Program Implementation in Schools

Evaluation of Program Outcomes

Process Outcomes
More instructional interactions with teachers
Fewer management interactions with teachers
More constructive interactions among students
Fewer disruptive behaviors
Decreased time spent waiting for teacher assistance
More time-on-task
Less distracted behavior
Students work well in groups and individually
Students work well under teacher direction and independently

Product outcomes
Achievement in basic skills (standardized achievement test scores)
Mastery of curriculum objectives
Task completion
Perceptions of self-competence and personal control
Social cooperation and friendship patterns
Teacher perceptions of student competence in academic learning, social, and self-management skills
Student and teacher perceptions of positive program impact

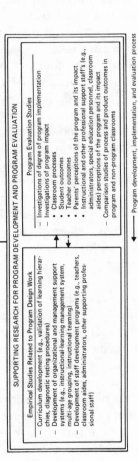

SUPPORTING RESEARCH FOR PROGRAM DEVELOPMENT AND PROGRAM EVALUATION

Empirical Studies Related to Program Design Work

– Curriculum development (e.g., validation of learning hierarchies, diagnostic testing procedures)
– Development of organizational and management support
  systems (e.g., instructional-learning management system,
  multi-age grouping, instructional teaming)
– Development of staff development programs (e.g., teachers,
  classroom aides, administrators, other supporting professional staff)

Program Evaluation Studies

– Investigations of degree of program implementation
– Investigations of program impact
  • Classroom processes
  • Student outcomes
  • Teacher outcomes
  • Parents' perceptions of the program and its impact
  • Instructional and other professional support staff's (e.g.,
    administrators, special education personnel, classroom
    aides) perceptions of the program and its impact
– Comparison studies of process and product outcomes in
  program and non-program classrooms

──────▶ Program development, implementation, and evaluation process

- - - - -▶ Program refinement process

Figure 9.1

A model of design, implementation, and evaluation research for adaptive instruction.

unlikely to lead to effective adaptive instruction. (See Wang, Catalano, and Gromoll 1983, for a discussion of the design and operation of the program dimensions.)

Development of the ALEM has been associated with two primary lines of supporting research. As outlined in the bottom box of Figure 9.1, this research has consisted of empirical studies related to design of the program and evaluation of implementation and outcomes. The first line of research—empirical studies related to program design— can be characterized as instructional experimentations associated with the development of program components. The focus of this research has been the operationalization and integration of what is known from psychological theories of learning, and from research on instructional methods and effective schooling practices, in the design of educational environments that successfully accommodate students' diverse needs. Examples of this work include development and validation of curricular hierarchies in the various basic skills areas (Resnick, Wang, and Kaplan 1973; Wang, Resnick, and Boozer 1971); development of diagnostic tests and procedures for monitoring student progress (Glaser 1967; Lindvall and Cox 1967; Wang and Fitzhugh 1978); development of a training program for student self-responsibility (Smith 1976; Stone and Vaughn 1976; Wang 1983a); and development of a data-based, staff development program (Wang 1981; Wang and Gennari 1983).

The second line of supporting research has addressed questions related to program implementation and evaluation. Specific research questions have dealt with the practicalities of implementing adaptive instruction in school settings and with program efficacy. Studies have focused on investigating what it takes to implement and maintain an adaptive instruction program, whether or not it is feasible to implement such a program widely in different school settings, and the manner and extent to which various components can be put together in complementary ways to form a cohesive and comprehensive program for school implementation. In addition, research in this area has been designed to characterize the actual operation of the ALEM for the purpose of answering basic questions relating to program development and refinement such as How can we do it better? and For whom, and under what conditions, is the program effective?

Essentially, the studies of program implementation and efficacy have been aimed at investigating (a) the extent to which implementation of various program components leads to the presence of those specific classroom processes that are hypothesized to support the provision of adaptive instruction; and (b) the extent to which the presence of those classroom processes leads to student achievement. Examples of such studies include analysis of program impact on teachers' and students' use of time (Wang, in press a; Wang and Walberg 1983) and evaluation of learning processes and outcomes in a variety of school sites (Wang, in press b; Wang and Birch 1984; Wang, Leinhardt, and Boston 1980; Wang, Peverly, and Randolph, 1984; Wang, Resnick, and Scheutz 1974; Wang and Walberg 1983).

PROGRAM IMPLEMENTATION AND RELATED EFFECTS: A SUMMARY OF MAJOR FINDINGS

Findings from four recent studies of implementation of the ALEM in a variety of school settings and its related effects are summarized in this section. These studies were designed to address the following three sets of questions.

1. Can a high degree of implementation of the critical dimensions of the ALEM be attained in classroom settings with different needs and contextual characteristics? In other words, is there evidence of the program's implementability or feasibility in varying school settings?

2. When the critical dimensions of the ALEM are in place, do the hypothesized patterns of classroom processes occur; and, to what extent do the classroom process patterns differ from, or concur with, the hypothesized trends?

3. Do the ALEM (as characterized by degree of implementation data) and its resulting classroom process patterns lead to expected student outcomes?

Briefly, Study I was designed to investigate program implementation and effects in 117 classrooms at six school sites where the ALEM was implemented in conjunction with the local school district's participation in the National Follow Through Program during the 1980-81 school year. (Follow Through is a nationwide compensatory education program sponsored by the U.S. Department of Education.) Study II was carried out during 1980-81 in twenty-one classrooms at school sites where the focus was on assessing the efficacy of the ALEM as the core educational program in regular classrooms in which mildly handicapped and gifted students were mainstreamed on a full-time basis. Study III was a replication of Study I; it was carried out at five collaborating school sites that participated in the National Follow Through Program during the 1981-82 school year. Study IV was a replication of Study II; it was conducted during the 1982-83 school year in twenty-eight mainstreaming classrooms in five schools within a large urban school system.

Discussion of the results from the studies is organized under two major headings: the degree of implementation of the ALEM in a variety of school settings; and impact of the program on classroom processes, teachers' use of time, and student achievement in mathematics and reading. While the four studies shared the overall goal of examining the school implementation and effects of the ALEM, different research questions were addressed. Thus, the specific variables included in the studies differed somewhat from one study to another, as did the measures. Discussion of results related to specific research questions, therefore, may not include data from all four studies. In each case, however, the reported data represent all that are available from all four studies.

Degree of Implementation

Data on degree of implementation were used to address four specific questions related to the implementability of the ALEM. These questions are: (a) To what extent was an overall high degree of implementation attained across a variety of school sites? (b) To what extent did the degree of implementation improve over time? (c) Were there significant differences in the patterns of implementation among classrooms with different overall degree of implementation scores? and (d) Were there differences in the degree of implementation of adaptive instruction in classrooms where the ALEM was implemented and classrooms where the program was not implemented?

Overall Degree of Implementation

The Implementation Assessment Battery for Adaptive Instruction (Wang 1980b) was used to obtain data on the degree of program implementation. The Battery, which is designed to assess the presence and absence of the critical dimensions of the ALEM, is based on a series of performance indicators that have been identified through systematic analysis of the program's structural and action domains. The structural domain consists of the resources, such as materials, space, facilities, time, and personnel, required to create the conditions under which adaptive instruction can be implemented effectively (that is, the support systems for program implementation in classroom settings). The action domain consists of the roles and behaviors of instructional staff (that is, the process related to provision of adaptive instruction) and students.

Table 9.1 provides a summary of the results from the analysis of degree of implementation data from all four studies. To investigate the extent to which a high degree of implementation of the ALEM was established in a variety of school sites (that is, program implementability), the mean degree-of-implementation scores (as shown in the last column under each study) for the spring period were examined. The implementability of the ALEM is suggested by the generally high spring degree-of-implementation scores across all twelve critical dimensions and by the overall spring scores for the four studies. As shown in the last row of the table, the overall average spring scores for all four studies were above 85 percent—the criterion level for a high degree of implementation.

Improvements in Program Implementation

A critical test of the implementability of the ALEM is the extent to which the degree of implementation at the participating sites improved over time. To this end, the mean scores for fall, winter, and spring for each study were examined. A consistent pattern of steady improvement in the implementation of the critical dimensions over time was noted in all four studies. Furthermore, as shown in Table 9.1, the differences in the changes in degree-of-implementation scores between fall and winter, and between fall and spring, were statistically significant in all cases.

In most cases, the greatest changes in degree of implementation occurred between the fall and winter data collection periods. In a way, this finding is an additional indicator of the program's implementability. It reflects one of the criteria for successful implementation of any school innovation that requires major programmatic changes—the reality is that teachers and students cannot cope for extended periods of time with the disruption that can be caused by initiation of an innovative school program. Successful implementation of new programs is unlikely unless critical dimensions of the programs

Table 9.1

Summary of Fall, Winter, and Spring Mean Degree-of-Implementation Scores in the ALEM's 12 Critical Dimensions Across All Participating Classrooms

Critical Dimensions	Study I Follow Through Classrooms (1980-81) N = 117						Study II Mainstreaming Classrooms (1980-81) N = 21						Study III Follow Through Classrooms (1981-82) N = 88						Study IV Mainstreaming Classrooms (1982-83) N = 26					
	Fall		Winter		Spring		Fall		Winter		Spring		Fall		Winter		Spring		Fall		Winter		Spring	
	Means	(S.D.)	Means	(S.D.)	Means	(S.D.)	Means	(S.D.)	Means	(S.D.)	Means	(S.D.)	Means	(S.D.)	Means	(S.D.)	Means	(S.D.)	Means	(S.D.)	Means	(S.D.)	Means	(S.D.)
Arranging Space & Facilities	91	(12)	95	(6)	94	(13)	77	(21)	93	(9)	96	(7)	92	(14)	95	(9)	96	(5)	81	(16)	93	(10)	95	(7)
Creating & Maintaining Instructional Materials	74	(23)	86	(15)	85	(18)	78	(11)	76	(15)	74	(13)	83	(17)	91	(13)	93	(8)	75	(17)	90	(16)	95	(14)
Establishing & Communicating Rules & Procedures	79	(12)	89	(10)	90	(8)	76	(15)	92	(7)	89	(8)	82	(11)	91	(10)	89	(11)	77	(18)	90	(17)	95	(13)
Managing Aides	98	(8)	99	(6)	99	(5)	94	(22)	96	(20)	98	(7)	95	(17)	95	(16)	95	(19)	90	(26)	98	(13)	100	(0)
Diagnostic Testing	98	(8)	98	(8)	98	(9)	98	(7)	100	(0)	100	(0)	96	(12)	98	(7)	100	(3)	89	(19)	94	(13)	95	(10)
Record Keeping	96	(14)	99	(7)	98	(11)	77	(36)	87	(27)	98	(7)	94	(20)	99	(6)	98	(11)	37	(35)	92	(22)	99	(7)
Monitoring & Diagnosing	89	(12)	94	(9)	94	(9)	82	(17)	92	(9)	93	(6)	86	(16)	91	(14)	92	(11)	83	(12)	97	(6)	100	(0)
Prescribing	97	(9)	98	(10)	97	(12)	93	(14)	99	(4)	100	(0)	99	(6)	99	(7)	100	(0)	76	(21)	90	(21)	97	(15)
Interactive Teaching	87	(27)	90	(23)	90	(24)	61	(41)	82	(38)	93	(18)	88	(31)	92	(22)	91	(23)	75	(22)	95	(14)	97	(9)
Instructing	87	(13)	92	(11)	92	(10)	71	(14)	80	(11)	79	(10)	89	(15)	90	(12)	90	(13)	77	(14)	95	(8)	97	(7)
Motivating	78	(17)	89	(17)	92	(11)	69	(19)	87	(18)	92	(13)	83	(20)	95	(10)	95	(15)	91	(17)	96	(14)	98	(9)
Developing Student Self-Responsibility	75	(22)	82	(21)	87	(19)	61	(32)	69	(30)	81	(25)	73	(22)	89	(19)	79	(25)	75	(22)	91	(18)	97	(11)
Overall Averages	88	(7)	93	(6)	93	(6)*	78	(11)	88	(10)	91	(5)*	88	(9)	94	(7)	93	(7)*	77	(10)	93	(8)	97	(6)*

Note. The differences in the scores between Fall and Winter, and between Fall and Spring, were statistically significant ($p \leq .01$).

are implemented at an acceptable level, and a reasonable implementation plan is established and maintained during the initial three months of their operation.

Patterns of Degree of Implementation

Another question of interest in examining the degree of program implementation is whether or not there is a consistent pattern of differences in the implementation of various program dimensions among classrooms at different overall degree-of-implementation levels. Scores in individual dimensions for classrooms grouped at high, average, and low degree-of-implementation levels were examined. A class is rated as being at a high degree-of-implementation level when a score at or above 85 percent is obtained in eleven or twelve of the critical dimensions. Average degree-of-implementation classrooms are those with criterion-level scores in six through ten of the dimensions. Classrooms at the low degree-of-implementation level have scores at or above 85 percent in five or fewer critical dimensions. Data from Spring 1981 for Studies I and II were used in the analysis. A summary of the mean degree-of-implementation scores for each of the twelve critical dimensions among the three groups of classrooms is presented in Table 9.2.

When the patterns of high mean degree-of-implementation scores for each critical dimension were examined, consistent differences among the three groups of classrooms were noted. Moreover, the differences suggest a hierarchy of teacher expertise in classroom implementation of adaptive instruction. As shown in Table 9.2, for example, the data suggest that all three groups had mean scores at or above 85 percent in four of the dimensions: Record Keeping, Prescribing, Diagnostic Testing, and Managing Aides. Given the nature of these dimensions, it can be said that, by the end of the school year, all teachers in the ALEM classes at the Follow Through and mainstreaming sites were able to achieve a high level of implementation of the basic mechanics of providing individualized instruction. The major differences between classes in the average and high degree-of-implementation groups and those in the low degree-of-implementation group were in critical dimensions related to classroom instruction and management. These dimensions are Arranging Space and Facilities, Establishing and Communicating Rules and Procedures, Monitoring and Diagnosing, Instructing, and Motivating.

Differences between the high degree-of-implementation group and

Table 9.2
Differences in Patterns of Mean Degree-of-Implementation Scores for Each Critical Dimension Among Classrooms at the High, Average, and Low Degree-of-Implementation Levels (Data from Spring, 1981 for Studies I and II)

Critical Dimensions	Mean Percentage Scores		
	High Degree-of-Implementation Classrooms (N=55)	Average Degree-of-Implementation Classrooms (N=78)	Low Degree-of-Implementation Classrooms (N=5)
Record Keeping	99	98	87
Prescribing	100	96	96
Diagnostic Testing	100	98	95
Managing Aides	100	98	100
Arranging Space and Facilities	98	93	77
Establishing and Communicating Rules and Procedures	93	87	79
Rules and Procedures			
Monitoring and Diagnosing	95	93	83
Instructing	96	87	77
Motivating	99	89	80
Creating and Maintaining Instructional Materials	92	78	62
Interactive Teaching	100	84	70
Developing Student Self-Responsibility	93	81	74
Mean Across All Dimensions	97	90	81

Dimensions for which mean scores at or above the 85% criterion level were achieved by all three levels of degree-of-implementation classrooms.

Dimensions for which mean scores at or above the 85% criterion level were achieved by the high and average degree-of-implementation classrooms, but not by the low degree-of-implementation classrooms.

Dimensions for which mean scores at or above the 85% criterion level were achieved by the high degree-of-implementation classrooms, but not by the average and low degree-of-implementation classrooms.

This table is taken from Margaret C. Wang and Herbert J. Walberg, "Adaptive Instruction and Classroom Time." *American Educational Research Journal* 20 (Winter 1983): 601-625. © 1983, American Educational Research Association, Washington, D.C.

the average and low groups, on the other hand, were found in three dimensions: Creating and Maintaining Instructional Materials, Interactive Teaching, and Developing Student Self-Responsibility. A high degree of implementation of these latter dimensions requires skill and simultaneous and spontaneous analyses of students' ongoing learning behaviors and needs, knowledge of the nature of the tasks to be learned, and ability to provide instructional resources and learning experiences for meeting individual student needs.

Thus, there seems to be a clear hierarchy of teacher expertise associated with implementation of the ALEM. All teachers— including those whose overall degree-of-implementation scores were considered to be at the "low" level—had scores at or above 85 percent (the criterion score) in dimensions related to the basic mechanics of individualizing instruction. However, teachers with overall low degree-of-implementation scores generally were below the 85 percent criterion in dimensions related to management of the classroom environment and instruction, as well as those related to the ongoing adaptations required for the instructional-learning process. For the latter skills, the 85 percent criterion was attained only by teachers with overall high degree-of-implementation scores.

Comparison of Implementation of Adaptive Instruction in ALEM and Non-ALEM Classrooms

To investigate the extent to which there were significant differences in the progress made by ALEM and non-ALEM teachers in implementing critical features of adaptive instruction, degree-of-implementation data for teachers from the two groups of classrooms were examined. Data from Study II (the only study that included a comparison group) were used in this analysis. The results are summarized in Table 9.3. The mean percentage scores in each of the critical dimensions for classrooms at each grade level, as well as the total mean scores for both groups of classrooms, are reported.

Two major findings are suggested by the data reported in Table 9.3. First, an overall high degree of implementation of the critical program dimensions was attained in the ALEM classrooms by the end of the school year (92 percent), while a comparatively much lower degree-of-implementation score was noted for the non-ALEM classrooms (46 percent)—a difference of 46 percentage points. Second, the differences in the degree-of-implementation scores for the ALEM and

Table 9.3

Summary of Changes (Ch.) In Mean Degree-of-Implementation Scores in the 12 Critical Dimensions For ALEM and Non-ALEM Classrooms: Fall (F) and Spring (S) of the 1980-81 School Year
(Data from Study II)

Critical Dimensions	ALEM Classrooms (N = 4)											Non-ALEM Classrooms (N = 5)								
	K		Grade 1		Grade 2		Grade 3		Total			Grade 1		Grade 2		Grade 3		Total		
	F	S	F	S	F	S	F	S	F	S	(Ch.)	F	S	F	S	F	S	F	S	(Ch.)
Arranging Space & Facilities	27	100	64	100	64	100	91	100	62	100	(+38)	46	46	55	51	41	59	47	43	(− 4)
Creating & Maintaining Instructional Materials	64	64	73	73	64	73	91	73	73	71	(− 2)	46	27	46	41	37	55	43	44	(+1)
Establishing & Communicating Rules & Procedures	41	93	74	100	70	93	89	100	69	97	(+28)	56	78	48	69	56	63	53	68	(+15)
Managing Aides	100	100	100	100	100	100	100	100	100	100	(0)	•		•		•		•		(+6)
Diagnostic Testing	100	100	100	100	100	100	100	100	100	100	(0)	25	0	13	25	0	13	13	19	(+6)
Record Keeping	33	100	100	100	100	100	33	100	67	100	(+33)	33	33	50	84	33	33	39	67	(+28)
Monitoring & Diagnosing	63	88	100	88	63	100	100	100	81	94	(+13)	38	50	26	44	44	57	32	50	(+18)

Prescribing	60	100	60	100	100	100	100	100	80	100 (+20)	40	40	40	30	50	40	43	36 (− 7)
Interactive Teaching	0	100	100	100	100	100	100	100	75	100 (+25)	50	0	0	75	0	25	17	40 (+23)
Instructing	57	79	86	71	71	86	86	93	75	82 (+7)	71	79	54	68	50	50	58	63 (+5)
Motivating	80	100	40	100	100	100	80	100	75	85 (+10)	40	60	40	70	30	50	37	60 (+23)
Developing Student Self-Responsibility	0	100	33	33	33	33	100	67	42	58 (+16)	67	0	17	50	17	0	34	20 (−14)
Total	52	94	78	90	80	90	89	94	75	92 (+17)	47	38	35	55	33	40	38	46 (+9)

non-ALEM classrooms included dimensions that are generally a part of effective instruction (for example, Establishing and Communicating Rules and Procedures).

Summary

To summarize, findings related to program implementation across all four studies consistently suggest the overall implementability of the ALEM. That is, they provide evidence of feasibility of establishing and maintaining a high degree of implementation of the critical program dimensions of the ALEM in a large number of diverse school sites that include students from disadvantaged backgrounds and students labeled as having "special" needs. In addition, the findings show that, in general, the ALEM teachers made significant improvements in degree of implementation over time, and differences in patterns of implementation were noted for teachers with overall high degree-of-implementation scores and those with comparatively lower scores. Furthermore, when the degrees of adaptive instruction in ALEM and non-ALEM classes were compared, the non-ALEM classes scored considerably lower, even in dimensions widely recognized as reflecting generic expertise associated with effective teaching.

Data on implementation of the ALEM in schools challenge current opinion on the implementability of adaptive instruction, or the potential for wide-scale implementation in school settings. The general consensus in the effective-teaching literature (for example, Bennett 1976; Brophy 1979) is that effective implementation of adaptive instruction requires considerable teacher expertise and resources. Many have concluded that even if adequate school organizational and resource supports could be provided, the knowledge base on how to develop the teacher expertise required for effective implementation of adaptive instruction in regular class settings is sorely lacking. Furthermore, successful demonstrations of adaptive instruction often have been attributed to unusual teachers and/or students. The underlying assumption is that it is extremely difficult to "reproduce" the special sort of teacher (or teacher expertise) required by such programs. Although some researchers and practitioners concede that individualized and small-group instruction might work under the guidance of master teachers and with adequate organizational and resource supports, and that the results under these circumstances could include positive classroom processes, most are quite skeptical.

Thus, the fact that, on the average, teachers in all four studies achieved or exceeded the criterion for a high degree of program implementation indicates that they can develop the expertise, and/or use the expertise they already possess, to implement effectively the critical program features of the ALEM. Findings from the studies suggest that, with systematic training, a large percentage of public school teachers can establish and maintain the kinds of school learning environments normally considered to be possible only with specially skilled teachers.

Degree of Implementation and Program Outcomes

A central issue in assessing the efficacy of the ALEM has been the extent to which implementing the critical dimensions of the program leads to intended outcomes. In other words, the question has been, Does the program work as predicted? Thus, the focus of analyses of the data on program implementation and outcomes has been on investigating the relationships between program implementation and (a) classroom processes, (b) teacher use of class time, and (c) student outcomes. Findings from these and related analyses are summarized in this section.

Program Implementation and Classroom Processes

Four separate questions were addressed in the analysis of the relationship between degree of implementation and classroom processes: To what extent did implementation of the critical dimensions of the ALEM lead to the patterns of classroom processes that the program is designed to achieve? Did differences in the overall degree of implementation lead to significant differences in classroom processes? Did improvements in implementation result in positive changes in classroom processes? and, Were the differences in classroom processes in ALEM and non-ALEM classrooms characterized by different degrees of implementation?

To investigate whether program implementation led to the desired patterns of classroom processes, the degree-of-implementation data and the observation data on classroom processes collected in all the first- and second-grade classrooms ($N = 72$) participating in Studies I and II were analyzed (Wang and Walberg 1983). The Student Behavior Observation Schedule (Wang 1974) was used to obtain the classroom process data. A significant overall relationship between implementation and classroom processes was suggested by the results from the canonical correlation analysis (canonical $R = .36$, $p < .01$). In addition to this overall relationship, the extent to which classrooms at the three different degree-of-implementation levels exhibited distinct patterns of classroom processes was analyzed. The results from this analysis are summarized in Table 9.4.

As with the implementation data, some consistent patterns of differences in classroom processes were noted among groups of classes at the three implementation levels. For example, the data on the differences in the frequency of management interactions between teachers and students suggest a pattern of lower degree of implementation associated with greater frequencies of observed management interactions between teachers and students. The data also suggest that the interactions among students were more constructive in classrooms at the higher degree-of-implementation levels and that students in the higher degree-of-implementation classrooms seemed to spend less time working in individual settings, compared to those in the average and low degree-of-implementation classrooms.

Differences also were found in the types of activities in which students engaged and the manner in which learning tasks were performed. Students in the high degree-of-implementation classrooms were observed to spend significantly more time on student-selected, exploratory learning tasks, compared to students in the average and low degree-of-implementation classrooms. In addition, students in the high degree-of-implementation classrooms exhibited more on-task behavior, and they were less distracted. (Note that statistical analyses of the differences were not performed, due to the large differences in the numbers of classes among the three degree-of-implementation groups.)

An alternate way of examining the relationship between classroom processes and degree of implementation is to analyze the extent to which concomitant changes in classroom processes were noted as program implementation improved from fall to spring. This was one of the questions addressed in Study II (Wang, Nojan, Strom, and Walberg, 1984). Results from the analysis, as shown in Table 9.5, suggest consistent patterns of changes from fall to spring in classroom processes in the hypothesized directions as the degree of implementation improved over time (as shown in Table 9.1). For example, student-initiated interactions with teachers increased significantly

Table 9.4
Mean Percentages of Observed Frequencies in Major Categories of Classroom Process Variables for Classrooms at Different Degree-of-Implementation Levels
(Data from Spring, 1981 for First- and Second-Grade Classes in Studies I and II)

| | Degree-of-Implementation Levels | | | | | |
| | High (N = 29) | | Average (N = 39) | | Low (N = 4) | |
Variables	Mean	(S.D.)	Mean	(S.D.)	Mean	(S.D.)
Interactions Between Teachers and Students						
Initiation						
Student	41.1	(1.7)	33.3	(1.4)	32.1	(1.9)
Teacher	58.9	(1.2)	66.7	(1.5)	67.9	(1.4)
Purpose						
Instruction	93.3	(2.3)	91.7	(2.0)	90.0	(1.7)
Management	6.7	(.6)	8.3	(.4)	10.0	(.4)
Interactions with Peers						
Sharing ideas, materials, activities, etc.	99.8	(2.3)	94.4	(2.8)	90.0	(1.8)
Disruptive	.2	(.2)	5.6	(.3)	10.0	(.3)
Setting						
Group: Interactive	5.1	(2.1)	3.0	(1.6)	3.0	(1.8)
Group: Parallel	5.1	(2.0)	2.0	(1.5)	0.0	(0)
Individual	89.8	(2.9)	95.0	(2.4)	97.0	(1.8)
Activity Type						
Prescriptive	84.7	(3.5)	96.0	(2.1)	98.0	(1.6)
Exploratory	15.3	(3.4)	4.0	(1.9)	2.0	(1.3)
Initiation						
Assigned	2.6	(3.6)	6.3	(3.7)	10.4	(3.0)
Self-initiated	97.4	(3.9)	93.6	(3.8)	89.6	(3.2)
Manner						
On-Task	86.0	(2.5)	81.0	(3.7)	76.0	(3.2)
Waiting	8.0	(1.9)	8.0	(2.7)	10.0	(2.3)
Distracted	6.0	(1.6)	11.0	(2.2)	14.0	(2.5)

This table is taken from Margaret C. Wang and Herbert J. Walberg, "Adaptive Instruction and Classroom Time." *American Educational Research Journal* 20 (Winter 1983): 601-625. © 1983, American Educational Research Association, Washington, D.C.

from fall to spring, while teacher-initiated interactions decreased. Teacher-student interactions occurred more frequently for instructional purposes and less frequently for management purposes. In addition, students were observed to spend increasingly greater proportions of their time on self-initiated tasks.

Classroom process data from Study II also were analyzed to investigate the extent of any differences in classroom processes between ALEM and non-ALEM classrooms (Wang, in press b). Some of the major hypothesized differences in classroom processes are suggested by the data (see Table 9.6). The ALEM students initiated interactions with teachers more often than did the non-ALEM students (a difference of 28.4 percentage points), and the ALEM students interacted with their teachers significantly more often for instructional purposes than for management purposes. While no major differences were noted between the two groups of students in terms of the percentages of time spent working in group and individual settings, the ALEM students were observed to be significantly more on-task than the non-ALEM students and to spend significantly less time waiting for teacher help.

Results from the analysis of classroom process data across the various studies discussed in this paper suggest that as critical program features were established, so were classroom processes that are hypothesized to facilitate successful student learning as portrayed in the effective teaching literature (for example, high rates of time-on-task, increased instructional interactions with teachers, low incidence of disruptive behavior). This finding is replicated in results from the analysis of differences in the data for fall and spring, the analysis of differences in classroom processes in classrooms with high degrees of implementation and those with comparatively lower implementation scores, and the analysis of differences in classroom processes for ALEM and non-ALEM classes.

One noteworthy implication is that it is possible, through the implementation of adaptive instruction, to attain classroom processes generally recognized as positive in the research on effective teaching. The manner in which students spend their school time and the nature and patterns of interactions between teachers and students are examples of such classroom processes. Among the most frequent criticisms of adaptive instruction programs is that they result in ineffective use of time by teachers and students. Many critics have argued that a major

Table 9.5
Mean Percentages of Observed Frequencies in Major Categories of Classroom Process Variables
(Data from Fall and Spring, 1980-81 for Study II)
(N = 21 classrooms)

| | Observation Periods | | | | Probability |
| | Fall | | Spring | | |
Variables	Mean	(S.D.)	Mean	(S.D.)	from t-test
Interactions Between Teachers and Students					
Initiation					
Student	12.86	(.7)	41.7	(1.1)	<.05
Teacher	87.01	(2.0)	58.3	(1.4)	<.05
Purpose					
Instruction	83.57	(2.1)	92.3	(1.7)	<.05
Management	15.55	(.6)	7.3	(.3)	<.05
Interactions with Peers					
Sharing ideas, materials,					
activities, etc.	97.33	(2.5)	100.00	(2.1)	<.05
Disruptive	2.67	(.1)	0	(0)	<.05
Setting					
Group: Interactive	27.16	(4.5)	69.0	(4.1)	N.S.
Group: Parallel	31.18	(4.0)	23.0	(3.8)	<.05
Individual	41.66	(3.0)	8.0	(2.1)	<.05
Activity Type					
Prescriptive	61.00	(3.9)	16.0	(3.5)	<.05
Exploratory	25.48	(3.8)	13.0	(3.0)	N.S.
Other	13.52	(4.5)	71.0	(4.2)	N.S.
Initiation					
Assigned	83.08	(4.3)	23.0	(3.8)	<.05
Self-initiated	15.39	(4.2)	77.0	(3.8)	<.05
Cannot determine	1.53	(.8)	0	(0)	<.05
Manner					
On-Task	83.91	(1.9)	86.0	(2.0)	N.S.
Waiting	5.60	(1.1)	8.0	(1.8)	N.S.
Distracted	10.48	(1.5)	5.0	(.9)	N.S.

This table is taken from Wang, M.C.; Nojan, M.; Strom, C.D.; and Walberg H.J. "The Utility of Implementation Measures in Program Evaluation and Implementation Research." *Curriculum Inquiry, 14*(3): 249-286.

Table 9.6

Mean Percentages of Observed Frequencies of Classroom Processes for ALEM and Non-ALEM Classrooms (Data from Spring, 1981 for Study II)

Comparison Variables	ALEM Classrooms (N=4)		Non-ALEM Classrooms (N=5)		Differences	Results from t-test
	$\bar{X}$%	(S.D.)	$\bar{X}$%	(S.D.)		
Interactions						
Interactions Between Teacher and Student						
Initiation						
Student	32.4	(1.0)	4.0	(.3)	28.4	18.9**
Teacher	67.6	(1.7)	96.0	(2.9)	28.4	6.17**
Purpose						
Instructional	95.2	(1.9)	88.1	(2.6)	7.1	1.45
Management	4.8	(.3)	11.9	(.6)	7.1	7.89**
Purpose of Interactions with Peers						
Instructional	100.0	(2.2)	99.0	(1.4)	1.0	.263
Disruptive	00.0	(0)	1.0	(.1)	1.0	.744
Activity Types						
Prescriptive	63.6	(4.3)	91.0	(3.0)	27.4	3.60**
Exploratory	26.0	(4.0)	5.5	(2.2)	20.5	3.11**
Other	10.4	(2.6)	3.5	(1.5)	6.9	.688
Setting						
Group Interactive	22.3	(3.7)	34.4	(4.4)	12.1	1.49
Group Parallel	25.1	(4.0)	20.5	(3.7)	4.5	.605
Individual	52.6	(4.7)	45.1	(4.7)	7.5	.798

Initiation						
Assigned	31.4	(4.5)	90.9	(3.9)	58.6	6.76**
Self-Initiated	68.2	(4.5)	9.0	(2.5)	59.2	7.89**
Cannot be Determined	00.4	(.3)	0.1	(.1)	.3	.638
Manner						
On-Task	90.1	(1.7)	80.0	(3.3)	10.1	1.98*
Waiting for Teacher Help	5.9	(1.5)	13.5	(1.0)	7.6	2.93*
Distracted	3.0	(.8)	6.0	(1.2)	3.0	1.50*

Note. *p ≤ .05
**p ≤ .01

This table is taken from Wang, M.C. "Effective Mainstreaming Is Possible. Provided That . . ." *Analysis and Intervention in Developmental Disabilities*, in press.

design flaw of such programs is the requirement that students spend large amounts of time working alone, and that time spent by students working independently generally has tended to be associated with lower rates of time-on-task. Data from the ALEM classrooms suggest findings to the contrary.

Program Implementation and Teacher Use of Class Time

Many practical problems have been encountered in efforts to establish adaptive instruction programs in school settings. Among those cited most frequently are the sometimes intractable demands on teachers' time and the lack of supports that would enable teachers to spend more time on instruction-related, rather than management-related, activities. Therefore, a major task in the design of adaptive instruction programs is the development of ways to increase the amount of school time teachers devote to instruction. This task has been central to the design and implementation of the ALEM.

To investigate the impact of implementing the ALEM on teacher use of class time, observation data from Study II on the manner in which teachers spent their school day in the ALEM mainstreaming classrooms were examined (Wang 1983b). The primary objective of the analysis was to characterize the distribution patterns for time actually spent by teachers performing various functions. The focus was on addressing four questions: What was the overall pattern of time distribution among the major teacher functions? Did patterns of teacher time use differ in classrooms with different degrees of program implementation? Did the amount of teacher time spent on different functions vary according to instructional grouping (that is, individual, small-group, or whole-class)? and, Did the amount of instructional and noninstructional time spent by teachers vary according to differences in student learning characteristics and needs (for example, according to whether students were identified as mainstreamed handicapped, academically gifted, or general education)?

Overall patterns of teacher time use. The percentages of class time spent by teachers on various instructional and noninstructional functions are summarized in Figure 9.2. As shown in the first pie chart in Figure 9.2, teachers in the ALEM classes were observed to spend averages of 81.1 percent (approximately 49 minutes per hour) of their time on instructional functions and 18.9 percent on noninstructional functions. Of the time devoted to instruction-related activities (shown in the second pie chart in Figure 9.2), 93.4 percent (approximately 46 minutes per hour) was spent actually instructing students. These activities included introducing, and providing instruction in, new tasks; conducting review lessons; and giving instruction-related management directions (for example, going over workbook directions, explaining how to get reference materials for specific learning tasks). In addition, teachers were observed to spend 2.8 percent of their instruction-related time on evaluation activities such as checking students' work, giving feedback, and assessing students' learning progress. Planning activities that included prescription of learning tasks and discussion of individual progress plans with students accounted for 3.8 percent of the time spent by teachers on instruction-related activities. Similarly, the third pie chart in Figure 9.2 shows the breakdown of the 18.9 percent of the time that teachers spent on non-instruction-related activities such as managing student behavior and engaging in informal conversations with students regarding personal or other non-instruction-related matters. The 39.1 percent of noninstructional time spent on "other activities" included conversations with school staff, parents, and visitors and unexplained temporary absences from the classrooms.

Degree of program implementation and patterns of teachers' use of time. A question of interest from the instructional design perspective was whether the degree to which critical program design dimensions were in place resulted in differences in teachers' use of time. Figure 9.3 provides a summary of the results from the analysis of time use by teachers in classrooms with overall degree-of-implementation scores at the high, average, and low levels. Statistically significant differences were noted in the overall patterns of instructional/noninstructional time use for the three groups of teachers. Furthermore, as shown in Figure 9.3, the percentage of time spent on instruction-related activities increased from the low to the high degree-of-implementation groups. In addition to the overall amounts of time spent by teachers on instructional and noninstructional functions, major differences were noted in the distribution of time for the various activities within each of the two categories. For example, teachers in the high and average degree-of-implementation classrooms were observed to spend more time prescribing and checking work than did teachers in the low

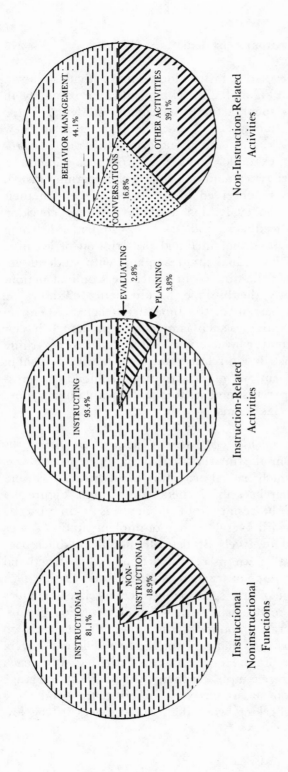

Figure 9.2

Summary of the distribution of teacher time use among instructional and noninstructional functions.*

(N = 28 classrooms; the mean number of observation minutes per teacher was 199.29.)

BEHAVIOR MANAGEMENT 44.1%

CONVERSATIONS 16.8%

OTHER ACTIVITIES 39.1%

Non-Instruction-Related Activities

EVALUATING 2.8%

PLANNING 3.8%

INSTRUCTING 93.4%

Instruction-Related Activities

INSTRUCTIONAL 81.1%

NON-INSTRUCTIONAL 18.9%

Instructional Noninstructional Functions

*Results reported in Figures 9.2 and 9.3 are from Study II.

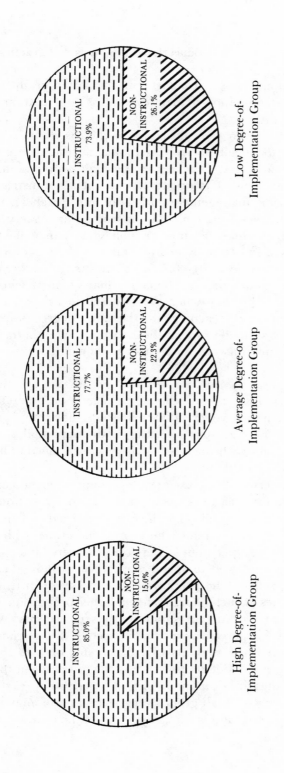

Figure 9.3

Summary of the distribution of teacher time use in classrooms at the high, average, and low degree-of-implementation levels. (N = 28 classrooms; the mean number of observation minutes per teacher was 199.29.)

degree-of-implementation classes. Teachers in the latter group of classes spent significant amounts of their evaluating and planning time doing record keeping.

Some major differences also were observed in the distribution of noninstructional time for teachers in classrooms at the different degree-of-implementation levels. Teachers in the high degree-of-implementation classrooms tended to spend less of their noninstructional time on behavior management. In addition, teachers in classrooms with high degree-of-implementation scores were observed to spend about equal amounts of time on behavior management whether students worked individually or in whole-class instructional situations; teachers in average degree-of-implementation classrooms were observed to spend more time on behavior management when students worked individually than when they worked in whole-class instructional situations; and teachers in the low degree-of-implementation classrooms seemed to spend the greatest amount of their behavior management time in whole-class instructional situations.

Instructional grouping and teachers' use of time. To investigate the extent to which the amounts of time spent by teachers on different types of instructional activities were related to instructional grouping, the manner in which time was spent working with individual students, in small groups, and with the whole class was examined. The results are summarized in Table 9.7.

Differences in the patterns of time use are suggested by the data on the percentages of time that teachers spent on the various functions across the three instructional groupings. (The ratios reported in Table 9.7 are based on 79.67 percent of the teachers' total class time, which is approximately 48 minutes per hour. Therefore, the percentage of time that teachers were observed to spend working with individual students, for example, reflects the proportion of time spent on this activity during 48 minutes of each hour.) While a larger proportion of the teachers' time spent working in small-group settings was expended on instructing (78.1 percent), when compared to the instructing time spent with individual students (57.18 percent) or with the whole class (61.26 percent), a different picture is suggested when the actual numbers of minutes are examined. The 78.1 percent of teachers' time spent instructing in small groups represents approximately 2.42 actual minutes per hour, and the 57.18 percent of the time spent

Table 9.7
Time Teachers Spent on Specific Functions During Interactions with Students in Different Instructional Groupings

| | Instructional Grouping | | | | | |
| | Individual (76.56) | | Small Group (5.17) | | Whole Class (18.27) | |
Teacher Function	Percent-age	Minutes Per Hour	Percent-age	Minutes Per Hour	Percent-age	Minutes Per Hour
Instructing	57.18	26.25	78.10	2.42	61.26	6.71
Giving Task-Specific Procedural Directions	29.44	13.52	18.73	.58	19.90	2.18
Behavior Management	3.15	1.45	3.17	.10	18.84	2.07
Checking Work	4.75	2.18	0	0	0	0
Prescribing	2.84	1.30	0	0	0	0
Conversations with Students for Personal Reasons	3.00	1.37	0	0	0	0

Note. Numbers in parentheses indicate the percentages of time spent in the particular instructional groupings.

providing instruction for individual students, on the other hand, is equal to approximately 26.25 minutes per hour. It is also noteworthy that teachers were observed to spend more time on behavior management functions when working with the whole class, compared to the time spent on this function in individual and small-group settings. Teacher functions such as checking work, prescribing, and conversing with students for personal reasons occurred only when working with individual students.

Student characteristics and teachers' use of time. Another factor of interest in analyzing teacher time use under the ALEM was the extent to which the nature and amount of instruction varied for students with different learning characteristics and needs. The contention here is that the extent to which teachers spent varying amounts of time on different types of instructional and noninstructional tasks with students who had different learning characteristics and needs would be an indicator of adaptive instruction. Results from the analysis are summarized in Table 9.8.

Table 9.8
Mean Percentages of Teacher Time Spent with Individual General
Education, Handicapped, and Academically Gifted Students on
Instructional and Noninstructional Functions

	Mean Percentages of Teacher Time Per Student		
Teacher Functions	General Education Students (N=672)	Handicapped Students (N=77)	Academically Gifted Students (N=35)
Instructional			
Instruction			
Instructing	3.64	3.20	3.40
Giving task-specific procedural directions	3.57	3.27	5.66
Planning	2.19	4.82	1.78
Evaluation	2.65	2.40	1.43
Non-Instructional			
Behavior Management	2.55	3.11	2.38
Conversations with Students (for personal and other non-instructional purposes)	3.56	.81	4.38
Total per-student time across functions	3.65	3.50	3.45

Note. Results reported in Tables 9.7 and 9.8 are from Study II.

As suggested by the data presented in the last row of Table 9.8, the differences in the total percentages of teacher time (instructional and noninstructional) spent with general education, mainstreamed handicapped, and academically gifted students were negligible. There were some notable variations, however, in the time teachers spent performing specific instructional and noninstructional functions with the three different types of students. For example, the teachers seemed to spend only slightly different percentages of time instructing the three types of students. However, when the per-student percentages of time spent on instructing were compared with the time spent giving task-specific procedural directions, major differences were noted. The teachers spent proportionately greater amounts of time giving task-specific procedural directions to the academically gifted students (5.66 percent per student), compared to the time spent instructing these same students (3.4 percent per student). By contrast, there was little difference between the time spent instructing the general education and handicapped students and the time spent giving task-specific procedural directions to these two groups of students.

Differences also were noted in the patterns of teacher time spent with individual students for planning and evaluating their learning. Teachers tended to spend more time with the handicapped students on planning activities (for example, prescribing tasks, record keeping) than with the academically gifted or general education students. In addition, more time was spent evaluating the work of the general education and handicapped students, compared to the amount of time spent evaluating the work of gifted students. Teachers also seemed to spend more time managing the behaviors of handicapped students, compared to the behavior management time spent with the academically gifted and general education students. Similarly, variations were noted in the amounts of time spent conversing with students about personal matters. Teachers tended to spend more time chatting with general education and gifted students than with handicapped students.

As suggested by the analyses discussed above, teachers' use of time in the context of the ALEM is considered to be both an independent and a dependent variable. As an independent variable, time is seen as an instructional design variable that can be manipulated (and should be manipulated) in order to respond adaptively to the needs of individual students. The varying patterns of teacher time use observed across different settings and among individual students with different learning characteristics are viewed, on the other hand, as an indicator of adaptive instruction at work and, therefore, as a dependent variable. Nevertheless, the descriptive nature of the data makes it impossible to draw any direct implications relating differences in teachers' use of time to student learning. The data can be interpreted only as descriptive of observed differences. For example, no assertions can be made about the meaning of the differences in the amounts and purposes of time spent by teachers with gifted students and with mainstreamed handicapped students. However, the data do provide a description of the way teachers use time under the ALEM.

Program Implementation and Student Outcomes

Analysis of the impact of the ALEM on student achievement in mathematics and reading focused on two questions: How did the achievement of ALEM students compare with that of non-ALEM students? and, Did students with varying prior achievement levels make comparable achievement gains under the ALEM? The latter question, in particular, was directed specifically at assessing the effects of adaptive instruction. The hypothesis is that if adaptive instruction provisions for effectively meeting the learning needs of individual students can be successfully achieved under the ALEM, then all students should be able to make expected, if not greater, achievement gains, despite individual differences in prior achievement and learning characteristics.

Scores on standardized achievement tests in mathematics and reading that are routinely administered by the school districts participating in the four studies as part of their annual assessment programs were used in analyzing the impact of the ALEM on student achievement. Three types of analysis were performed: comparison of students' achievement scores in mathematics and reading with the national norm, comparison of achievement test results for ALEM and non-ALEM students, and comparison of achievement results for students with varying learning characteristics and needs. Achievement results from both the Follow Through sites (Studies I and III) and the mainstreaming sites (Studies II and IV) were included in the analysis.

Comparisons with the national norm and with non-ALEM comparison groups. Results from Studies I and II showed that the mean scores for students from the ALEM Follow Through classrooms were well above the estimated population norms (Branden and Weis 1977) for students from similar low-income families. Furthermore, the mean percentile scores in mathematics and reading, in general, were found to be consistently at or above the national norm, despite the predicted below-national-norm achievement average for Follow Through students (Wang and Walberg 1983). For example, the achievement data from Study I showed that, overall, more than the expected 25 percent of students had scores in mathematics and reading that were at or above the 75th percentile. (According to the national norm, 25 percent of the students could have been expected to have scores at or above the 75th percentile.) The percentages of students with percentile ranks at or above 75 ranged from 17 (third-grade reading) to 46 (first-grade mathematics). Likewise, examination of the distribution of scores in the bottom quartile showed that, in every case, less than 25 percent of the students were found to have scores below the 25th percentile (25 percent being the national norm). The range of percentile ranks was 10 (first-grade mathematics) to 23 (third-grade mathematics). In addition, comparison of students' achievement scores for two consecutive years (Study I: Spring 1981; Study III: Spring 1982) suggests improvement over time. Increases were noted in the numbers of students with achievement scores at or above the 75th percentile, and decreases were noted in the numbers of students with scores at or below the 25th percentile.

Comparable positive achievement results under the ALEM were replicated in Studies II and IV. Data from Study IV showed, for example, that statistically significant gains in mathematics and reading were made by both the general education students and the mainstreamed special education students (Wang, Peverly, and Randolph 1984). The mean percentile ranks in reading for the general education students in this study were 60.7 for the second grade, 65.0 for the third grade, and 66.1 for the fourth grade. The mean percentile rank scores for these students in mathematics were 71.0 for the second grade, 75.7 for the third grade, and 66.1 for the fourth grade. It is particularly noteworthy that considerable percentages of the special education students had achievement scores that fell at or above the 75th percentile (according to the test norm). For example, 42.3 percent of the fourth-grade special education students had mathematics scores ranked in the upper quartile, and 28.6 percent had reading scores at or above the 75th percentile.

Comparisons of mathematics and reading achievement for ALEM and non-ALEM students were based on the standardized achievement test results from one of the sites in Study II where a control group was set up specifically for comparison purposes. General education and special education students in the school were randomly assigned to either ALEM classrooms or classrooms where handicapped students were pulled out each morning to attend a resource-room program. The data suggest a consistent pattern of greater achievement gains for the mainstreamed handicapped and gifted students in the ALEM classrooms, compared to the achievement gains for students in the non-ALEM, comparison classrooms (Wang, in press b).

Comparison of students with varying learning characteristics and needs. An ultimate goal of adaptive instruction is to increase the chances for all students to be successful in school, despite individual differences in prior achievement level and related learning characteristics. A basic contention is that, if instructional programs are well adapted to student differences, all students, in spite of varied learning needs, should be able to make achievement gains that are at or above the expected levels. Thus, one criterion for testing the efficacy of an instructional program aimed at adapting to individual differences is the extent to which all students make expected achievement gains.

Data from Study IV were used to investigate whether general education and special education students in the ALEM mainstreaming classrooms made expected, or greater, achievement gains. The results showed that the average gains for both groups of students were at or above the expected one year in grade equivalent. The mean gains for general education students were 1.87 in mathematics (which is significantly different from the expected gain of 1.00, $p < .001$) and 1.19 in reading ($p < .01$). The achievement gains for the mainstreamed special education students were 1.08 in mathematics and 1.04 in reading. While the achievement gain scores for the special education students were not found to be significantly beyond the expected norm of one year, they were significantly greater in both reading ($t = 2.62$, $p < .01$) and mathematics ($t = 2.62$, $p < .01$) than the expected gains for students with comparable special education classifications. The average achievement gain for students in the district with similar classifications was six months. Further evidence of the program's impact is found in the fact that approximately 30 percent of the mainstreamed special education students in Study IV were recommended by their teachers as potential candidates for decertification. The average decertification rate in the school district for special education students with similar classifications who are placed in self-contained, special education classes is 2.8 percent. Thus, the overall achievement results seem to suggest the positive impact of the ALEM on the achievement of students with varied prior achievement levels and learning characteristics.

Analysis of Causal Links Among Program Implementation, Classroom Processes, and Student Outcomes

A final analysis of the data on the implementation and effects of the ALEM was an attempt to examine the extent to which program implementation was related to the observed classroom processes and achievement outcomes. Figure 9.4 shows a theoretical causal model of adaptive instruction. As shown in the figure, relationships among six major constructs were hypothesized. Three of the constructs are related to the design of the ALEM. They are classroom organization, instructional planning and classroom management, and teaching and learning functions. Of the three remaining constructs, one is related to student learning characteristics (prior achievement), and two are program outcome constructs (classroom processes and post achievement).

The construct of students' prior achievement included measures of students' standardized achievement scores from the previous school year. The classroom organization construct included measures of the degree of implementation for three of the critical program dimensions of the ALEM—Arranging Space and Facilities, Establishing and Communicating Rules and Procedures, and Managing Aides. The construct, instructional planning and classroom management, included measures of degree of implementation for five critical dimensions of the ALEM—Creating and Maintaining Instructional Materials, Diagnostic Testing, Monitoring and Diagnosing, Prescribing, and Record Keeping. The construct, teaching and learning functions, included measures of the degree of implementation for four of the critical program dimensions of the ALEM—Developing Student Self-Responsibility, Instructing, Interactive Teaching, and Motivating. The classroom processes construct included observational data related to the manner in which students spent their class time (for example, on-task, distracted, waiting for teacher direction or help). Finally, students' post achievement was measured by standardized achievement tests administered by the school districts at the end of the school year.

Path analysis procedures (Pedhazur 1975) were applied to test the hypothesized causal links shown in Figure 9.4. Mathematics data from Study IV were used to examine the relationship between program implementation and classroom processes and student post achievement. Overall, the data suggest that, after controlling for the effects of

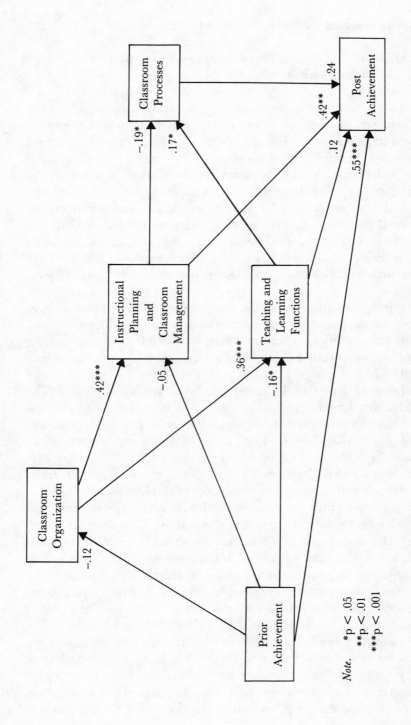

Figure 9.4

A causal model of adaptive instruction, classroom processes, and student achievement. (Results reported are from Study IV.)

Note. *p < .05
**p < .01
***p < .001

prior achievement in mathematics, the four program-related constructs—classroom organization, instructional planning and classroom management, teaching and learning functions, and classroom processes—were found to have significant positive effects on students' post achievement in mathematics. Results from further analysis of the relationships among the constructs are reported in Figure 9.4

A number of significant causal relationships are suggested by the data. Prior achievement in mathematics, as would be expected, had a large significant effect on post achievement. In addition, several of the hypothesized causal linkages between program design, classroom processes, and student achievement are supported by the data. Some interesting examples are the positive relationship between the instructional planning and classroom management construct and post achievement in mathematics (Beta $= .42, p < .01$), and the moderate (Beta $= .24, p < .10$) but positive relationship between classroom processes and post achievement. The findings also indicate that the classroom organization construct was significantly related to the instructional planning and classroom management construct and the teaching and learning functions construct (Beta $= .42$ and $.36$, respectively). Furthermore, the teaching and learning functions construct was found to have a significant positive effect on classroom processes (Beta $= .17, p < .05$). It also should be pointed out that two significant negative relationships were found: the effect of the instructional planning and classroom management construct on classroom processes (Beta $= -.19, p < .05$), and the effect of prior achievement on teaching and learning functions (Beta $= -.16, p < .05$).

While results of the path analysis suggest an overall positive causal relationship between program implementation and hypothesized program outcomes, they also indicate the need for further analysis, particularly insofar as some of the confounding and seemingly counterintuitive findings are concerned (for example, the significant negative effects of instructional planning and classroom management on classroom processes and their significant positive effects on student achievement). Thus, a cautionary note regarding the path analysis findings is in order. Since they represent a preliminary examination of hypothesized causal relationships among the major program design and outcome constructs, they are considered to be only suggestive. Further investigations involving replication of the causal model, analyses of variables within and across constructs included in the model, inclusion of other outcome measures of attitudes and academic achievement, and testing of rival hypotheses and alternative causal models are the necessary next steps. Additional work in this area is seen as crucial for empirical validation of the hypothesized impact of the ALEM on student outcomes.

SUMMARY AND DISCUSSION

In summary, it can be stated that the results discussed in this chapter provide substantial support for three major conclusions. First, it is possible to establish and maintain average to high degrees of implementation of the ALEM on a large-scale basis in a variety of school settings. This is clearly substantiated by the replication of findings across the four studies. Second, as critical features of the ALEM are established, so are classroom processes that are hypothesized to facilitate effective adaptive instruction in classroom settings. Finally, implementation of the ALEM and the presence of desired classroom processes of adaptive instruction seem to facilitate student achievement. While, admittedly, further analysis of the causal relationships among these variables is needed, the overall results from the four studies seem to suggest a consistent pattern of higher achievement scores for ALEM students, when compared with those for non-ALEM students. Particularly noteworthy are the data on the higher-than-expected percentages (based on the national norm of 25 percent) of ALEM students who had achievement scores at or above the 75th percentile (including some of the mainstreamed handicapped students and students from the Follow Through program); and the finding that mainstreamed handicapped students in ALEM classrooms made an average gain of a little over one year in grade equivalent scores in mathematics and reading achievement, compared to the average gain of six months for students with similar handicapping labels. These achievement test results may be regarded as one indicator of adaptive instruction at work. That is, they demonstrate the possibility that students with poor prognoses for academic achievement can succeed in their school learning through the provision of the type of adaptive instruction imbedded in the design of the ALEM. Thus, despite the limitations of attempting to generalize the implications of findings from studies of a single program, there seems to be substantial evidence to support making educational provisions for individual differences in regular classroom settings.

In addition to the data on program efficacy, perhaps the most noteworthy work on the development and evaluation of the ALEM includes identifying critical programming features and specifying required conditions for effective adaptive instruction. The development of systematic procedures for evaluating the degree of program implementation has greatly facilitated efforts directed to program refinement, while also helping to increase understanding of the workings of adaptive instruction. The results from periodic "readings" and systematic analysis of the degree of program implementation provide information not only for program validation and refinement purposes, but also for use by school personnel in planning individually tailored, staff development activities for improving program implementation.

Work on development and evaluation of the ALEM has raised several methodological issues related to evaluation design and analytical procedures, as well as some instructional design questions. Three lines of research are clearly suggested: The first two relate to furthering understanding and development of a theory of adaptive instruction and refinement of adaptive instruction practices in schools; the third relates to refining methods of research into the implementation of innovative educational programs in school settings in general and the subsequent consequences of such implementation.

The first line of suggested research centers on a fundamental question that has guided past work and probably will be the basis of instructional design research on adaptive instruction for years to come. The question is: Given that we have been able to create and maintain an educational program which exemplifies quite closely our design specifications, does the program work as it ought to; and, how do we know? Summaries of research findings presented in this chapter and elsewhere suggest that at a rather gross level, when the critical program dimensions of the ALEM are in place, certain of what Glaser (1982a) has termed the "large practical variables" of effective schooling are observed to be present. Such variables, including efficient use of time by teachers and students and increased interactions between teachers and students on instructional matters, in turn seem to lead to certain desired student outcomes. Several findings from the analysis of the impact of the ALEM, however, clearly indicate the need for further analysis and empirical validation. For example, while some of the relationships (for example, the relationship between the program's structural dimensions, such as classroom organization, and student achievement in mathematics) were found to be quite strong, others were moderate and, in a few cases, indicated quite puzzling negative effects.

These results suggest that analysis of the interrelationships among critical program dimensions and the resulting classroom processes and student outcomes will require much more fine-grained, micro-level analyses than have been utilized thus far in the study of the ALEM. Such analyses are likely to result in further delineation of the causal relationships among the variables within and across critical program dimensions and, perhaps even more important, in the development of alternative models that deal with rival hypotheses about these relationships. One example of further work in this area is the inclusion of variables that are known to be associated with student achievement but have not been included in the analytical model used for the conceptualization and evaluation of adaptive instruction (for example, resource utilization, quality of instruction, nature of the learning task). Another example is the investigation of whether, and to what extent, specific program design dimensions, and/or particular performance indicators within given dimensions, are differentially predisposed to producing a range of desired classroom processes and student achievement and attitudinal outcomes.

Research to examine closely the quality of instruction as it is related to student achievement seems particularly timely, given the present state of the art of research on subject-matter learning (for example, Anderson 1976; Greeno 1980; Resnick and Ford 1981); recent developments in cognitive-instructional psychology (for example, Calfee 1981; Glaser 1982a, b; Simon 1981); and continuing developments in the research on effective teaching in general and the provision of adaptive instruction in particular (Wang and Lindvall 1984). A program of research that seeks ways to incorporate recent advances in these areas into the refinement of instructional-learning adaptations would be a fruitful approach to improving student capabilities, as well as to improving the quality of education for all students through adaptive instruction.

The second line of research is related to delineation of instructionally relevant, individual difference variables. Modern models of schooling have come to recognize that dual adaptation is required for the instructional-learning process—that is, adaptation in the instructional process to accommodate student differences (that is, modification of the learning environment), and adaptation in the ability of individual students to respond successfully to task demands (that is, modification within the learner). Nevertheless, even in the case of widely recognized, research-based programs of adaptive instruction, little work has been done to date on the actual nature of those adaptations that are required if the individual learner is to succeed. The designs of such extant programs, including the ALEM, tend to be concerned with a limited number of individual difference variables. Furthermore, very few of these variables are incorporated in planning and the actual instructional process, despite the research suggesting a wide range of individual difference variables as correlates of learning (Wang and Lindvall 1984).

The third line of research suggested by the work described here is related to refining and improving research methodologies for the analysis and evaluation of innovative schooling practices. Several quite complex problems have been raised. Although these problems are not new, their resolution seems even more critical given the state of the art of the design and study of adaptive instruction in classroom settings.

One problem has to do with the difficulty of obtaining controls for conducting instructional experimentations or intervention studies in naturalistic settings and the scientific credibility of findings from descriptive field research of the type discussed in this chapter. Experience in the implementation and study of the ALEM and the work of others have shown that the participation of schools and teachers in an innovative program tends to be a matter of choice rather than assignment by central administrators. While such identification of sample populations can portend well for program implementation, it precludes the evaluation of randomized program treatments. One common solution to this design problem is use of the replication strategy. The basic contention is that results on program impact can be inferred from quasi-experimental studies or correlational studies, if they are repeated under a variety of conditions. Nevertheless, while the replication strategy adopted in the study and analysis of the impact of the ALEM has provided intuitively sound evidence of support for the particular adaptive instruction approach reflected in the program's design, the research associated with the design and evaluation of the ALEM can be characterized only as suggestive at best.

Another related technical problem has to do with the fact that, in cases where a high degree of program implementation is maintained (a desired outcome of any innovative school improvement program), there is very little variance in the implementation measures. This low variance has been identified as a persistent psychometric problem with analyses of relationships between program implementation and hypothesized program outcomes. There is an obvious need to identify and develop alternative designs and methodologies for obtaining empirical evidence to answer the fundamental questions: Does the program work? and How do we know?

From the methodological perspective, the importance of greater technical sophistication in the study of adaptive instruction programs is clear. Much work is needed in the development of procedures for examining nonlinear effects and nonrecursive relationships, as well as interactive and contextual effects that typically are associated with instructional design and program validation and evaluation research of the type discussed in this chapter. Research designs incorporating multiple indicators or triangulation data-collection procedures are indicated for future investigations of innovative programs.

REFERENCES

Anderson, John R. *Language, Memory, and Thought*. Hillsdale, N.J.: Lawrence Erlbaum Associates, 1976.

Bennett, Neville. *Teaching Styles and Pupil Progress*. Cambridge, Mass.: Harvard University Press, 1976.

Bloom, Benjamin S. *Human Characteristics and School Learning*. New York: McGraw-Hill, 1976.

Branden, Ann, and Weis, Lynn. "Alternative Presentation of the MAT Data: Follow Through National Evaluation." Paper presented to the Office of Planning and Evaluation, Elementary and Secondary Education Programs, U.S. Office of Education, Washington, D.C., 1977.

Brophy, Jere. "Teacher Behavior and Its Effects." *Journal of Educational Psychology* 71 (December 1979): 733-50.

Calfee, Robert. "Cognitive Psychology and Educational Practice." In *Review of Research in Education*, vol. 9, edited by David C. Berliner. Washington, D.C.: American Educational Research Association, 1981.

Glaser, Robert. *Criterion-referenced Testing for Measurement*. LRDC Publication Series

R41. Pittsburgh, Pa.: Learning Research and Development Center, University of Pittsburgh, 1967.

Glaser, Robert. *Adaptive Education: Individual Diversity and Learning.* New York: Holt, Rinehart & Winston, 1977.

Glaser, Robert, editor. *Advances in Instructional Psychology*, vol. 2. Hillsdale, N.J.: Lawrence Erlbaum Associates, 1982 (a).

Glaser, Robert. "Education and Thinking: The Role of Knowledge." Paper presented as the Edward L. Thorndike Award Address at the annual meeting of the American Psychological Association, Washington, D.C., 1982 (b).

Greeno, James G. "Psychology of Learning, 1960-80: One Participant's Observations." *American Psychologist* 35 (August 1980): 713-28.

Johnson, David W.; Maruyama, Geoffrey; Johnson, Roger T.; Nelson, Deborah; and Skon, Linda. "Effects of Cooperative, Competitive, and Individualistic Goal Structures on Achievement: A Meta-analysis." *Psychological Bulletin* 89 (January 1981): 47-62.

Lindvall, C. Mauritz, and Cox, Richard C. "A Rationale and Plan for the Evaluation of the Individually Prescribed Instruction Project." Paper presented at the annual meeting of the American Educational Research Association, New York, 1967.

Marshall, Hermine H. "Open Classrooms: Has the Term Outlived Its Usefulness?" *Review of Educational Research* 51 (Summer 1981): 181-92.

National School Public Relations Association. *Good Teachers: What to Look For.* Arlington, Va.: National School Public Relations Association, 1981.

Pedhazur, Elazar J. "Analytic Methods in Studies of Educational Effects." In *Review of Research in Education*, vol. 3, edited by Fred N. Kerlinger. Itasca, Ill.: F.E. Peacock, 1975.

Peterson, Penelope L. "Direct Instruction Reconsidered." In *Research on Teaching: Concepts, Findings, and Implications*, edited by Penelope L. Peterson and Herbert J. Walberg. Berkeley, Calif.: McCutchan, 1979.

Resnick, Lauren B., and Ford, Wendy W. *The Psychology of Mathematics for Instruction.* Hillsdale, N.J.: Lawrence Erlbaum Associates, 1981.

Resnick, Lauren B.; Wang, Margaret C.; and Kaplan, Jerome. "Task Analysis in Curriculum Design: A Hierarchically Sequenced Introductory Mathematics Curriculum." *Journal of Applied Behavioral Analysis* 6 (Winter 1973): 679-710.

Rosenshine, Barak V. "Content, Time, and Direct Instruction." In *Research on Teaching: Concepts, Findings, and Implications*, edited by Penelope L. Peterson and Herbert J. Walberg. Berkeley, Calif.: McCutchan, 1979.

Simon, Herbert A. *The Sciences of the Artificial.* Cambridge, Mass.: MIT Press, 1981.

Smith, Elaine. "Implementation of the Self-Schedule System: The Teacher's Perspective." In *The Self-Schedule System for Instructional-learning Management in Adaptive School Learning Environments*, edited by Margaret C. Wang. LRDC Publications Series 1976/9. Pittsburgh, Pa.: Learning Research and Development Center, University of Pittsburgh, 1976.

Stone, Ruth, and Vaughn, Larry. "Implementation and Evaluation of the Self-Schedule System in an Adaptive School Learning Environment." In *The Self-Schedule System for Instructional-learning Management in Adaptive School Learning Environments*, edited by Margaret C. Wang. LRDC Publications Series 1976/9. Pittsburgh, Pa.: Learning Research and Development Center, University of Pittsburgh, 1976.

Walberg, Herbert J. "Synthesis of Research on Teaching." In *Third Handbook of Research on Teaching*, edited by Merlin C. Wittrock. Washington, D.C.: American Educational Research Association, 1984.

Wang, Margaret C., editor. *The Use of Direct Observation to Study Instructional-Learning Behaviors in School Settings*. LRDC Publications Series 1974/9. Pittsburgh, Pa.: Learning Research and Development Center, University of Pittsburgh, 1974.

Wang, Margaret C. "Adaptive Instruction: Building on Diversity." *Theory Into Practice* 19 (Spring 1980): 122-28. (a)

Wang, Margaret C. *The Degree of Implementation Assessment Measures for the Adaptive Learning Environments Model*. Pittsburgh, Pa.: Learning Research and Development Center, University of Pittsburgh, 1980. (b)

Wang, Margaret C. *The Use of the Data-Based Staff Development Program to Improve Program Implementation*. Pittsburgh, Pa.: Learning Research and Development Center, University of Pittsburgh, 1981.

Wang, Margaret C. "Development and Consequences of Students' Sense of Personal Control." In *Teacher and Student Perceptions: Implications for Learning*, edited by John M. Levine and Margaret C. Wang. Hillsdale, N.J.: Lawrence Erlbaum Associates, 1983. (a)

Wang, Margaret C. "Time Use and the Provision of Adaptive Instruction." In *Time and School Learning*, edited by Lorin W. Anderson. London: Croom Helm Ltd., 1983. (b)

Wang, Margaret C. "An Analysis of Program Design Implications for Teacher and Student Use of School Time." In *Perspectives on Instructional Time*, edited by Charles Fisher and David Berliner. New York: Longman, in press. (a)

Wang, Margaret C. "Effective Mainstreaming is Possible—Provided That . . ." *Analysis and Intervention in Developmental Disabilities*, in press. (b)

Wang, Margaret C., and Birch, Jack W. "Effective Special Education in Regular Classes." *Exceptional Children* 50, no. 5 (1984): 391-99.

Wang, Margaret C.; Catalano, Rita; and Gromoll, Erika. *Training Manual for the Implementation Assessment Battery for Adaptive Instruction*, vol. 1. Pittsburgh, Pa.: Learning Research and Development Center, University of Pittsburgh, 1983.

Wang, Margaret C., and Fitzhugh, Robert C. "Planning Instruction and Monitoring Classroom Processes with Computer Assistance." *Educational Technology* 18 (February 1978): 7-13.

Wang, Margaret C., and Gennari, Patricia. "Analysis of the Design, Implementation, and Effects of the Data-Based Staff Development Program." *Teacher Education and Special Education* 6, no. 4 (1983): 211-26.

Wang, Margaret C.; Leinhardt, Gaea; and Boston, M. Elizabeth. *Individualized Early Learning Program*. LRDC Publications Series 1980/2. Pittsburgh, Pa.: Learning Research and Development Center, University of Pittsburgh, 1980.

Wang, Margaret C., and Lindvall, C. Mauritz. "Individual Differences and School Learning Environments: Theory, Research, and Design." In *Review of Research in Education*, vol. 11, edited by Edmund W. Gordon. Washington, D.C.: American Educational Research Association, 1984.

Wang, Margaret C.; Nojan, Meyran; Strom, Charles D.; and Walberg, Herbert J. "The Utility of Degree of Implementation Measures in Program Evaluation and Implementation Research." *Curriculum Inquiry* 14, no. 3 (1984): 249-86.

Wang, Margaret C.; Peverly, Stephen; and Randolph, Robert. "An Investigation of the Implementation and Efficacy of a Full-time Mainstreaming Program." *Journal of Remedial and Special Education* 5, no. 6 (1984): 21-32.

Wang, Margaret C.; Resnick, Lauren B.; and Boozer, Robert F. "The Sequence of Development of Some Early Mathematics Behaviors." *Child Development* 42 (December 1971): 1768-78.

Wang, Margaret C.; Resnick, Lauren B.; and Scheutz, Patricia R. *PEP in the Frick Elementary School: Interim Evaluation Report 1969-70*. LRDC Publications Series 1974/13. Pittsburgh, Pa.: Learning Research and Development Center, University of Pittsburgh, 1974.

Wang, Margaret C., and Stiles, Billie. "An Investigation of Children's Concepts of Self-Responsibility for Their School Learning." *American Educational Research Journal* 13 (Summer 1976): 159-79.

Wang, Margaret C., and Walberg, Herbert J. "Adaptive Instruction and Classroom Time." *American Educational Research Journal* 20 (Winter 1983): 601-25.

Team-Assisted Individualization: A Cooperative Learning Solution for Adaptive Instruction in Mathematics

Robert E. Slavin

The issue of whether and how to adapt instruction to individual differences in student ability or achievement has been one of the most long-standing controversies in American education. At various times, such practices as tracking, within-class ability grouping, programmed instruction, computer-assisted instruction, and mastery learning have

This chapter is based on research funded by grants from the National Institute of Education and by the Office of Special Education, U.S. Department of Education. The opinions expressed are mine and do not represent official policy.

The research reported here was done in collaboration with Marshall Leavey, Nancy Madden, Sabine Oishi, and Reva Bryant.

been favored as ways to insure that the needs and abilities of every student are taken into account. The need for individualized instruction has been perceived as particularly great in mathematics, where learning of each skill depends in large part on mastery of prerequisite skills.

The rationale behind individualizing mathematics instruction is that students enter class with widely divergent knowledge, skills, and motivation. When the teacher presents a single lesson to a diverse group, it is likely that some students will not have the prerequisite skills to learn the lesson, and will fail to profit from it. Others will already know the material, or will learn it so quickly that additional time spent going over the lesson will be wasted for them. Karweit (1983) and Slavin (1984a) have hypothesized that small, inconsistent effects of time-on-task on achievement (net of ability) are due at least in part to a lack of correspondence in group-paced instruction between what is taught and students' levels of readiness and individual learning rates.

It is clear that teaching a single lesson at a single pace to a heterogeneous class is in some ways inefficient in the use of instructional time. In theory, maximum instructional efficiency should be achieved when material presented to students is exactly appropriate to their levels of readiness and proceeds at as rapid a pace as students can assimilate information. The substantial effects of one-to-one tutoring on student achievement (see, for example, Glass, Cahen, Smith, and Filby 1982) probably arise in part from the ability of the adult tutor to establish a level and pace of instruction that is closely tailored to the needs of the individual student being tutored.

However, students for the most part are taught in class groups, not in individual tutoring sessions. Individualizing instruction in class groups entails costs in instructional efficiency that may equal or exceed the inefficiencies of a single level and pace of instruction. For example, programmed instruction provides complete individualization of instruction, allowing students to proceed at their own rates on materials appropriate to their level of prior knowledge. Yet programmed instruction inevitably reduces the amount of time teachers can spend in direct instructional activities and increases the amount of time students spend doing seatwork. In studies of group-paced instruction, time spent on seatwork has typically been negatively associated with learning, while time spent on direct instruction has had positive effects on learning (see Brophy 1979; Good 1979). Time spent checking materials and managing the program is largely time lost from instruction. Motivation is often lacking in programmed instruction, as students may place little value on progress for its own sake, and may become bored with endless interaction with written materials alone (see Kepler and Randall 1977; Schoen 1976, for discussions of the problems of programmed instruction).

Reviews of research on programmed instruction in mathematics (for example, Miller 1976; Schoen 1976) uniformly conclude that programmed instruction is no more effective than traditional methods in increasing student achievement. Given the costs and difficulties of implementing programmed instruction, one might argue that this approach should be abandoned as unworkable and ineffective.

Yet the problems of student heterogeneity that programmed instruction was designed to address will not go away. If anything, classes are becoming more, not less heterogeneous as a consequence of such movements as mainstreaming, desegregation (which sometimes brings about abandonment of tracking), and shrinking school size (which restricts possibilities for tracking). Tracking itself is increasingly being questioned as an effective means of dealing with the problem of student heterogeneity. Studies of tracking find few achievement benefits for this practice (see Esposito 1973; Good and Marshall 1984; Kulik and Kulik 1982), except perhaps for gifted students (but see Slavin, 1984b, for criticism of this research).

Rather than abandon programmed instruction, we began a project at the Johns Hopkins Center for Social Organization of Schools to attempt to resolve as many of the problems of programmed instruction as possible. We hoped to reap the achievement benefits of providing instruction appropriate to the needs and skills of individual students by reducing the time and management costs of programmed instruction and increasing the amount of direct instruction teachers could deliver in coordination with the individualized program. Our plan was to have the students themselves handle the routine management and checking required for the individualized program in small, heterogeneous teams, and to reward the teams based on the number and accuracy of units completed by all team members. In a decade of research on group-paced cooperative learning methods (see Slavin 1980, 1983), we had found that team incentives were effective in motivating students to help and encourage one another to achieve, and thus were consistently effective in increasing student achievement. We now wished to apply the same principle to motivate students to help and encourage one another to do individualized units quickly and accurately.

By having student teams take responsibility for routine management and checking, for helping one another with problems, and for encouraging one another to achieve, we felt it would be possible to free the teacher to provide direct instruction to small, homogeneous groups of students drawn from the heterogeneous teams. We intended this instruction to focus on the concepts behind the algorithms students were learning in their individualized work, and we thus hoped to integrate the teacher's instruction to the homogeneous teaching groups with the individualized work.

In addition to solving the problems of management and motivation in programmed instruction, we hoped to create a method that would take advantage of the considerable socialization potential of cooperative learning. Previous studies of group-paced cooperative learning methods have consistently found positive effects of these methods on such outcomes as race relations and attitudes toward mainstreamed academically handicapped students (see Slavin 1980, 1983). We thus had good reason to expect that similar outcomes could be achieved in a method combining cooperative learning and individualized instruction.

TEAM-ASSISTED INDIVIDUALIZATION

To solve the theoretical and practical problems of programmed instruction, we set out to create a method that would satisfy the following criteria:

— The teacher would be minimally involved in routine management and checking.

— The teacher would spend at least half of his or her time teaching small groups.

— Program operation would be so simple that students in grades three and up could manage it.

— Students would be motivated to proceed rapidly and accurately through the materials, and could not do so by cheating or finding shortcuts.

— Many mastery checks would be provided so that students would rarely waste time on material they had already mastered or run into serious difficulties requiring teacher help. At each mastery checkpoint, alternative instructional activities and parallel tests would be provided.

— Students would be able to check one another's work, even when the checking student was behind the student being checked in the instructional sequence, and the checking procedure would be simple and not disruptive to the checker.

— The program would be simple to learn for teachers and students, inexpensive, and flexible, and would not require aides or team teachers.

— The program would, by having students work in cooperative, equal-status groups, establish conditions for positive attitudes toward mainstreamed, academically handicapped students and among students of different racial or ethnic backgrounds.

The Team-Assisted Individualized program (TAI) that was developed to meet the above criteria was first piloted in a single class, extensively revised, studied in two full-scale but brief (eight and ten weeks, respectively) field experiments, revised again, and studied in a large-scale, twenty-four-week field experiment in a suburban school district and two smaller-scale experiments in inner-city Baltimore. It was then completely revised and further evaluated in two final field experiments of sixteen and eighteen weeks' duration, respectively. The TAI program as applied in the field experiments consisted of the following components.

1. *Teams.* Students were assigned to four- to five-member teams by the project staff. Each team consisted of a mix of high, average, and low achievers as determined by a placement test, boys and girls, and students of any ethnic groups in the class represented in the proportion they made up of the entire class. Students identified as receiving resource help for a learning problem were evenly distributed among the teams. Every eight weeks, students were reassigned to new teams by their teachers according to the same procedures.

2. *Placement test.* The students were pretested at the beginning of the project on mathematics operations. Students were placed at the appropriate point in the individualized program based on their performance on the placement test.

3. *Curriculum materials.* During the individualized portion of the TAI process, students worked on prepared curriculum materials

covering addition, subtraction, multiplication, division, numeration, decimals, fractions, word problems, and introduction to algebra. These materials had the following subparts:

— An Instruction Sheet explaining the skill to be mastered and giving a step-by-step method of solving problems.

— Several Skillsheets, each consisting of twenty problems. Each skillsheet introduced a subskill that led to final mastery of the entire skill.

— A Checkout, which consisted of two parallel sets of ten test items.

— A Final Test.

— Answer Sheets for Skillsheets, Checkouts, and Final Tests.

4. *Team Study Method.* Following the placement test, students were given a starting point in the individualized mathematics units. They worked on their units in their teams, following these steps:

— Students formed into pairs or triads within their teams. Students located the unit they were working on and brought it to the team area. Each unit consisted of the Instruction Sheet, Skillsheets, and Checkout stapled together, and the Skillsheet Answer Sheets and Checkout Answer Sheets stapled together.

— Students exchanged Answer Sheets with partners within their teams.

— Each student read his or her Instruction Sheet, asking teammates or the teacher for help if necessary, and then began with the first Skillsheet in his or her unit.

— Each student worked the first four problems on his or her own Skillsheet and then had his or her partner check the answers against the Answer Sheet. If all four were correct, the student could immediately go on to the next Skillsheet. If any were wrong, the student had to try the next four problems, and so on until he or she got one block of four problems correct (asking teammates or the teacher for help if needed).

— When a student got four in a row on the last Skillsheet, he or she could take Checkout A, a ten-item quiz that resembled the last Skillsheet. On the Checkout, students worked alone until they were finished. When they were finished, a teammate scored the Checkout. If the student got eight or more items correct, the teammate signed the Checkout to indicate that the student was certified by the team to take the Final Test. If the student did *not* get eight correct, the teacher was called in to explain any problems the student was having. The teacher would then ask the student to work again on certain Skillsheet items. The student then took Checkout B, a second ten-item test comparable in content and difficulty to Checkout A. Otherwise, students skipped Checkout B and went straight to the Final Test. No student would take the Final Test until he or she had been passed by a teammate on a Checkout. When a student "checked out," he or she took the Checkout to a student monitor from a different team to get the appropriate Final Test. The student then completed the Final Test, and the monitor scored it. Two or three students served as monitors each day, rotating responsibility among the class every day.

5. *Team Scores and Team Recognition.* At the end of each week, the teacher computed a team score. This score was based on the average number of units covered by each team member, with extra points for perfect or near-perfect papers. Criteria were established for team performance. A high criterion was set for a team to be a "SUPER-TEAM," a moderate criterion was established for a team to be a "GREATTEAM," and a minimum criterion was set for a team to be a "GOODTEAM." The teams meeting the "SUPERTEAM" and "GREATTEAM" criterion received attractive certificates.

6. *Teaching Groups.* Every day, the teacher worked with groups of students who were at about the same point in the curriculum for five-to-fifteen-minute sessions. The purpose of these sessions was to prepare students for major concepts in upcoming units and to go over any points with which students were having trouble. Teachers were instructed to emphasize concepts rather than algorithms in their instruction, as the individualized materials were considered adequate for teaching algorithms but not concepts. Teaching groups were recommended in the first five studies of TAI but were much more strongly emphasized in the sixth and seventh studies.

RESEARCH ON TAI

Seven field experiments have been conducted to evaluate the effects of TAI on student achievement, attitudes, and behavior. The principal features and results of these studies are summarized in Table 10.1 and discussed in more detail in the following sections. To avoid confusion, the studies will be referred to as "Experiment 1," "Experiment 2," and so on. The actual references for the studies appear in Table 10.1.

Research Strategies

All of the TAI studies used either random assignment of classes (Experiments 4, 5, 6, and 7) or schools (Experiment 1), or matched experimental and control classes (Experiments 2 and 3). In all cases, teachers who had volunteered to use TAI were then assigned to use TAI immediately or to serve as teacher of a control group and use TAI later. Analyses of covariance or equivalent multiple regression procedures were used to control for any initial differences between students and to increase statistical power. In three of the studies (Experiments 3, 6, and 7), the numbers of teachers involved were large enough to allow for nested analyses of covariance, which are essentially equivalent to conservative class-level analyses. In Experiment 6, the "control group" was the Missouri Mathematics Program, or MMP (Good, Grouws, and Ebmeier 1983), a whole-class instructional method that emphasizes a high ratio of active teaching to seatwork and other principles derived from research on direct instruction. Experiment 7 compared TAI both to the MMP and to an untreated control group. All other studies compared TAI and untreated control groups only. Teacher training for each experiment involved a three-hour workshop, followed by classroom visits to insure faithful implementation. The settings for the studies ranged from inner-city Baltimore and Wilmington, Delaware, to suburban and rural Maryland, and grade level from three to six. Implementation periods varied from eight to twenty-four weeks (median=sixteen weeks).

Academic Achievement

Academic achievement outcomes were assessed in six of the seven studies. In Experiment 5, our original intention was to assess achievement outcomes, but the dropping out of a teacher upset the

Table 10.1
Summary of Research on Team-Assisted Individualization

Study and Major Reports	Setting and Design Characteristics						Measures and Results[1]	
	No. of Students	Grade Levels	Duration (weeks)	Kinds of Schools	Experimental Design	Mathematics Achievement	Attitudes	Behavior Ratings
Experiment 1: Full Sample (Slavin, Leavey, and Madden 1984)	506	3-5	8	Suburban	Randomly Assigned Schools	CTBS Computations +	Liking of Math Class + Self-Concept in Math +	Classroom Behavior + Self-Confidence + Friendships + Neg. Peer Behavior +
Experiment 1: Academically Handicapped Students (Slavin, Madden, and Leavey 1984a)	117	3-5	8	Suburban	Randomly Assigned Schools	CTBS Computations 0	Liking of Math Class (+) Self-Concept in Math 0 "Best Friend" Choices + "Rejection" Choices +	Classroom Behavior + Self-Confidence + Friendships + Neg. Peer Behavior +
Experiment 2 (Slavin, Leavey, and Madden 1984)	320	4-6	10	Suburban	Matched Schools	CTBS Computations +	Liking of Math Class 0 Self-Concept in Math 0	Classroom Behavior 0 Self-Confidence + Friendships + Neg. Peer Behavior 0
Experiment 3: Full Sample (Slavin, Madden, and Leavey, in press)	1371	3-5	24	Suburban	Matched Schools	CTBS Computations + CTBS Concepts & Applications +		
Experiment 3: Academically	113	3-5	24	Suburban	Matched	CTBS Computations +		

Experiment	N	Grades	Schools	Location	Assignment	Achievement Measures		Attitude/Sociometric Measures	
Handicapped Students (Slavin, Madden, and Leavey, in press)						CTBS Concepts & Applications	+		
Experiment 4 (Oishi, Slavin, & Madden (1983)	160	4-6	16	Urban	Randomly Assigned Classes	CAT Computations	0	Cross-Race:	
						CAT Concepts & Applications	0	Friends	+
								Rejects	+
								Nice	0
								Not Nice	+
								Smart	0
								Not Smart	(+)
Experiment 5 (Oishi, 1983)	120	4-6	16	Urban	Randomly Assigned Classes			Cross-Race:	
								Friends	0
								Playmates	+
								Nice	0
								Not Nice	+
								Smart	+
								Not Smart	0
Experiment 6 (Slavin & Karweit, in press)	354	4-6	18	Urban	Randomly Assigned Classes	CTBS Computations	+	Liking of Math Class	+
						CTBS Concepts & Applications	0	Self-Concept in Math	+
Experiment 7 (Slavin & Karweit, in press)	480	3-5	16	Rural	Randomly Assigned Classes	CTBS Computations	+	Liking of Math Class	+
						CTBS Concepts & Applications	0	Self-Concept in Math	0

[1] + = TAI students scored significantly higher than control students on the indicated measure, p < .05 or better.

(+) = Same as above, but p < .10

From Robert E. Slavin, "Team-Assisted Individualization: Combining Cooperative Learning and Individualized Instruction in Mathematics." In *Learning to Cooperate, Cooperating to Learn*, edited by Robert Slavin, Shlomo Sharan, Spencer Kagan, Rachel Hertz-Lazarowitz, Clark Webb, and Richard Schmuck (New York: Plenum, forthcoming).

comparability of the experimental and control groups in terms of prior achievement, so achievement was not assessed. The posttest achievement data were scores on district-administered California Achievement Tests (CAT) in Experiment 4, but in all other studies, the Comprehensive Test of Basic Skills (CTBS) was used. CTBS scores were also used as covariates to control for initial performance level in Experiments 1 and 2, and district-administered CAT scores served this purpose in Experiments 3, 4, 6, and 7. The Mathematics Computations scale was used in all studies, and in all but the first two, Mathematics Concepts and Applications scales were also given.

In five of the six achievement studies, TAI students significantly exceeded control students in Computations. Similar effects were found for Concepts and Applications in only one of the four studies in which this variable was assessed (Experiment 3), but in all four studies means for Concepts and Applications favored the TAI group. The one study in which statistically significant effects on neither achievement measure were found was Experiment 4 (Oishi, Slavin, and Madden 1983), which took place in a Baltimore City public school. Poor implementation (particularly failure to use teaching groups) may account for this anomalous finding. In the five studies in which the treatment effects for Computations were statistically significant, they were also quite large. Even in the relatively brief Experiments 1 and 2, the TAI classes gained twice as much in terms of grade equivalents as did control students. The TAI-control differences were 42 percent of a grade equivalent in Experiment 3, and in Experiment 6, TAI exceeded the Missouri Mathematics Program (MMP) by 93 percent of a grade equivalent. In Experiment 7, TAI exceeded MMP by 30 percent of a grade equivalent and exceeded the control group by 75 percent of a grade equivalent. The remarkable effects found in Experiments 6 and 7 (in only eighteen and sixteen weeks, respectively) may be due in part to a complete revision of the curriculum materials just before Experiments 6 and 7, and perhaps more importantly to an increased emphasis on regular use of teaching groups for concept instruction in these studies.

Searches for interactions between treatment and various student attributes failed to find any consistent patterns. Experiments 1 and 3 failed to find any interactions between academically handicapped/ nonhandicapped status and treatment effect. There was an interaction between ability (pretest) and treatment in Experiment 1 favoring TAI effects for low achievers, but this was almost certainly due to a ceiling effect on the tests used; no such interactions were found in Experiments 2, 3, 6, or 7. An exhaustive search for interactions was conducted in Experiments 6 and 7; no significant interactions were found between treatment and absolute prior performance level, prior performance relative to class means, sex, or (in Experiment 7) race.

Attitudes

Two general attitude scales were used in Experiments 1, 2, 6, and 7. These were eight-item experimenter-made scales assessing Liking of Math Class and Self-Concept in Math. Statistically significant effects favoring TAI were found for Liking of Math Class in Experiments 1, 6, and 7, but not in Experiment 2. For Self-Concept in Math, positive effects were found in Experiments 1 and 6 but not Experiments 2 or 7. However, in no case did means for these variables favor a control treatment.

Behaviors

In Experiments 1 and 2, teachers were asked to rate a subset of their students (all academically handicapped students plus six randomly selected nonhandicapped students) on six scales: Classroom Behavior, Self-Confidence Behavior, Friendship Behavior, and Negative Peer Behavior (for example, fighting). In Experiment 1, statistically significant effects favoring TAI students were found on all four scales. Experiment 2 replicated these findings for Self-Confidence and Friendship behaviors, but not for the other two scales (though the means were in the same direction).

Race Relations

The primary purpose of Experiments 4 and 5 was to assess the effects of TAI on race relations, to discover whether the frequently found positive effects of cooperative learning in general on attitudes between blacks and whites (see Slavin and Hansell 1983) would also be found for TAI. In Experiment 4, positive effects of TAI were found on cross-racial nominations on two sociometric scales, "Who are your friends in this class?" and "Who would you rather *not* sit at a table with?" No effects were found on cross-racial ratings of classmates as "nice" or "smart," but TAI students made significantly fewer cross-racial ratings as "not nice" and marginally fewer as "not smart." In

Experiment 5, no effects were found on cross-racial "friendship" nominations, but TAI students named significantly more students of another race as playmates at recess than did control students. Positive effects were also found on cross-racial ratings as "smart" and on reductions in ratings as "not nice." Interestingly, the effect on "smart" ratings was due primarily to increases in whites' ratings of black classmates.

Effects on Academically Handicapped Students

One principal impetus for the development of TAI was to develop a means of meeting the instructional needs of academically handicapped students in the context of the regular class while providing these students with the cooperative experiences found in earlier research to improve the acceptance of academically handicapped students by their nonhandicapped classmates (see Madden and Slavin 1983). Effects of TAI on academically handicapped students have been positive on several dimensions. No achievement differences for the academically handicapped subsample were found in Experiment 1, which involved an eight-week intervention, but significant and strong achievement effects were found in the longer (twenty-four weeks) Experiment 3, where academically handicapped students gained 52 percent of a grade equivalent more in Computations than did their control counterparts. In Experiment 1, academically handicapped students in TAI gained more than control students in sociometric choices as "best friends" received from their nonhandicapped classmates, and they were less often checked neither as "best friends" nor as "o.k." They were also rated much more positively than control students on all four behavior rating scales.

DISCUSSION

The results of the field experiments evaluating Team-Assisted Individualization (TAI) clearly indicate that this method increases students' mathematics achievement more than traditional instructional methods. On every Computations measure in all six studies in which achievement was assessed, the TAI students gained more than their control counterparts, although the differences were not statistically significant in Experiment 4. Significant effects for Concepts and

Applications were found in one of the four studies in which it was assessed, although the means were in the same direction in all four studies.

In operation, TAI was found to satisfy most of the criteria outlined earlier in this paper. In all seven studies, students were able to take on routine maintenance and checking functions. In fact, students' abilities to carry out responsibly the various program activities, including checking partners, routing themselves, recording scores, and serving as monitors exceeded our initial expectations. The team reward system did seem to be very motivating, and students greatly enjoyed both the program itself and making progress in it. Several teachers reported difficulty getting students to go to the next class; many students asked to do mathematics all day!

One criterion that was only partially met was that teachers would be able to spend at least half of their time teaching small groups. In the first five experiments, most teachers worked with individuals rather than small groups most of the time. We felt that this provided students with inadequate direct instructional time. Before Experiments 6 and 7, we changed the procedure to make teaching groups easier to manage and emphasized teaching groups more in teacher training. Most teachers in these studies spent at least half of their class time teaching small groups of students. This change could account for the remarkable effects of TAI on student achievement in these studies.

Teachers have responded very favorably to TAI, and approximately 80 percent of all teachers who used TAI in the experimental studies continued to do so in the following school year.

One important theoretical issue is posed by the results of Experiment 1. In that study, the use of the individualized materials and all procedures except the cooperative teams increased student achievement (as compared to control students) almost as much as the full TAI program. Besides the materials themselves, this individualized instruction (II) treatment retained the student-managed aspect of TAI, including student monitors and self-routing, freeing the teacher to work with individuals and small groups (as in TAI). This result suggests that the cooperative teams may not be essential to TAI, but that the positive achievement effects seen for TAI are due either to student management of an individualized program or to the particular individualized materials themselves. However, Experiment 1 lasted only eight weeks. A longer study comparing TAI with and without cooperative incentives (Cavanagh 1984) did find greater achievement due to the cooperative incentives.

The results of Experiment 1 for the academically handicapped subsample indicate that TAI can have a strong positive effect on the social acceptance and behavior of academically handicapped students. The sociometric findings mirror effects of group-paced cooperative learning methods (see Madden and Slavin 1983). The behavioral rating effects are particularly dramatic. All academically handicapped students were rated as much worse in behavior than their nonhandicapped classmates at the beginning of the study. By the end, ratings of academically handicapped students in the TAI classes were nearly identical to ratings of nonhandicapped students in the control classes! Experiment 3 also showed that TAI can have a strong positive effect on the achievement of academically handicapped students.

However, it is important to note that on most of the sociometric and behavior rating measures, the II group performed almost as well as the TAI group. This was even more surprising than the parallel finding for achievement. Meece and Wang (1982) also found positive effects of an individualized program without cooperative groups on acceptance of academically handicapped students. Slavin, Madden, and Leavey (1984a) and Madden and Slavin (1983) discuss these findings at some length, suggesting that we may have underestimated the social benefits of individualized instruction. The II condition did not contain the cooperative work groups hypothesized to be the principal factor explaining the success of cooperative learning methods in improving relationships among diverse students (see Slavin and Hansell 1983). However, it does have other features that should have similar effects, particularly as regards acceptance of academically handicapped students. First, it removes (or certainly reduces) individual competition between students. Noncompetition has been found to reduce the degree to which students form a "pecking order" based on perceived intelligence characteristic of the traditional competitive class (see Ames, Ames, and Felker 1977). Second, in the context of individualized instruction, it may be difficult or impossible to pick out the academically handicapped students. They are engaging in activities similar to those of their classmates, and are likely to experience success, as they are working on materials appropriate to their needs. This may make it possible for academically handicapped students to blend in behaviorally with their nonhandicapped classmates to a degree that would be unusual in a traditional classroom, where these students must either be set apart to receive different stigmatizing tasks, or must often experience public failure (see Madden and Slavin 1983). Finally, students are allowed to interact in individualized instruction, and this amount of interaction may be enough to create the positive social effects that are characteristic of cooperative learning methods.

Two of the studies, Experiments 4 and 5, investigated the effects of TAI on race relations. Both studies found that TAI improved attitudes and friendships among black and white students in Baltimore classrooms. Interestingly, the effects were stronger for decreasing negative attitudes than for increasing positive ones (though both outcomes were found). However, our experience implementing TAI in Baltimore elementary schools makes us cautious in recommending this method for use in low-achieving urban settings. In most of the classes involved in these studies, neither students nor teachers appeared to be able to handle the increased responsibility and autonomy given to students in TAI. High concentrations of students with serious reading and behavior problems made the program difficult to implement. On the other hand, Experiment 6, which took place in inner-city Wilmington, Delaware schools, indicates that TAI can be implemented well in urban settings; the achievement effects found in Experiment 6 were the largest of all the studies. Wilmington has an extensive metropolitan desegregation plan that mixes students of diverse backgrounds in every class, avoiding the concentrations of low achievers seen in many of the Baltimore City classes. However, it is also possible that changes in the TAI procedures to make the program more manageable and to emphasize teaching groups more may have made the program effective in inner-city settings.

Research on TAI is currently at an intermediate stage. The basic achievement effects of the program have been demonstrated in five field experiments, and a number of positive social and attitudinal effects have been found. Research and development are continuing to improve the program (and hopefully improve program outcomes further), to explore effects other than achievement, and to resolve remaining theoretical and practical issues raised by the earlier experiments. However, at this point we can conclude that we were correct in our initial assumption: if the problems of management, motivation, and direct teaching characteristic of previous programmed instruction could be solved, the benefits of providing instruction appropriate to students needs could finally be realized.

REFERENCES

Ames, Carole; Ames, Russell; and Felker, Donald W. "Effects of Competitive Reward Structure and Valence of Outcome on Children's Achievement Attributions." *Journal of Educational Psychology* 69 (February 1977): 1-8.

Brophy, Jere E. "Teacher Behavior and Its Effects." *Journal of Educational Psychology* 71 (December 1979): 733-50.

Cavanagh, Barbara R. "Effects of Interdependent Group Contingencies on the Achievement of Elementary School Children." Unpublished doct. dissertation, University of Maryland, 1984.

Esposito, Dominick. "Homogeneous and Heterogeneous Ability Grouping: Principal Findings and Implications for Evaluating and Designing More Effective Educational Environments." *Review of Educational Research* 43 (Spring 1973): 163-79.

Glass, Gene V; Cahen, Leonard; Smith, Mary Lee; and Filby, Nikola. *School Class Size: Research and Policy.* Beverly Hills, Calif.: Sage Publications, 1982.

Good, Thomas. "Teacher Effectiveness in the Elementary School." *Journal of Teacher Education* 30 (March/April 1979): 52-64.

Good, Thomas; Grouws, Douglas; and Ebmeier, Howard. *Active Mathematics Teaching.* New York: Longman, 1983.

Good, Thomas, and Marshall, Susan. "Do Students Learn More in Heterogeneous or Homogeneous Groups?" In *The Social Context of Instruction: Group Organization and Group Processes,* edited by Penelope L. Peterson, Louise Cherry Wilkinson, and Maureen Hallinan. New York: Academic Press, 1984.

Karweit, Nancy. "Time-On-Task: A Research Review." Baltimore, Md.: Center for Social Organization of Schools, Johns Hopkins University, 1983.

Kepler, Karen, and Randall, Jill W. "Individualization: The Subversion of Elementary Schooling." *Elementary School Journal* 77 (May 1977): 358-63.

Kulik, Chen-Lin, and Kulik, James. "Ability Grouping: A Research Synthesis." *Educational Leadership* 39 (May 1982): 481-84.

Madden, Nancy A., and Slavin, Robert E. "Mainstreaming Students with Mild Handicaps: Academic and Social Outcomes." *Review of Educational Research* 53 (Winter 1983): 519-69.

Meece, Judy, and Wang, Margaret C. "A Comparative Study of Social Attitudes and Behaviors of Mildly Handicapped Children in Two Mainstreaming Programs." Paper presented at the annual meeting of the American Educational Research Association, New York, 1982.

Miller, Richard L. "Individualized Instruction in Mathematics: A Review of Research." *Mathematics Teacher* 69 (May 1976): 345-51.

Oishi, Sabine. "Effects of Team-Assisted Individualization in Mathematics on Cross-Race and Cross-Sex Interactions of Elementary School Children." Doct. dissertation, University of Maryland, 1983.

Oishi, Sabine; Slavin, Robert; and Madden, Nancy. "Effects of Student Teams and Individualized Instruction on Cross-Race and Cross-Sex Friendships." Paper presented at the annual meeting of the American Educational Research Association, Montreal, 1983.

Schoen, Harold L. "Self-paced Mathematics Instruction: How Effective Has It Been?" *Arithmetic Teacher* 23 (February 1976): 90-96.

Slavin, Robert E. "Cooperative Learning." *Review of Educational Research* 50 (Fall 1980): 315-42.

Slavin, Robert E. *Cooperative Learning*. New York: Longman, 1983.

Slavin, Robert E. "Component Building: A Strategy for Research-based Instructional Improvement." *Elementary School Journal* 84 (January 1984): 255-69. (a)

Slavin, Robert E. "Meta-Analysis in Education: How Has It Been Used?" *Educational Researcher* 13 (October 1984): 6-15, 24-27. (b)

Slavin, Robert E., and Hansell, Stephen. "Cooperative Learning and Intergroup Relations: Contact Theory in the Classroom." In *Friends in School*, edited by Joyce Epstein and Nancy Karweit. New York: Academic Press, 1983.

Slavin, Robert E., and Karweit, Nancy. "Effects of Whole-class, Ability-grouped, and Individualized Instruction on Mathematics Achievement," in press.

Slavin, Robert E.; Leavey, Marshall; and Madden, Nancy A. "Combining Cooperative Learning and Individualized Instruction: Effects on Student Mathematics Achievement, Attitudes, and Behaviors." *Elementary School Journal* 84 (March 1984): 409-22.

Slavin, Robert E.; Madden, Nancy A.; and Leavey, Marshall. "Effects of Cooperative Learning and Individualization on Mainstreamed Students." *Exceptional Children* 50 (February 1984): 434-42.

Slavin, Robert E.; Madden, Nancy A.; and Leavey, Marshall. "Effects of Team-Assisted Individualization on the Mathematics Achievement of Academically Handicapped and Nonhandicapped Students." *Journal of Educational Psychology* 76 (October 1984b) 813-19.

A Retrospective and Prospective View of Bloom's "Learning for Mastery"

Lorin W. Anderson

In 1968 Benjamin Bloom published his ideas on "Learning for Mastery" (LFM) in a newsletter, *UCLA Evaluation Comment*. In essence Bloom suggested that the model of school learning proposed by John Carroll (1963) could be extended and applied to a wide variety of school settings and situations. Based on his understanding of Carroll's model, Bloom was able to contend that virtually all students could learn what was being taught in schools if instruction was approached systematically and sensitively, and if extra time and help were provided as necessary.

Professor Benjamin Bloom's comments on an earlier draft of this chapter are greatly appreciated.

In the years since the publication of Bloom's article, a large number of papers have been written about the concept of learning for mastery. Some of the papers have been theoretical; others have been practical. Some have been quite positive; others extremely critical. Some have been empirically based; others based more on opinion. Whatever the nature of the papers it is apparent that much interest has been generated by the set of ideas contained in that 1968 newsletter. The purposes of this chapter are to (1) review the essential features of Bloom's "Learning for Mastery," (2) contrast it with other approaches to adaptive instruction, (3) discuss a number of successes and failures in attempting to implement LFM programs, and (4) speculate on the future of LFM in American education.

THE PRIMARY TRADE-OFF: FIXED TIME FOR FIXED ACHIEVEMENT

Schools typically are structured and organized around fixed-time allocations. A variety of academic subjects, enrolled in for a specified number of years, is necessary for the awarding of a high school diploma. A certain number of days per year are allocated to formal schooling. Finally, a fixed number of minutes per day are given to the study of particular subject matters (for example, fifty-minute mathematics class periods).

Students enter schools differing widely in their preparation for school, academically, socially, and emotionally. Some students already know how to read; others do not know their alphabet. Some are eager to learn; others are more interested in the social aspects of schooling.

In combination, the *fixed-time orientation* of schools and the differences in the characteristics students possess upon entry into schools produce a predictable result. Under these *fixed-time conditions* student differences in entering characteristics are transformed into student differences in achievement. The strength of the relationship between prior achievement and subsequent achievement has been documented extensively (Bloom 1976). And, after several years of schooling, these differences in achievement increase greatly (Carroll 1974).

In developing his model of school learning Carroll basically hypothesized a *fixed-achievement orientation* of schools. That is, schooling could be defined not only in terms of time spent, but alternatively in terms of whether or not students achieved the learning tasks assigned to them. Under such *fixed-achievement conditions* Carroll suggested that student differences in entering characteristics (particularly aptitude and ability to understand instruction) would be transformed into student differences in the amount of time students would need in order to learn. Furthermore, students would learn well provided they actually spent the amount of time they needed to spend in order to learn. Thus, depending on whether one holds time or achievement constant, one *causes* initial student differences to be transformed into *either* differences in achievement *or* differences in time needed to learn. As a consequence, if the trade-off of fixed time for fixed achievement is made, if sufficient time for learning is provided to all students, and if students can be encouraged to spend the time necessary for them to learn, then virtually all students will learn what is being taught in schools.

In order to make such a trade-off Bloom suggested that several preconditions and operating procedures would need to be in place. Quite obviously it was necessary to fix achievement, or as Bloom put it, define mastery. Someone had to specify what the students were expected to learn, how they were to demonstrate that learning, and what level of performance would be accepted as indicating they had learned. Thus, programs based on the ideas underlying the concept of learning for mastery would need to have (1) clearly stated objectives, (2) valid assessment procedures, and (3) mastery performance standards.

Since students would need different amounts of time in order to achieve mastery, some mechanism must be made available to provide different amounts of time for different students while at the same time helping students make better use of the time already available. The primary mechanism recommended by Bloom was the provision of periodic feedback on the quality of student learning and corrective instruction for those students not learning as expected or desired. Based on the results of relatively short, highly valid assessments of student learning, students would be informed of their progress (or lack of progress) on the specified objectives (feedback). Once students were so informed, efforts would be made to correct the specific errors and misunderstandings identified by the assessments before they could accumulate and interfere with future learning (correctives).

Finally, both learning and failing to learn were believed to be cumulative; similarly, and quite obviously, not all course content or objectives can be taught or learned at the same time. As a consequence, Bloom suggested that courses or subjects be broken down into learning units. These units—which would correspond with chapters in textbooks or major course topics—would be analyzed into their constituent elements (for example , important facts, concepts, principles, and skills). The units themselves would then be placed in order from the beginning to the end of the course or subject.

One more point is necessary to make if one is to understand the nature and development of Bloom's LFM. Bloom had been discouraged by the ineffectiveness of attempts in this country at large-scale curricular revisions and large-scale changes of school structure and organization. Thus, he suggested that LFM programs be implemented within the context of existing curriculums and school organization. Specifically, he recommended that LFM be implemented in a group-based, teacher-paced format with teachers teaching whatever they currently taught in whatever ways they felt appropriate and comfortable, and with grades being assigned based on standards used by teachers in the past. In this way, LFM programs would require minimum change in schooling, thereby enhancing their adoption and retention.

In Bloom's expansion and application of the Carroll model, then, we see the essential features of the concept of LFM and of LFM programs. In summary these features are:

1. Clearly specified learning objectives;

2. Short, highly valid assessment procedures;

3. Preset mastery performance standards;

4. A sequence of learning units, each comprised of an integral set of facts, contents, principles, and skills;

5. Provision of feedback of learning progress to students; and,

6. Provision of additional time and help to correct specified errors and misunderstandings of students who are failing to achieve the preset mastery learning standards.

Any instructional program containing *all* six of these features can be rightfully referred to as an LFM program, or, more appropriately, a proper application of Bloom's "Learning for Mastery."

LEARNING FOR MASTERY AND ADAPTIVE INSTRUCTION

The relationship between learning for mastery and adaptive instruction is not altogether clear. Bloom (1983), for example, contends that mastery learning is not a form of adaptive instruction. The nature of the relationship between mastery learning and adaptive instruction is clouded by the variety of definitions that have been attributed to both instructional programs. If one accepts Glaser's (1977) essential characteristics of adaptive education, learning for mastery programs could not be considered as adaptive instructional programs since there is not a one-to-one correspondence of essential program characteristics.

On the other hand, LFM programs do share many features with adaptive instructional programs (including "true believer" proponents and hypercritical opponents). Furthermore, one of the prime concerns of LFM programs is finding ways of accommodating initial differences among learners so that virtually all of them actually learn. This concern appears paramount among proponents of adaptive instructional progams as well. At the same time, however, several features differentiate LFM from most approaches to adaptive instruction. Three of the most important differences are described below.

The Adaptive Mechanism

Different approaches to providing adaptive instruction contain different ways of accommodating student differences; that is, different approaches have different *adaptive mechanisms*. Some approaches begin with the identification of learner aptitudes or learning styles. Differences in learners can be accommodated by putting each learner in contact with the most appropriate method or teaching style given his or her aptitudes or learning style.

Some approaches permit the learners to move through a highly sequenced, materials-based curriculum at a rate or pace determined by the learners themselves. These approaches attempt to accommodate differences in learning rate by giving control of the pacing of the instruction and learning to the learners. Still other approaches provide a variety of learning goals, instructional materials, and/or learning activities. The availability of such a variety of goals, materials, and activities is believed to accommodate a diversity of learner interests, reading skills, and other psychosocial characteristics.

Finally, some approaches include several of these adaptive mechanisms. Such eclectic approaches, for example, may match learner aptitudes with teaching methods while at the same time permitting student choice of goals, materials, and activities, and student control of the pacing of the instruction and learning.

LFM programs attempt to accommodate individual differences among learners by providing them with task-specific feedback coupled with appropriate instruction designed to correct identified errors before they accumulate and interfere with future learning. Accommodations to student differences are made *only when* the evidence suggests that students are having difficulty learning from the instruction as presented. Thus, LFM differs from most approaches to adaptive instruction in both the *nature* and *timing* of the adaptive mechanism. The adaptive mechanism of LFM is the feedback/corrective component, which is used only as necessary.

One additional point must be made before moving on to the next section. A number of what may be termed "eclectic LFM programs" do exist. These programs typically include additional adaptive mechanisms, most often learner control of the pacing of instruction and learning (Cohen 1981). Since such programs do include a feedback/corrective component, they are by definition LFM programs. It must be pointed out, however, that the presence of a periodic feedback/corrective component is both a *necessary* and *sufficient* adaptive mechanism within the context of LFM.

The Modifiability and Alterability of Learners

Inherent in Bloom's LFM is his belief that learners can be changed greatly by the educational process. Furthermore, if education is to have long-term benefits for learners, they should be helped to change in ways that will enable them to adapt to a variety of future schooling and life situations, especially those they will most likely encounter frequently. Quite obviously, then, instructional programs initially must be sensitive to differences among learners but only for as long as it takes learners to develop or acquire knowledge and skills that allow them to succeed in a wide variety of settings and situations. The importance of the feedback/corrective component in LFM programs is based at least partly on this set of beliefs. If the feedback/corrective component is effective and if the learning goals are worthwhile, increasing numbers of learners should be able to benefit from more traditional instructional conditions as they become more similar in the knowledge, skills, and abilities necessary for school survival. At the beginning of each new learning unit in LFM programs, therefore, all learners are placed into contact with fairly traditional instructional procedures, techniques, and conditions. The responsibility for accommodating, then, rests alternatively with the instructional program and the learner.

This alternating sequence of instructional accommodation—learner accommodation—instructional accommodation—learner accommodation is reasonable only within the context that learners are alterable. If the characteristics of the learners to which the instruction is designed to adapt are believed to be highly stable, instruction must *continually* accommodate differences among learners if it is to be effective. Thus, for example, if learner aptitudes, learning styles, learner interests, and learning rates are highly stable, then the overall effectiveness of the instructional program depends entirely on the ability of the program continuously to accommodate these differences.[1]

In many ways, then, Bloom's LFM is a more optimistic instructional approach since learners are believed to be adaptable or alterable, and are given frequent opportunities to develop and demonstrate that adaptability.[2] The ultimate effectiveness of LFM, then, is achieved when LFM is no longer necessary to ensure high levels of student learning.

The Awareness and Acceptance of School Constraints

Much of the discussion about LFM in the early 1970s was concerned with whether it was an *evolutionary* or a *revolutionary* approach to school improvement (see, for example, Block 1974). Quite clearly LFM was intended to be used initially with existing curriculum ("whatever the schools have to teach"), within existing school organization, and with available teachers (providing original instruction in whatever ways they believed appropriate). Equally clearly, however, many of these conditions often serve as constraints to the effectiveness of LFM programs. Nonetheless, Bloom believed that the key to getting LFM into a large number of schools was to make it suitable to a variety of schooling conditions. And, if LFM programs were not in schools, they obviously could not be effective at all. Once LFM programs are in place, their effectiveness may spawn curriculum and course revisions that ultimately would result in qualitative changes in learning.

In contrast to LFM, most approaches to adaptive instruction either require or strongly encourage changes in schooling conditions. Permitting student choice of goals, materials, and/or activities, for example, requires changes in classroom organization and teaching strategy. Student control over the pacing of instruction typically requires large-scale curricular revision since the instruction must come primarily from the curriculum materials or some form of instructional technology. A single teacher in a classroom of thirty students cannot possibly provide direct instruction to thirty unique learners. Advocates of so-called "outcome-based instructional programs" recommend massive changes in the grading/certification process of the schools if adaptive instructional programs are to be maximally effective (see, for example, Spady 1981).

Schools have been stable social institutions in this country for well over a century. The nature and structure of schools do, in fact, impose constraints on the activities that occur within them. In essence, this is the argument of the ecological psychologists (see, for example, Barker 1968). Rightly or wrongly, LFM was initially designed to improve classroom instruction and school learning within the context of typical schools. As a consequence, only rarely have LFM programs produced the 95 percent rate of "mastery" suggested as an upper limit by Bloom. Nevertheless, a much larger proportion of students do learn in LFM programs than in non-LFM programs under these constraints (see, for example, Burns 1979). We now turn to an examination of the successes and failures of LFM programs.

SUCCESS AND FAILURES OF LFM

In a recent encyclopedia entry Anderson and Block (1985) present and discuss three generalizations that can be derived from the current body of research on LFM. First, LFM programs are effective. Second, the key to their effectiveness lies within the feedback/corrective component. Third, LFM programs are differentially effective for different types of learners. Each of these generalizations is described briefly below.

LFM Programs Are Effective

"Beginning with the early studies which were small-scale, used laboratory-like learning tasks, and occurred in rather contrived classroom

settings (for example, programmed instruction) and continuing
to the present studies which are large-scale (often involving entire
school districts in the United States, or entire countries, such as the
Republic of Korea and Indonesia), use school-related learning tasks,
and take place in naturally occurring classroom settings, the effectiveness of mastery learning programs has been demonstrated repeatedly
(about 90 percent of the time, in fact)" (Anderson and Block 1984, p. 24).

The effectiveness of LFM has been defined and measured in a
number of ways. In addition to the traditional criterion of immediate
achievement, measures of retention, learning rate, attitudes, and
self-esteem have been used. Over all the studies that have been
conducted in a variety of settings, LFM students have outperformed
non-LFM students on all of these measures. With respect to immediate achievement, for example, the average mean difference between
LFM and non-LFM students is of the magnitude that the average
student in an LFM class would perform as well or better than would
80 to 85 percent of the students in a non-LFM class (Burns 1979). The
consistency of the results combined with the magnitude of the differences support the overall effectiveness of LFM programs.

The Key to Effectiveness Is the Feedback/Corrective Component

Several essential features of the feedback/corrective component
have been identified in the research. Two of the most essential tend to
be (1) the *level* at which the mastery performance standard is set, and (2)
the effective *use* (rather than mere provision) of corrective instruction.

"The results of the research on standard setting suggest the standard must be set sufficiently high so as to ensure that the desired
learning has occurred. Capricious standard setting may result in no
real, functional standards at all" (Anderson and Block 1984, p. 26).
The results of at least two studies suggest that setting the performance
standard at 75 percent correct results in no substantial improvement
in learning (Block 1972; Chan 1981). Overall, the research evidence
indicates standards somewhere between 85 percent and 95 percent
correct are most appropriate (see also Davis 1975).

The provision *and* use of corrective instruction has been the focus of
several studies. The significance of the results of each study to the present discussion can be briefly described in a series of generalizations.

1. Corrective instruction tends to be more important to the overall

effectiveness of LFM than the clarity of the original instruction, the mere provision of extra time to learn, and a variety of other instructional factors (Block and Burns 1976; Nordin 1980).

2. Students must make use of the corrective instruction if it is to have any effect (Jones, Gordon, and Schechtman 1975). [The moral of this generalization is that one must observe the implementation of LFM programs, not just the design, if one is to understand their effectiveness or lack of effectiveness].

3. For instruction to *function* as corrective instruction it must be preceded by the gathering of evidence concerning the quality of student learning. Corrective instruction, by its very nature, must be targeted toward particular learners and particular learning problems or difficulties (Rochester 1982).

The Differential Effects of LFM

"One of the questions posed to proponents of mastery learning is whether students at all ability levels benefit equally well from mastery learning or whether the (improved) learning of lower ability students is purchased at cost of decreased learning of (higher) ability students" (Anderson and Block 1984, p. 28). At least four studies have been conducted to address this question.

In two of the studies, students at all ability levels benefited by participating in an LFM program (Kim 1969; Detheux, Leclerq, Paquay, and Thirion 1974). "The results of the Detheux et al. study suggested that while the (LFM) program was especially beneficial for the underprivileged students, all three (ability) groups benefited from the program" (Anderson and Block 1984, p. 28). In the remaining two studies lower ability LFM students outperformed their non-LFM counterparts while the performances of high-ability students in the LFM and non-LFM programs were virtually identical (Anderson and Reynolds 1979; Chan 1981). Furthermore, although some critics may attribute the comparable performances of high-ability LFM and non-LFM students in these last two studies to the "ceiling" of the achievement test used, Chan employed a latent trait vertical equating procedure to create a "ceilingless" test.

Recent school-based studies of LFM programs have begun to examine the impact of LFM on students of different ages and grades (Abrams 1981, Cohen 1981). Although the studies are quasi-longitudinal in design (involving different cohorts of students in grades one through eight), the results are intriguing. The effectiveness of LFM programs appears to be relatively minor at grades one through three. Beyond grade three, however, the effectiveness is notable, often approaching differences between LFM and non-LFM students of more than two grade levels on traditional standardized norm-referenced achievement tests. One reason for these results may be that the clear specification of what is to be learned, how the learning is to be demonstrated, what the learning errors are, and what should be done to correct the errors becomes increasingly important as the subject matter increases in both scope and complexity. The more finite and simple the subject matter being learned, the more likely it is that students will be able to decipher for themselves the answers to these questions. In any case the results of these studies raise some doubt as to the validity of the contention, made by both proponents and critics of LFM, that LFM programs are likely to be especially effective when they are introduced very early in the schooling process, and when they are employed in the teaching of simple, "closed" subjects rather than more complex, "open" subjects.

Despite the "success story" described in the previous several paragraphs it is only fair to point out that not all attempts to implement LFM programs have been successful. Those attempts that have not been successful have tended to be severely flawed either in design or implementation. Anderson and Jones (1981) have pointed out several common flaws:

Flaw 1.   Failure to establish priorities among instructional objectives. In many programs all objectives are seen as equally important. Given the realities of subject matter (and classroom instruction), some instructional objectives are (and must be seen as) more important than others. Setting priorities among objectives has implications for the time allotments for instructional units, the setting of performance standards, and the evaluation and grading of students.

Flaw 2.   Failure to organize objectives into instructional units and to order/ sequence the units based on rational or empirical considerations. "Less than successful" mastery programs often progress objective-by-objective without regard to sequencing, thereby destroying the structure of the subject matter and the structure of the student learning.

Flaw 3.   Failure to properly orient students to the mastery learning program; failure to specify in advance the duration of the instructional units, the tentative date of the formative test, and the amount of time to be devoted to corrective instruction/learning (both in-class and out-of-class). Given that one purpose of mastery learning programs is to make explicit the goals, objectives, tests, performance standards, and the like, it is surprising that the ways in which the goals/objectives will be attained remains implicit in many programs.

Flaw 4. Failure to make rational, justifiable decisions about performance standards. Rather, quick and dirty figures of 80 per cent are used. Performance standards should be set based on answers to the question, "What evidence will I (we) accept that learning has occurred?" As a consequence, performance standards should be set *after* careful examination of the objectives and the appropriate items on the formative and summative tests and may differ from objective to objective based on the complexity of the objective (from a psychological perspective) and the difficulty of the test items (from a psychometric point of view).

Flaw 5. Tendency to over-test. Formal testing (such as paper and pencil formative tests) should occur only after the completion of an instructional unit (for example, every five to twelve days). This is recommended for at least three reasons. First, the focus in mastery learning programs should be on instruction rather than testing. Yet some programs spend as much time on testing as they do on teaching. Second, learning takes time. Few, if any, objectives can be attained in fifty minutes. Third, testing students too often may create unnecessary feelings of being tested *ad nauseum* and testing may come to be seen as an end in itself.

Note that the above comments refer only to formal testing. Informal testing (such as teacher questions and short worksheets on a particular objective) should be integrated into the instructional process as is now being done by highly skilled teachers. (pp. 122-23)

Two major implications follow from the presence of such flaws. First, the design of particular LFM programs must be compared to the concept of LFM described earlier. This comparison is best made on an "essential feature" by "essential feature" basis. Essential features of the concept of LFM not present in the LFM program should be noted. Furthermore, nonessential or extraneous features of the LFM program that may impact on the program's effectiveness also should be noted.

Second, the implementation of LFM programs must be monitored with close attention paid to the "fidelity of implementation," that is, the extent to which the program is implemented as designed. Since LFM is in essence an approach to *planning* sound, effective instruction, the fidelity of implementation can be determined primarily by examining the lesson plans and the availability of appropriate instructional support materials (for example, formative tests). A few classroom observations will be necessary to monitor the appropriate use of the plans.

THE FUTURE OF LFM RESEARCH AND PRACTICE

Although much has been learned about the nature and effectiveness of LFM during the past fifteen years, additional information is sorely needed. Future research should focus on two key questions. First, under what conditions is LFM more or less effective? These studies would examine the nature of classrooms, teachers, administrators, as well as students themselves. Since no approach to adaptive instruction is likely to be effective under all conditions, such research (if conducted on all approaches to adaptive instruction) would result in the development of a repertoire of adaptive instructional approaches that could be matched with a variety of schooling conditions to yield maximum effectiveness.

Second, what are the upper limits of student learning that can be achieved using LFM programs? This research would address the overall educability of the children enrolled in our schools. If an ideal LFM program was devised, what proportion of students currently in schools would learn excellently? Similarly, if an optimum approach to adaptive instruction was devised, what proportion of students could achieve excellence in their learning? Such research would go a long way toward increasing our understanding of the nature of individual differences in relation to school learning.

From a more practical perspective, three future directions appear important if teaching and learning are to improve substantially in our schools. First, the key elements of LFM should be incorporated into curriculum materials. Formative tests, alternative learning materials, and structural diagrams of learning units must become a regular part of curriculum and course design. This already has been done in several countries outside of the United States. Second, preservice teachers will be taught to teach for mastery as part of their course work in schools of education. An integration of LFM with the results of teacher effectiveness research will aid greatly in this regard. Third, educators will begin to explore the preventative power of LFM (Block 1983). To date, the major use of mastery learning has been remedial rather than preventive (Block 1979). That is, LFM models have frequently been implemented in school settings where a "quick fix" to educational ills is sorely needed. It may be possible to introduce LFM early in a child's educational career to immunize him or her from future problems and failure. Such an immunization may in fact be present in the quasi-longitudinal studies mentioned earlier, accounting in part for the large jump in achievement differences in the middle grades. Finally, such an immunization is consistent with the philosophy underlying the development of LFM as an instructional strategy. For, if such an immunization occurs, we will have produced intelligent, adaptable learners.

REFERENCES

Abrams, Joan D. "Precise Teaching Is More Effective Teaching." *Educational Leadership* 39 (November 1981): 138-39.

Anderson, Lorin W., and Block, James H. "Mastery Learning." In *Handbook on Teaching Educational Psychology*, edited by Donald Treffinger, J. Kent Davis, and Richard Ripple. New York: Academic Press, 1976.

Anderson, Lorin W., and Block, James H. "The Mastery Learning Model of Teaching and Learning." In *International Encyclopedia of Education: Research and Studies*, edited by Torsten Husén and T. Neville Postlethwaite. Oxford, England: Pergamon Press, 1985.

Anderson, Lorin W., and Jones, Beau F. "Designing Instructional Strategies Which Facilitate Learning for Mastery." *Educational Psychologist* 16 (Fall 1981): 121-38.

Anderson, Lorin W., and Reynolds, Amelia. "The Effect of Mastery Learning on the Achievement of High Ability Students and the Academic Self-Concept of Low Achieving Students." Paper presented at the annual meeting of the American Educational Research Association, San Francisco, 1979.

Barker, Roger G. *Ecological Psychology*. Stanford, Calif.: Stanford University Press, 1968.

Block, James H. "Student Learning and the Setting of Mastery Performance Standards." *Educational Horizons* 50 (Summer 1972): 183-91.

Block, James H., editor. *Schools, Society, and Mastery Learning*, New York: Holt, Rinehart & Winston, 1974.

Block, James H. "Mastery Learning: The Current State of the Craft." *Educational Leadership* 37 (November 1979): 114-17.

Block, James H. "Learning Rates and Mastery Learning." *Outcomes* 2 (Winter 1983) 18-25.

Block, James H., and Burns, Robert B. "Mastery Learning." In *Review of Research in Education*, Vol. 4., edited by Lee S. Shulman. Itasca, Ill.: F. E. Peacock Publishers, 1976, pp. 3-49.

Bloom, Benjamin S. "Learning for Mastery." *Evaluation Comment* 1 (May 1968): np.

Bloom, Benjamin S. *Human Characteristics and School Learning*. New York: McGraw-Hill, 1976.

Bloom, Benjamin S. Personal communication, 1983.

Burns, Robert B. "Mastery Learning: Does It Work?" *Educational Leadership* 37 (November 1979): 110-13.

Carroll, John B. "A Model of School Learning." *Teachers College Record* 64 (May 1963): 723-33.

Carroll, John B. "Fitting a Model of School Learning to Aptitude and Achievement Data over Grade Levels." In *The Aptitude-Achievement Distinction*, edited by Donald R. Green. Monterey, Calif.: CTB/McGraw-Hill, 1974.

Chan, Kim Sang. "The Interaction of Aptitude with Mastery versus Nonmastery Instruction: Effects on Reading Comprehension of Grade Three Students." Doct. dissertation, University of Western Australia, 1981.

Cohen, S. Alan. "Dilemmas in the Use of Learner Responsive Delivery Systems." Paper presented at the annual meeting of the American Educational Research Association, Los Angeles, 1981.

Davis, Michael L. "Mastery Test Proficiency Requirement Affects Mastery Test Performance." In *Behavior Research and Technology in Higher Education*, edited by James M. Johnston. Springfield, Ill.: Charles C. Thomas, 1975.

Detheux, M.; Leclerq, E.; Paquay, J.; and Thirion, A. M. "From Compensatory Education to Mastery Learning." *London Educational Review* 3 (Autumn 1974): 41-50.

Glaser, Robert. *Adaptive Education: Individual Diversity and Learning*. New York: Holt, Rinehart & Winston, 1977.

Jensen, Arthur R. "How Much Can We Boost IQ and Scholastic Achievement?" *Harvard Educational Review* 39 (Winter 1969): 1-123.

Jones, Emmett L.; Gordon, Howard A.; and Schechtman, Gilbert L. *Mastery Learning: A Strategy for Academic Success in a Community College*, Topical Paper no. 53. Los Angeles: ERIC Clearinghouse for Junior Colleges, University of California, 1975.

Kim, Hogwon, et al. *A Study of the Bloom Strategies for Mastery Learning*. Seoul, Republic of Korea: Korean Institute for Research in the Behavioral Sciences, 1969.

McCombs, Barbara L. "Motivational Skills Training: Helping Students Adapt by Taking Personal Responsibilities and Positive Self-Control." Paper presented at the annual meeting of the American Educational Research Association, Montreal, 1983.

Nordin, Abu Bakar. "Improving Learning: An Experiment in Rural Primary Schools in Malaysia." *Evaluation in Education: An International Review Series* 4, no. 2 (1980): 143-263.

Rochester, Margot. "An Analysis of the Formative Testing and Corrective Instruction Components of LFM Programs." Doct. dissertation, University of South Carolina, 1982.

Spady, William G. "Outcome-based Instructional Management: A Sociological Perspective." Unpublished paper, American Association of School Administrators, Arlington, Virginia, 1981.

Wang, Margaret C., editor. *The Self-Schedule System for Instructional-Learning Management in Adaptive School Learning Environments*. Pittsburgh, Pa.: Learning Research and Development Center, University of Pittsburgh, 1976.

CHAPTER
12

Adaptive Education: Policy and Administrative Perspectives

Richard C. Wallace, Jr.

Individualized education programs have been a part of the American educational scene for the past twenty years. These programs, which were designed to alter significantly the education of American youth, have met with limited success. The reasons for success or failure may not be clear. But one thing is clear — we must still pursue the goal of adaptive/individualized education if we are to fulfill the potential and the promise of American public education.

---

[1] Jensen's (1969) recommendation to develop different instructional treatments which could accommodate the differences in genetically determined abilities among students of different races is, in fact, consistent with the principles of adaptive instruction when coupled with his strong belief in the stability or unalterability of these abilities.
[2] Several approaches to adaptive instruction also emphasize the need to develop adaptive learners. See McCombs (1983) and Wang (1976) for descriptions of other approaches.

In preparing this chapter I reviewed my own personal involvement in individualized instruction programs over the past twenty years. During the 1960s and 1970s I was involved at varying times in national efforts such as Project PLAN, Individually Guided Education (IGE), and Aptitude-Treatment Interaction (ATI) studies. At the local district level, I developed an individualized instruction program called the "Reading Continuum" while I was an elementary school principal in the early 1960s. Later in the 1960s, while I was a director of elementary and middle school education, I developed Process and Knowledge Inventories for middle school students as a means of verifying individualized learning outcomes. More recently I have been involved in the development of achievement-monitoring systems that are designed to insure that learners master the fundamental processes of learning; this work has been an important part of my role as superintendent of schools. My twenty-year personal odyssey in pursuit of individualized or adaptive instructional programs has yet to be fully realized. I am still seeking ways to deliver individualized education efficiently and effectively.

As I reflected further on individualized education, I thought of my experience with special education programs under a comprehensive special education law in Massachusetts known as Chapter 766, and in Pennsylvania under Public Law 94-142, I have recently become actively involved in shaping a new individualized program for secondary gifted students called "Centers for Advanced Study." The more I reflect upon my experience with these special education programs, the more it appears to me that they embody all of the basic principles of adaptive education. Upon further examination, I found an almost one-to-one correspondence between the concepts espoused by adaptive education and the practices of special education. Then I began to consider the possibility of applying the principles and practices of special education to all educational levels in the public schools as a means of adapting instruction to individual pupils.

In the remainder of this chapter I shall explore the characteristics of special education and adaptive education. Then I will raise the policy and administrative implications that would be involved if educators were to apply the principles of special education to the education of the mainstream student body in the public schools.

SPECIAL EDUCATION: COMPONENTS AND CHARACTERISTICS

The basic components of special education include the following: diagnosis, prescription, program implementation, reevaluation, and assessment of outcomes.

Diagnosis is the heart of the special education process. Each child who is referred for special education is the subject of intensive study. All relevant achievement data, family and child growth data, aptitude, interest, motor and speech development, and other relevant psychological and medical information are gathered to provide the best possible profile of strengths and weaknesses of each individual child. Through a core evaluation or staffing conference, all parties who have an interest in the welfare of the pupil participate in the analysis of the data gathered. Teachers, principals, counselors, psychologists, and other specialists confer with parents for the purpose of gaining comprehensive understanding about the child's learning potential and learning problems. The results of this analysis lead to the development of an individualized educational program (IEP) for each student.

The IEP specifies what the child is expected to learn in the academic, social-emotional, or motor/speech areas over a period of time. The parents acknowledge the IEP to be appropriate for the child and they, along with school authorities, sign the plan, acknowledging its validity as providing the level of expected development of the individual child after a specific time period (usually one year).

The implementation of the program is carried out by those teachers, specialists, and paraprofessionals who are assigned the responsibility. The program is monitored carefully and feedback is provided; periodically the program is adapted depending upon the day-to-day successes or failures that each child experiences with the plan devised for him or her. An important part of the educational program for each child and the parents is the annual reevaluation and redesign of the program. In each case the parents review and reaffirm their agreement with the program; typically, programs specify the roles and responsibilities of parents as well as of educational professionals and specialists.

The outcomes to be achieved by the development of an appropriate educational program for each pupil center on maximizing the potential of each individual student as a learner. Among the major outcomes is the assurance to the parent that the schools, in collaboration with the parent, will help each child to achieve that level of self-actualization consistent with the child's potential or handicap. One of the major goals is to make each handicapped child as independent as possible. Each child must become as self-directing and self-correcting as can be expected in order to maximize his or her potential.

Special Education Teachers

As one observes special education teachers and engages in discussion with them, three attitudes are readily perceived. The attitudes can be expressed as propositions (a) that every child can learn something; (b) that every special education teacher is responsible for the learning of *every* child assigned to him or her; (c) that every special education teacher is responsible for demonstrating growth for each and every student assigned (Zigmond 1983). These attitudes often stand out in dramatic contrast when compared with the attitudes of mainstream classroom teachers at the elementary, middle, and secondary school levels (Zigmond and Sansone 1981).

Special educators typically have classroom management routines or controls "down to a science." They appear to be expert in the use of motivational strategies; they have a "bag of tricks" at their command to excite students about learning and to motivate them to achieve. Typically they treat each student differentially and are not afraid to do so. They will (a) vary the pace of instruction depending on the child's level and progress; (b) vary reinforcement intervals based on the individual youngster's need; (c) reteach skills to insure that students attain mastery. Perhaps most importantly they are accustomed to making data-based instructional decisions.

What one tends to observe in effective special education classrooms is the combined science and artistry of teaching. The "science" found in special education teachers tends to manifest itself in a data orientation, the tendency to use explicit motivational reinforcement and reteaching techniques. The "artistry" of special education is found in the ability of special education teachers to orchestrate their classes with a high degree of positive enthusiasm combined with the uncanny ability to manage a variety of activities.

Special Education Teachers Compared with Regular Classroom Teachers

Special education teachers take full responsibility for demonstrating the growth in learning of their pupils. Oftentimes regular classroom teachers take the attitude that students cannot learn effectively for a variety of reasons; mainstream teachers tend to believe that they cannot be held responsible for lack of student learning. Often cited by mainstream classroom teachers for the failure of students to learn are the following: lack of ability; lack of prerequisite knowledge or skill; socioeconomic background; racial composition of the learning group. What is so remarkable about special educators on the contrary is the positive attitude they project toward the ability of pupils to learn. That same positive attitude toward students and their ability to learn by mainstream teachers could make a significant impact on their students.

As a general rule, skills of differential treatment of students such as pacing and reinforcement are lacking in the repertoire of regular classroom teachers at the elementary, middle, and secondary levels. Regular classroom teachers tend to deny or ignore differences and "homogenize" their classes. Rarely do regular classroom teachers attempt to differentiate instruction. At best they may vary the pace of (accelerate) certain pupils through the *same instructional material* used for all pupils (Zigmond and Sansone 1981).

One of the most salient features of special education instruction is the emphasis on growth and achievement. The grading of the students' work tends to be nonpunitive. Special education teachers strive to demonstrate individual pupil growth toward particular goals established for an individual student; they tend not to compare a student's growth with some arbitrary standard for an age group or grade level. On the contrary, regular education teachers tend to use rather rigid, arbitrary "grade level" standards to judge pupil progress and assign grades.

ADAPTIVE EDUCATION: CHARACTERISTICS AND COMPONENTS

When one compares the characteristics of special education to those of adaptive education the similarities are striking. Included among the characteristics of adaptive education are the following: (1)

observable and measurable outcomes of instruction; (2) diagnosis of learner competencies prior to instruction; (3) the provision of instructional alternatives matched to the performance of the learner; (4) the monitoring and adjusting of the educational program based on feedback to the learner; (5) self-initiated and self-guided instruction; and (6) a mutual support system (Glaser 1977).

Usually adaptive education systems involve organizational supports in the form of multiage grouping, team teaching, and parental involvement (Wang 1980). Perhaps the most salient feature of adaptive systems is the emphasis placed on the development of self-management skills in pupils.

Comparison Between Adaptive and Special Education

The characteristics of adaptive and special education are remarkably similar. In fact, the work of Wang (1980) and others in developing Adaptive Learning Environment Models (ALEM) demonstrates the efficacy of combining adaptive and special education students in the same learning environment; it is difficult in such an ALEM environment to identify the differences among mainstreamed, handicapped, gifted, or remedial students.

Leinhardt, Bickel, and Pallay (1982) propose that compensatory and special education students be served by a single system; their proposal is based on an analysis of goals, program comparison, and outcomes of both forms of education. My position is that special education, compensatory education, and regular education should emanate from the same assumptions, principles, and values and should embrace the same or similar practices.

SPECIAL EDUCATION APPLIED: POLICY IMPLICATIONS

Special educators appear to apply, with success, the salient principles of adaptive education. From a policy and administrative perspective, what would happen if we were to implement in all schools, at all educational levels, the basic principles of special education? What implications would this have for curriculum? For teaching and learning? For classrooms and school buildings? For staffing patterns? Perhaps most importantly, what kind of staff development for both teachers and administrators would be required to bring about this change? And finally, what kind of training would have to occur for prospective teachers and administrators?

Curriculum

A special education approach for all pupils would require that specific learning outcomes be established for each subject matter area with respect to both skill and knowledge outcomes. There would have to be a detailed set of learner outcomes at the level of skills, concepts, and generalizations; additionally there would have to be accompanying measures of achievement to verify student achievement of those outcomes. Alternative ways to present information must be available for all skill and knowledge outcomes. We could not assume that every learner would master a skill or achieve a knowledge outcome in the same way, at the same pace, or by using the same materials for instruction. Alternatives would have to be available to be used when teachers judged a particular modality was not effective for a particular student.

In order to maximize the learning potential of all students, and specifically the more able students, extensive use of community resources would be required. In addition to a wide use of field trips, expanded opportunities for learning would have to be available in the form of mentorships, internships, and independent study in collaboration with business, industry, college and university resources, governmental and social agencies. Older students at the middle and secondary levels must have opportunities to pursue independent study programs using the community as a learning resource; the community would be viewed as an equally valid learning resource in combination with the multimedia resources available within the school building. This would allow for an expansion of exciting learning opportunities similar to what will be implemented in the Pittsburgh Center for Advanced Study for gifted secondary students. The "community-based curriculum" would be designed to provide a positive and stimulating learning environment for students.

Classrooms and School Buildings

As in special and adaptive education classrooms, the conventional classroom would have to have flexible space and the potential for a variety of learning stations. One would expect to find individual study spaces, clustered groupings of desks and tables, interest centers, and a wide variety of instructional materials. Each classroom would need to be adaptable to differential pacing of instruction and various modes of instruction including: (a) direct instruction to the total group of students, (b) small-group instruction for short-term purposes, (c) student peer learning, (d) tutorial instruction, (e) independent study.

Within the entire school building a variety of places where students can engage in learning activities must be provided. Spaces that would allow for large- and small-group instruction, individual study, instructional material centers, seminar rooms, centers for computer-assisted instruction, and centers where computers are used for programming purposes and simulations should be available.

Teaching and Learning

Instruction in the school would be data based, that is, it would be based on a thorough analysis of the student's current achievement profile and an individual educational plan prepared for each student.

Individualized instruction would not necessarily mean that students will work only by themselves. It may mean that groups of students will work together on similar learning outcomes that are unique to their developmental stage at a given time. For teaching and learning to be maximally efficient, direct instruction to large, medium, and small groups must be part of the teaching-learning environment. Additionally, individual tutorial instruction and independent self-guided study would be expected.

One would also expect to find the use of computer-assisted instruction for specific skill development and for drill and practice to reinforce skills. Students would use personal computers for simulation; the computer would be used as a tool to perform certain information-generation or retrieval tasks. Most of the record keeping, which is a fundamental part of the diagnostic orientation to instruction, would be computer managed. The records for tracking student attainment and progress must be available on a computer record. The key instructional role for the teacher would be to use the data gathered on the student profile to make intelligent decisions and design the next learning steps for pupils

Finally, one would expect to find that students have acquired and implemented self-management skills appropriate to their developmental level; skills of independent inquiry would enable each student to enhance and enrich his or her personal self-development and facilitate the attainment of specified educational outcomes.

Most importantly the teaching and learning environment would project a positive attitude toward learning. Teachers would take the responsibility for the personal achievement of each child. No excuses would be given for the failure of a pupil to make progress. Rather, personal consultation services would be available in the school to help teachers modify approaches to learning for individual students to insure that learning occurs.

Grading and Promotion

Special educators grade, or report progress of students, in relation to the individual growth expectation for each individual pupil as specified in the IEP. No fixed, arbitrary, grade-level standards are imposed. In conventional classrooms the opposite condition prevails. Pupils are graded, promoted, or retained in relation to "externally referenced standards." Schools would have to find effective means of communicating *growth* to parents that reflect the positive orientation toward pupil learning. The norms of conventional education, promoted from within the school and readily accepted by parents, fly in the face of special and adaptive educational programs. The problems of grading and reporting to parents present significant obstacles for schools, especially at the secondary level.

Staffing Requirements

The staffing for such a school would not have to be as expensive as one might expect. All teachers would be expected to perform the diagnosis and the assessment in order to place youngsters appropriately within the curriculum with respect to growth in knowledge and skills. One should not underestimate the magnitude of the changes that would have to occur in order for this to happen. Given appropriate training, the classroom teacher would probably be in the best position to make these assessments.

Each school and department would have to provide consultation to teachers, helping them to define problems, manage and analyze data, and adapt instruction for students who are not learning well and for those who are learning beyond expectations. The conventional types of instructional services for slow or handicapped learners would also have to be available in schools as they now are. One might expect to find a complement of parent volunteers and paraprofessionals who would assist teachers in the management of materials or the collection of data. However, one would not expect dramatic increases in staffing in order to implement special programs.

Teacher In-service Training

The in-service training of teachers is probably the most significant problem to be faced. Teachers would have to acquire a thorough knowledge of child and adolescent development, develop the skills of diagnosis with respect to the skills and the knowledge expected of students at a particular level, use assessment data for instructional planning, create systems for monitoring student progress, and employ a variety of classroom and contingency management techniques (Zigmond 1983). In all probability, teachers would have to work in collaborative relationships with their professional peers and therefore would have to develop team planning skills.

As part of the in-service training experience, it may be important for teachers to conduct case studies of the learning of one or two students in order to gain an understanding of the dynamics of the learning process.

Administrative In-service Training

Administrators of the school would also have to acquire knowledge related to the instructional process. Administrators should have a command of child and adolescent growth and development. They would need to have some knowledge of instructional theory and of learning problems and their remediation. Administrators should also have a command of organizational development skills in order to enable them to work effectively with their staff in analyzing and solving instructional and administrative problems and developing plans to improve the schools and the educational process.

The principal would have to have considerable expertise in data analysis and instructional management skills in order to provide assistance to teachers. Educational leadership must be the most important component of the principal's role. Finally, since this type of individualized education involves parental consent as well as involvement, it is important that the administrator be skillful in involving parents.

CONCLUSION

The position taken here is that (1) special education and adaptive education embody the same values and practices; (2) special education is the most widely implemented form of adaptive education in the nation's schools; (3) all levels of mainstreamed education could become adaptive if the principles and practices of special education were to be applied; (4) all students in the nation's schools would benefit from the application of the best practices and principles of special education; (5) the goals of adaptive education can be achieved best by converting mainstream educational practices to reflect the practices and principles of special education.

The policy and administrative perspectives presented in this chapter are not new or profound. However, their implementation in all classrooms of the nation's elementary, middle, and secondary schools would be radical! To change the habits, attitudes, and skills of teachers and administrators will not be easy, as professionals in research and development have discovered. However, effective models do exist in our special education programs. Perhaps a federal law like PL94-142 would be required to bring about the changes implicit in this proposal. If we are going to get beyond the classroom door (Goodlad 1983) and modify the curriculum and instructional practices in the school, some type of legal mandate may be required. To implement such a mandate would require knowledge and skill in personal and institutional dimensions of the dynamics of change; it would also require application of instructional and classroom management techniques that have been absent in most American classrooms.

REFERENCES

Glaser, Robert. *Adaptive Education: Individual Diversity and Learning* (New York: Holt, Rinehart & Winston, 1977).

Goodland, John. "What Some Schools and Classrooms Teach." *Educational Leadership* 40 (April 1983): 8-19.

Leinhardt, Gaea; Bickel, William; and Pallay, Allan. "Unlabeled But Still Entitled: Toward More Effective Remediation." *Teachers College Record* 84 (Winter 1982): 391-422.

Wang, Margaret C. "Adaptive Instruction: Building on Diversity." *Theory Into Practice* 19 (Spring 1980): 122-28.

Zigmond, Naomi. "Teacher Center Experience for Secondary Special Education
Teachers." Unpublished manuscript, Special Education Department, University
of Pittsburgh, 1983.
Zigmond, Naomi, and Sansone, Jan. "What We Know about Mainstreaming from
Experience." In *Mainstreaming: Our Current Knowledge Base*, edited by Percy Bates.
Minneapolis, Minn.: National Support System Project, University of Minnesota, 1981. ED 213-232.

CHAPTER

13

Time Spent, Time Needed, and Adaptive Instruction

Nancy Karweit

Adapting instruction to individual differences is a fundamental problem faced by all schools. This chapter examines the use of time under different approaches to adaptive instruction. Because most techniques for adapting instruction to individual differences involve some form of grouping or individualization, this chapter is primarily concerned with the use of time in the major methods of organizing students for instruction, namely whole-class, within-class ability grouped, and individualized approaches.

The numerous investigations of the effects of grouping or of individualization have not found consistently positive effects for these techniques compared to traditional methods. For improving educational practice and advancing educational theory, it is important to understand more thoroughly this phenomenon of inconsistent effects. Although many studies suffer from methodological difficulties of one sort or another, it is highly unlikely that these problems alone account for the lack of positive effects. It seems useful, then, to examine the properties of the methods themselves to locate features that could produce equivalent results. In this examination, we focus on how each method uses instructional time.

In this chapter, then, we ask how it is that seemingly disparate ways of providing adaptive instruction may in fact produce roughly comparable achievement results. We address this question by describing the use of time under different classroom organizational arrangements. In particular, the chapter focuses on the nature of time spent and time needed under whole-class grouping, within-class ability grouped instruction, and individualized instruction. Because student diversity and classroom management are major determinants of time needed and time spent, these features of classroom life are emphasized.

We begin by discussing whether comparability of results implies that the techniques are equally effective or ineffective. In this discussion, recent reanalyses of the effect of time on learning are interpreted to suggest that the methods are equally inefficient. An examination of how each technique addresses time needed and time spent, the components affecting efficiency, is then presented. This discussion also suggests likely avenues for improving the efficiency and effectiveness of instruction under whole-class, within-class ability grouping, and individualized approaches.

EQUALLY EFFECTIVE OR INEFFECTIVE?

Comparisons of alternate ways of organizing classrooms for instruction with traditional methods have not produced consistent evidence of the superiority of any particular technique. For example, when contrasted in an experimentally valid manner with traditional classroom organization, individualized instruction has not been shown to be consistently effective (Miller 1976, Schoen 1976). Nor has tracking, another organizational approach, been shown to be consistently more effective than traditional classroom arrangements (Esposito 1973; Heathers 1969). Studies that simultaneously compare tracking, within-class grouping, and individualization to a control group could assess the relative effects of these alternate organizational forms. Lacking such studies, we interpret the separate studies of individualization, of within-class grouping, and of tracking to mean that these techniques are equivalent to traditional instruction and are also equivalent to each other in achievement effects.

This equivalence could mean that the methods are equally efficient or equally inefficient. If they are equally efficient, then the instructional design task has been solved and schools simply need to have more time to carry out instruction. If they are equally inefficient, then more time is not an appropriate response, while improving efficiency is.

Carroll's (1963) view of learning as a function of time provides a useful definition of instructional efficiency. According to Carroll, learning can be expressed as the ratio of time spent to time needed. This view can be extended to suggest when efficient instruction will occur. Learning will be maximized when time spent and time needed are equivalent. When the student spends less time on a learning task than is needed, learning efficiency will be reduced. When the student spends more time on a learning task than is needed, learning efficiency will also be reduced. Thus, instructional processes that provide the student with either less time or more time than is needed are not efficient, while instructional processes that match time needed and time spent are efficient.

In actuality, little serious attention has been paid to time needed, despite its twin import in Carroll's model. For example, recent assessments of the effect of instructional time have focused only on time spent. Elsewhere, we have argued (Karweit 1983) that time spent, *by itself*, is not a strong predictor of achievement. This lack of consistent effects of time spent is important for assessing efficiency of existing classroom practices. If time spent, without controlling for time needed, were highly important for achievement, then time needed by definition would have to be similar to time spent. Because time spent is not highly related to achievement, with time needed omitted, time spent and time needed are of necessity not equivalent. And, because learning efficiency is maximized when time needed and time spent are equivalent, the weak effects for time spent suggest that existing instructional processes are not efficient.

Defining efficient instruction as the condition when time needed and time spent are equivalent also helps clarify how quite different patterns of time usage may result in comparable achievement results. Each grouping technique has its own typical pattern of time use, affecting time needed and time spent through such factors as classroom management, quality of instruction, motivation, and amount of instructional time. Figure 13.1 indicates the relative emphasis (low to high) on factors related to time needed and time spent for different grouping arrangements. Individualized instruction places a high emphasis on time needed—its purpose is to provide the exact amount of time needed for each student to accomplish the learning task—but it does not emphasize time spent, that is, total instructional time is often reduced to accomplish needed management tasks. Conversely, whole-class instruction emphasizes time spent for instruction. It uses little management time but does not emphasize time needed, so that most students get either too little or too much time to learn a task. Within-class ability grouping may be the compromise between the two, offering somewhat more appropriate instruction than whole-group instruction, but having less time available for instruction because of the procedural time needed to group and regroup students.

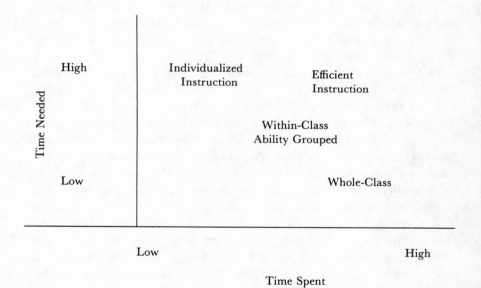

Figure 13.1
Emphasis on Time Needed and Time Spent in Three
Organizational Approaches

Efficient instruction is, by definition, concerned with both time spent and time needed. Operationally, for a technique to be effective, it must attend to motivating the students (time spent), to managing classroom activities (time spent), to providing adequate instructional time (time spent), and to providing an appropriate level and pace of instruction (time needed). The next sections examine in greater detail how different grouping arrangements affect time spent and time needed, primarily through their effect on student diversity and classroom management practices.

WHOLE-CLASS INSTRUCTION

Whole-class instruction is a widely used method of organizing students for instruction, especially for subjects other than reading in the elementary school and for most subjects in secondary and junior high schools. Tracked and nontracked classes present different instructional problems for whole-class instruction and are treated separately in the discussion that follows.

Time Spent

In whole-class instruction, the time a student actually spends actively engaged with learning a particular topic is determined by the amount of time allocated to the topic, the amount of the allocated time that is used for instruction, and the amount of time the student pays attention to instruction. There is appreciable variation in all three factors so that the amount of active learning time may vary widely from student to student. For instance, in one study, we determined that teachers in the same school differed by about 100 hours per year in the amount of time allocated to mathematics instruction (Karweit 1980). In addition, classrooms differ in the amount of allocated time that is actually used for instruction.

Interruptions, procedural and management activities, and disciplinary actions all take away from allotted instructional time, so that the amount of instructional time is actually less than the allotted time. Estimates vary, but the loss of instructional time to these activities may consume as little as 3 percent or as much as 30 percent of the allotted time. The size of the classroom and the heterogeneity of the students as well as the teacher's skill as a manager appear to affect the amount of noninstructional time (Evertson 1980). Finally, students do not always pay attention, and the nature of the activity and the setting influence these attentive levels. Gump(1974) found that students pay more attention in small-group instruction than in large-group recitation periods and argues that participation by each student is more important in smaller settings than in larger ones.

Whole-class instruction presents an interesting paradox for teacher planning. Because of the diversity of student abilities in the classroom, for instruction to be effective there must be a good deal of careful planning and attention to the details of instruction. But, because instruction is being conducted with the entire class, it is quite possible to survive the daily class routine without much planning at all, by a sort of muddling through, instructing when needed, answering questions here and there, and using the time in a haphazard manner. Effective whole-class instruction depends upon careful planning, but whole-class instruction can certainly be carried out without such planning.

This criticism of whole-class instruction does not imply that effective whole-class instruction is impossible or that all or even most teachers use their instructional time poorly. There are several examples of effective whole-class programs, such as Good's Missouri Mathematics Effectiveness Project, which focus explicitly on these issues of management, pace, and coordination. However, unless there is specific attention to these details of management, planning, and coordination, whole-class instruction can degenerate into mediocre instructional sessions where little is accomplished.

Time Needed

Time needed to master a particular concept or to attain a certain skill depends upon student aptitude and previous achievement and upon the quality of instruction. A poorly organized and noninformative lesson is of little benefit for any student. A well-organized and carefully thought-out lesson benefits students to the extent that they are prepared for it. The basic problem in structuring time needed in whole-class instruction is simply that instruction at a single level and pace is too advanced for some students, too slow for others, and about right for some. How many students benefit and how well they benefit from instruction probably depends upon the type of material being learned and how appropriate the level of the instruction is for them. Classrooms contain an amazing variety of skill deficits and masteries.

For example, a typical fifth-grade classroom may contain students who score at the third- to seventh-grade level on a standardized achievement test. Such variation makes the provision of appropriate instruction for all students very problematic. In particular, lower-performing students, who attain the same score on the standardized tests, may be deficient in totally different sets of skills. Providing appropriate instruction to a classroom of students with a patchwork of learning deficits may be quite problematic during whole-class instruction.

One response to diversity within the context of whole-class instruction is to assign students to classes on the basis of ability, or to track students between classes. Although a pervasive practice, tracking has not produced consistent evidence of its superiority over traditional instructional groupings. The inconsistent results may be interpreted variously: (a) heterogeneity is not a problem, (b) heterogeneity is a problem but tracking does not reduce it enough to be effective, (c) heterogeneity is a problem effectively dealt with by tracking, but tracking introduces other problems or ignores essential components necessary for instructional effectiveness.

These interpretations may actually all be relevant, but in different situations. For example, the first argument suggests that diversity may be overrated as a source of difficulty for effective instruction. There are two situations in which this may be true. In learning noncumulative subject matters such as history or social studies, previous knowledge should not have the same impact as in learning a very hierarchical subject such as mathematics. Second, the assumption that a major problem with instruction is the failure to match instruction precisely with learning levels may not be valid, especially for elementary school students. A much more serious problem may be the need to provide systematic instruction, sustained practice, feedback, and review, that is, thorough and complete instruction, until the skill is *firmly* mastered. Systematic information about the way that students receive, process, retain, and forget information during instruction and practice would help inform this question.

The second interpretation suggests that grouping may not be effective because diversity cannot be reduced enough. This argument is similar to the class size argument, which points out that class size may not make a difference simply because class size has not been reduced enough to make a difference. Studies of grouping have not typically controlled for the extent of diversity within the classroom, so it is not possible to tell empirically if diversity does condition the effect of grouping. Hallinan and Sorensen (1983) suggest that the extent of heterogeneity is a factor affecting the effectiveness of grouping.

The third interpretation holds that tracking reduces diversity enough to make instruction effective, but introduces new problems or ignores other critical features important for classroom functioning. This argument may be particularly salient for students in the low-ability track. Students who are tracked into the bottom ability track do not seem to fare as well as students of comparable ability who are in a low group in a within-class ability grouped situation (Rowan and Miracle 1983). Life in a low-track classroom may be fundamentally different from life in a within-class grouped situation, primarily because the concentration of low-performing students affects the norms, expectations, and standards for behavior, academic and otherwise. In this important sense, reducing diversity introduces more problems than it may solve, especially for the low-ability students.

We can look at tracking and its effects in terms of time spent and time needed. In theory, tracking should make time needed to learn less variable in the classroom, thus allowing the instructional level to be more appropriate for the students and bringing time spent on instruction more closely into line with time needed to learn. But, in low-track classrooms, instructional time is reduced by time spent in maintaining discipline and order. At the same time, time needed to learn is increased by student's low expectations and by interruptions to concentration. Thus tracking, instead of bringing time spent and time needed into equilibrium, actually forces the two farther apart and produces less efficient instruction.

Although the fundamental problem with whole-class instruction has been viewed as its inability to adapt to student diversity, this aspect may in fact not be the only or even the most serious problem. The fact that tracking of students, which does reduce diversity, does not consistently improve achievement, suggests that either diversity was not reduced enough or that by reducing diversity significant other problems were introduced that nullified any benefits from less heterogeneous classes. Additionally, management problems associated with whole-class instruction, such as pacing instruction at an inappropriate level, failure to use instructional time in an organized manner, and failure to integrate the seatwork and practice sessions with instruction, seriously affect the quality and quantity of instructional time.

WITHIN-CLASS ABILITY GROUPING

Within-class grouping refers to the practice of dividing students into smaller groups within the classroom for reading or other instruction. These groups may be stable with some movement among them or may be skill-based or mastery-based groups, where membership is flexible, at least in theory (Bossert, Barnett, and Filby, forthcoming). In elementary school classrooms, dividing students into ability groups for instruction is a common practice. Weinstein (1976) indicates that about 80 percent of reading instruction in large districts takes place in the context of grouped instruction. Mathematics instruction, especially at the lower grades, seems less likely to use grouping.

A typical grouping pattern for reading instruction uses three instructional groups among which the teacher divides his or her time equally. While the teacher instructs one group, the other two groups carry out independent seatwork. Assessments of within-class ability grouping suggest inconsistent results for this method in comparison to traditional instruction, although there are more positive than negative or no-effects findings (Begle 1975). As will be discussed next, whether within-class grouping is more effective than traditional instruction, most likely depends upon the adequacy of the management system and the successful integration of seatwork with the active teaching portion of the lesson.

Time Spent

Instructional time for each group is divided between direct instruction and independent seatwork time. The actual amounts of instructional and seatwork time depend upon the skill of the teacher in establishing smooth and automatic routines in the classroom. The two most difficult problems are the need to ensure the smooth transition of groups between activities and the need to have students work independently with a minimum of teacher monitoring.

If not adequately planned, the transition between activities can be very disruptive. The transition needs to be viewed as an orderly point connecting two segments of instruction and not as a time-out when chaos erupts. Often students arrive at their group and have nothing to do but wait for the teacher, who is still busy with another group. Once the teacher does arrive, the students are not ready for instruction as they still need to settle down, shift gears, and then turn their attention to the lesson.

One effective solution to this part of the transition problem is to post work for students to start on immediately upon arrival into their groups. These "starter problems" should be meaningfully related to the lesson and should not contain confusing or trick material that needs clarification from the teacher. The use of these starter problems (see Slavin and Karweit 1983) can be effective in making smooth transitions and engaging students in independent seatwork without direct teacher involvement.

Another management difficulty involves the use of time during independent seatwork. Because students in within-class grouping typically spend about two-thirds of the instructional period doing seatwork, the effective use of this time is obviously critical. Engagement rates tend to be lower in seatwork (68 percent) than they are in direct instruction (84 percent; Rosenshine, 1980). Whether these differences are related to the lack of direct supervision and teacher involvement or the nature of the task itself is unclear. Another problem with seatwork is that teachers often do not assign enough, so that students finish early and are left with nothing else to do.

One effective strategy for making seatwork more meaningful instructional time is found in the Missouri Mathematics Effectiveness Project (Good and Grouws 1979). The heart of this strategy involves making a smooth transition from direct instruction to seatwork. Basically, the successful transition is ensured by careful development of the lesson during the active teaching time, and by the use of controlled practice to assess accurately student comprehension and readiness to practice the skills on their own. By carefully planning for the transition from development to controlled practice to independent work, seatwork can become a meaningful time for practicing skills.

The use of grouping also alters how teachers use their time. While each group of students receives less direct instructional time in within-class grouping, the teacher is actually using more of the period for teaching than in traditional methods. Comparing the amount of time teachers spent in direct instruction in whole-class and ability-grouped classes, Slavin and Karweit (1984) found that teachers using grouping were teaching 87.2 percent of the allocated time in contrast to control teachers who were teaching 57.3 percent of the time. The high demands in preparation time, in teaching time, and in managerial skills may make within-class grouping a difficult arrangement to sustain day in and day out.

Student effort as well as teacher effort may be altered under within-class ability grouping. The existence of groups that are known as high-, average-, and low-ability groups often creates unwanted status distinctions within the classroom, which may in turn create serious motivational problems for the students in the low groups. The stigmatizing effect of membership in a low group may be more or less strongly felt depending upon how meaningful this membership becomes for teacher praise, condemnation, and expectations. Despite these potential negative effects, being a member of the low group in a heterogeneous class may be preferable to either whole-class or tracked whole-class instruction. For example, Rowan and Miracle (1983) found that low-ability students in within-class grouping benefited more from faster-paced instruction than did low-ability students in homogeneously tracked classrooms. The faster pace may result from smaller groups, from the use of a different "steering group" (Dahllof 1971), or from different expectations for performance of low-ability students in within-class ability grouped classrooms.

Time Needed

In within-class grouping, the actual instructional time for any one student is greatly diminished in comparison to whole-class instruction. For within-class grouping to be successful, the gains in appropriateness of instruction must offset these losses in instructional time. Whether they do or not probably depends upon how diverse the groups are and how integrated the independent seatwork is with the instructional portion of the lesson. The smaller sized instructional groups and the reduced heterogeneity may allow such gains in efficiency. But diversity is ever present in the classroom, and grouping may not be able to reduce diversity enough to make up for the loss of instructional time. In addition, teachers appear not to be guided by the need to reduce diversity in the way they make up groups. Hallinan and Sorensen (1983) point out that teachers seem more concerned with establishing equal-sized groups than in reducing diversity within groups. If in keeping the groups of equal size, the groups are still highly heterogeneous, not much may have been gained by grouping.

The nature of the learning task also has a large impact on the use of time. For example, in learning to read, reading aloud is an important skill, but one that is difficult to practice in group instruction. In a group of ten students during a twenty-five minute reading lesson, where reading occurs nonstop, each child could read aloud less than three minutes each.

Effectiveness of within-class grouping depends not only on time use during direct instruction, but also on the appropriateness of *instructional tasks* during seatwork. Frequently, seatwork may have little to do with the lesson; it is indeed busy work. Or, the seatwork may be on the right topic, but be too difficult or too easy for the students to use as meaningful practice. Another difficulty is that seatwork in and of itself may not be all that interesting as an activity day in and day out. Most seatwork involves a single student in a single type of activity, which day after day may become less interesting.

Locating effective ways of grouping is important, however, as grouping is at present a pervasive way of organizing classrooms and one not likely to become extinct. Even if other methods are made more effective, teachers may choose to group because they have done it in the past and because other arrangements, such as individualization, may be inappropriate for either the students or the subject at hand.

INDIVIDUALIZATION

Individualized systems of instruction provide, at least in theory, the opportunity for students to learn appropriate material and to learn it at an appropriate rate. Although exact figures on the present use of individualized systems are not to our knowledge available, it is probably accurate to say that individualization has declined in usage from the previous decade. Part of this decline may be due to the fact that individualization, at least at the elementary level, has not been effective.

Individualization has been justified on the belief that the primary difficulty with instruction is the extent of diversity in the classroom and that, by providing instruction at the right level and pace, the major difficulty with instruction in groups can be solved. However, assessments of existing individualized programs have been disappointing (Miller 1976; Schoen 1976). The failure of individualization to secure consistent effects is of fundamental importance for the design of future instructional systems. We need to understand the sources of this failure more clearly. Specifically, we need to know if the premise guiding the formation of individualized systems is incorrect or whether the implementations of existing systems are flawed in some systematic fashion. In examining the implementation issue, it is useful to focus on time needed and time spent on instruction.

Time Spent

Individualization requires a management system to support the multiple activities that are simultaneously occurring in the classroom. There must be a way to assess achievement, to determine what materials are needed, to get the right materials to the right student, to provide instruction in the new material, to assess student progress, and so on. Because each student in the classroom may be at a different point in this instructional loop, and because there is typically only one teacher in the classroom, the resolution of this management task is difficult. Often, individualization results in a massive queuing problem where students spend the majority of their time not working, but waiting for the teacher to check their work or to explain a misunderstood portion of the lesson. Many individualized systems have a definite structure built-in to handle this problem. Some have special flags or other signals to alert the teacher that a student needs assistance and that other students need activities to do while waiting for the teacher to get to them. Teachers are instructed often not to take too long with any individual student, say no more than a minute, so that the backup of students waiting for teacher assistance will not become too long. Students who need more time are then supposed to receive additional instructional or remedial help during a specific group or instructional time. In practice, it is often difficult for teachers to segment their time in this fashion, moving rapidly from one to the next, so that the inevitable queuing problem remains. Also, it may be difficult for a student, concentrating on completion of an activity, to drop it, start something else, and then return to the original activity when the teacher gets to him. As a result the "wait time" is still dead time. Even when these "wait periods" and other management activities are anticipated and planned for, there will of necessity be a reduction in instructional time to accomplish the management tasks.

The extent to which individualization succeeds probably depends upon the balance of the trade-off between time lost to manage instruction and the gains in effectiveness for targeting materials at a more appropriate level and rate. At first glance, the major difficulty with individualization would seem to be getting the management tasks under control. But, as Carroll's model reminds us, time spent is only half the story. The other half of the story is time needed, which is often not handled well under individualized approaches.

Time Needed

The quality of individualized instruction is often regarded as superior to group-paced models precisely because instruction can be geared to the level needed by the student. But the provision of adequate instructional materials, once this level is successfully determined, is a difficult task. Typically, individualized materials are derived from existing text series that have been designed for use in conjunction with teacher-directed instruction. The "individualization" of these materials amounts to little more than reducing a chapter into bite-sized nuggets of text, hardly adequate either as a self-instructional tool or as a review of instruction. The development of concepts, the assessment of comprehension, the periods of controlled practice, the review of other related materials, may be woefully inadequate in this sort of material.

Also, for many students, the presentation of a lesson via written text may be a very ineffective means of first exposure or continued exposure to material to be learned. Students who experience difficulties in reading mechanics or reading comprehension will obviously have difficulty in benefiting from instruction that assumes an inappropriate level of reading ability.

Direct instruction from the teacher, especially for the introduction and development of new concepts, may still be the best way to provide sound instruction. In many individualized approaches, the direct teaching component is either missing altogether or not systematically incorporated into an assessment, teaching, practice loop. Oftentimes the instructional groups are formed when the teacher perceives a need for instruction and may thus be a very hit-or-miss sort of enterprise.

Providing prescribed periods of direct instruction is one of the key components of the Team-Assisted Individualization (TAI) approach that has been found to be a highly effective method for elementary mathematics instruction (Slavin, Madden, and Leavey, in press). In TAI, teaching groups comprised of students at roughly comparable skill levels meet one week out of every four for regular instruction. The provision for instruction in these groups is a systematic, not haphazard, part of the program. The teaching groups are one way in which

TAI successfully provides appropriate instruction. In addition, review and adequate targeted practice times are provided.

A recent study (Slavin and Karweit 1984), which compared TAI to to an ability-grouped model and a whole-class model, raises some interesting questions about the extent to which the success of TAI is due to aspects of individualization or other features of the program. In this experiment, conducted in two cities, the achievement results were virtually identical for the ability-group model and the TAI classrooms. Here the ability-grouped classes used only two groups, scarcely overattention to individual differences. The performance of the TAI classes were not surprising, given previous studies and the fact that the TAI system effectively deals with major components related to time needed and time spent. The comparability of the ability-grouped classes was surprising, given the long-standing view of the necessity of accommodation to individual differences. One interpretation of these results is that there may be a broader range of aptitudes and abilities that can profit from instruction than is typically thought. However, replication and extension of this study manipulating the extent of individualization is needed to address this important issue directly.

DISCUSSION

One long range goal for research and practice should be to establish multiple ways of providing adaptive instruction where the suitable choice of technique depends upon the requirements of the learning situation and learners and the resources available in that situation. This goal explicitly recognizes that schools differ and classroom teachers differ, and that what is workable in one setting may be less than satisfactory in another. Hopefully, we are working toward the establishment of a menu of effective educational strategies where the selection is guided by knowledge of the requirements of the learning situation, the resources available to the teacher, and the applicability of the technique under those circumstances. The first step would surely seem to be to provide effective techniques for whole-class instruction, for within-class grouping, and for individualization. This chapter is an attempt to understand more thoroughly how the various techniques operate at present and how they might be made more effective in the future.

The point of view taken here is that improving the effectiveness of instruction can best be accomplished by changing structural features of instruction and classrooms. Given this orientation, the concern is not so much with locating appropriate teacher behaviors and teaching functions for effective instruction but more with locating possible classroom organizations and instructional strategies that facilitate and structure effective teaching. Time spent and time needed provide a úseful framework for examining the effectiveness and possible effectiveness of these different strategies. While many commission reports that have examined school quality seem to favor a strategy of increasing time spent, hopefully this chapter can suggest strongly that such a strategy will not be effective unless it is coupled with serious attempts to address the issue of quality of instruction. Time needed and time spent are together necessary components of effective instruction, and to focus on one without understanding the other is likely to result in continued inefficient instruction, but at a greater expense.

A more reasonable strategy would be to continue the research into effective teaching and classroom practices and to complete this cycle by the development and packaging of effective whole-class, within-class, and individualized programs. No one approach will be applicable for all grade levels, all teachers, or all students. But by carefully engineering programs to focus on time needed and time spent, we may be able to supply a selection of packages from which schools and teachers can choose.

REFERENCES

Begle, Edward G. *Ability Grouping for Mathematics Instruction: A Review of the Empirical Literature*. Stanford, Calif.: Stanford Mathematics Education Study Group, Stanford University, 1975.

Bossert, Stephen T.; Barnett, B. G.; and Filby, Nikola N. "Grouping and Instructional Organization." In *Instructional Groups in the Classroom: Organization and Processes*, edited by Penelope L. Peterson, Louise C. Wilkinson, and Maureen T. Hallinan. New York: Academic Press, forthcoming.

Carroll, John B. "A Model of School Learning." *Teachers College Record* 64 (May 1963): 723-33.

Dahllof, Urban S. *Ability Grouping, Content Validity, and Curriculum Process Analysis*. New York: Teachers College Press, 1971.

Esposito, Dominick. "Homogeneous and Heterogeneous Ability Grouping: Principal

Findings and Implications for Evaluating and Designing More Effective Educational Environments." *Review of Educational Research* 43 (Spring 1973): 163-79.

Evertson, Carolyn M.; Emmer, Edmund T.; and Clements, Barbara S. *The Junior High Classroom Organizational Study: Summary of Training Procedures and Methodology.* Report No. 6101. Austin: Research and Development Center for Teacher Education, University of Texas at Austin, 1980.

Good, Thomas L., and Grouws, Douglas A. "The Missouri Mathematics Effectiveness Project: An Experimental Study in Fourth Grade Classrooms." *Journal of Educational Psychology* 71 (June 1979): 355-62.

Gump, Paul V. "Operating Environments in Schools of Open and Traditional Design." *School Review* 82 (August 1974): 575-93.

Hallinan, Maureen, and Sorenson, Aage B. "The Formation and Stability of Instructional Groups." *American Sociological Review* 48 (December 1983): 831-51.

Heathers, Glen. "Grouping." In *Encyclopedia of Educational Research*, 4th ed., edited by Robert Ebel. New York: Macmillan, 1969.

Karweit, Nancy. "Time in School." In *Research in Sociology of Education and Socialization: An Annual Compilation of Research.* Greenwich, Conn.: JAI Press, Inc., 1980.

Karweit, Nancy. *Time-on-task: A Research Review*, Report No. 332. Baltimore, Md.: Center for Social Organization of Schools, Johns Hopkins University, 1983.

Miller, Richard L. "Individualized Instruction in Mathematics: A Review of Research." *Mathematics Teacher* 69 (May 1976): 345-51.

Rosenshine, Barak V. "How Time Is Spent in Elementary Classrooms." In *Time to Learn*, edited by Carolyn Denham and Ann Lieberman. Washington, D.C.: National Institute of Education, U.S. Department of Health, Education, and Welfare, 1980.

Rowan, Brian, and Miracle, Andrew W., Jr. "Systems of Ability Grouping and the Stratification of Achievement in Elementary Schools." *Sociology of Education* 56 (July 1983): 133-44.

Schoen, Harold L. "Self-paced Mathematics Instruction: How Effective Has It Been?" *Arithmetic Teacher* 23 (February 1976): 90-96.

Slavin, Robert E., and Karweit, Nancy. *Ability Grouped Active Teaching (AGAT): Teacher's Manual.* Baltimore: Center for Social Organization of Schools, Johns Hopkins University, 1983.

Slavin, Robert E., and Karweit, Nancy. "Within-class Ability Grouping and Student Achievement: Two Field Experiments." Paper presented at the annual meeting of the American Educational Research Association, New Orleans, 1984.

Slavin, Robert E.; Madden, Nancy A.; and Leavey, Marshall. "Effects of Team-Assisted Individualization on the Mathematics Achievement of Academically Handicapped and Nonhandicapped Students." *Journal of Educational Psychology*, in press.

CHAPTER
14

Comments on Part Two

A. How Is Adaptive Education Like Water in Arizona?

David C. Berliner

I was pleased when asked to respond to a set of papers billed as summaries of the "major elements in the design, development, implementation, and evaluation of adaptive instruction programs and practices." I thought that by accepting this task as discussant/critic I would learn about the new and exciting events related to the continuing commitment of the schools to adapt instruction to individual differences among students. I am, however, very disappointed in these papers. What I learned from them is that the concept of adaptive instruction has much in common with the concepts of motherhood and apple pie. Adaptive education is one of those wonderful concepts in education that everyone loves and talks about, but they find it difficult to define, to find in practice, to maintain over time, to document, and to validate.

To me, adaptive education is a way for schools to accommodate individual differences. One can design an instructional program and require that children partake of that form of instruction, as schools so often do, and virtually ignore the fact that differences between students are of enormous magnitude on virtually every psychoeducational variable that we can measure. One can also make marginal accommodations to individuals by, for example, tutoring a slow student, assigning special remedial or enrichment activities for other special students, and forming homogeneous groups with still other students. In these cases, however, the instructional form is not adapted very much to students. Rather, students are "tuned" or modified in some way, in order to fit better the standard instructional situation. Truly adaptive education, where individual differences among students are seriously considered in instructional design, is shown only when markedly different forms of instruction are prescribed for different kinds of children. The premise that underlies most educational programs in American schools is that we have adaptive children. Adaptive education is based on a different premise. Adaptive education requires that the schools assimilate and accommodate to the children. It stands in opposition to the kinds of programs we usually have that require children to assimilate and accommodate to the system of schooling already developed. These are vastly different premises about the way a school system should operate.

My understanding of this concept or philosophy of education is *not* idiosyncratic. I expect papers on adaptive education to be concerned, in some way, with the matching of instruction to students with different aptitudes. Aptitudes should be broadly defined to include virtually any individual difference variable. Margaret Wang agrees with this notion when she says in her writings that adaptive education is education suited to a student's needs. Le Cronbach and Richard E. Snow would bring in the concept of ATI, aptitude-treatment-interaction. In talking about this phenomenon, David Hunt would discuss the concept of matching models in education. I actually prefer the TTTI model, which is concerned with the interaction of traits, tasks, and treatments. Whatever the form and language used when we discuss adaptive education, we are talking of treatments matched to students. We are not talking about students being fit to treatments.

The philosophy of adaptive education has been well stated in the ancient Jewish Passover service. The readers of the service are reminded that the story of Passover must be told differently to different kinds of children at the table. To the wise son you explain the service down to the last detail. To the contrary son, a different way is used to explain the service. To the simple son, a third way is devised, and to the son who does not know how to ask questions, still a fourth way to explain the Passover service is devised. And in keeping with the times, to the young woman at the service, you tell nothing! One may, of course, question these practices because of concerns about equity and mainstreaming. Nevertheless, they are truly adaptive practices. Adaptive education is seen, therefore, as a very old philosophy and practice of education.

With these thoughts about adaptive education in mind, let us now examine the papers in this section. To begin with, Johnson and Johnson report a series of studies about cooperative learning. Their work and the work of other investigators in this area (for example, Shlomo Sharan and Robert Slavin) should make us all proud that educational research has produced a technology that *systematically affects the cooperative behavior* of school children. Unfortunately, what Johnson and Johnson have to say about adaptive education is surprisingly little. For example, although they pay lip service to the idea that competitive, individualistic, and cooperative learning structures should all be used in classrooms, the paper really makes a strong case *against* using some styles of instruction. It appears that each time a research study suggested an advantage for another style of instruction, Johnson and Johnson undertook a new study to show that cooperative learning was really better, and better for all levels of ability, handicapped and nonhandicapped students, girls and boys, and so forth. This is a search for the one best way to teach and *not* a search for methods that work best for different kinds of students.

Unless research questions are deliberately framed to push methods to the extreme, and to study novel kinds of individual differences, one can never find out the limits of an instructional method or technique for different kinds of students. For example, have cooperative, competitive, and individual learning structures been studied with such individual difference variables as field-independent and field-dependent students? I would find a study like that very interesting. I would also like to know about students whose attributions for failure favor internal stable events, such as lack of ability, and whose attributions for success suggest external unstable events, such as luck. That is, I would like to ask questions about the long-term adaptive nature of cooperative learning and, say, individual learning strategies of students showing learned helplessness.

The philosophy of adaptive education is to *tailor* instruction, not to search for the one best way or even to search for a variety of ways in which a technique can be used. Johnson and Johnson seem to believe that by pointing to a variety of ways that a technique can be used they are involved in adaptive education. They list various options for modifying cooperative learning environments, but they really do not tell us what options go with what kinds of individual differences. They simply point out in their section on adaptiveness how varied kinds of learning can take place in cooperative learning structures (for example, the structures allow for iconic or symbolic learning). Adaptive education has to do with tailoring the kinds of instruction we use, not simply providing choices and variety in one kind of instructional method. Variations on a theme still imply that there is one best way to teach. Adaptive education requires that there should be many ways to teach the same things, that is, many different forms or kinds of instruction, each of which is beneficial to students of a certain type.

I must also point out how the section on adaptiveness seems almost pinned on to the paper by Johnson and Johnson. It appears to me that the tone of the paper seems to change from social science writing to the kind of writing characteristic of the methods courses in some colleges of education. I believe this is shown when Johnson and Johnson make statements like "within cooperative learning groups members typically develop considerable liking for each other and attachment to being a member of the group." This strikes me as a perfectly legitimate and important summary statement based on scientific research. But then they also go on to make a statement about adaptiveness like this: "Students with different achievement histories can be given assignments within the division of labor that take their abilities into account. The only limit on adaptiveness that may be structured into a cooperative group is the creativity of the teacher." I personally believe that one of the failures of methods courses in this country is that they promote pet programs such as adaptive education (which they often support) by pointing out that the teacher's creativity is the key variable in implementing such a program. People who have not been in classrooms in a long time forget that teachers are rather overwhelmed by real life events. They are often tired. Teachers work in large classes with children who often do not wish to be there, and with children of varied intellectual ability and language ability. The reason we are concerned at all with adaptive education is because of the variations among students in different classes. To then go on to tell teachers that their creativity allows them to modify a particular learning technique is to tell them nothing at all! We need scientific investigations of how to adapt techniques of learning to individual differences. We do not have to leave it to happenstance and creativity.

From the paper by Johnson and Johnson I conclude that I have learned nothing new about adaptive education. Nevertheless, I am convinced that cooperative learning structures deserve our serious attention.

In Tobias's report on computer-assisted instruction I thought we would read about adaptive education in all its glory. Surely, teachers get tired and overwhelmed in their classes. But computers have infinite patience, can make split-second decisions, and can keep extensive histories on each student. The computer puts truly adaptive education within our reach. But again I am disappointed. This review shows me that computers are not, for the most part, being used very wisely for CAI (computer-assisted instruction), let alone adaptive CAI. In the best of the instructional programs the rate of instruction is adapted to individual differences in speed of learning or rate of learning. Content is sometimes adapted to individual differences through branching programs, as the computer takes into account the history of responses that subjects make. They chart new paths through the materials based on the history of students' responses. It appears, then, that the best instructional programs can adapt on rate and content. But only the best seem to do so. Most instructional programs used in computer-assisted instruction have only one path through the material and allow only for a modification of rate. Perhaps someday we will get the tutorial programs described by Tobias, such as those of Burton, who developed the interactive buggy program (IDE-BUGGY). Perhaps in a decade or so we will see these in schools. Perhaps then we will have truly adaptive education, that is, instruction tailored to some individual differences in students. The buggy algorithm programs will adapt to the logic of the answer that students give, hypothesize students' mental operations, and adjust the program accordingly. We do not yet have anything like this sophistication in the programs we currently see in classes.

I think a key point in Tobias's paper is his concern about increased computer literacy for teachers. I agree with him that more BASIC or PASCAL will not get better computer usage in school. Only better software, that is, *proven* better software, can do that. Most medical doctors learn how to prescribe the new wonder drugs. They really do not, anymore, know how the molecular structure of a chemical is changed by dipping it into a cryogenic bath. What they do know is how and when to dispense that drug. Similarly, our teachers do not really need programming for designing graphics. They need interactive, tutorial, dialoging adaptive programs that work, and an instruction manual that tells them how to use these programs.

Some things not addressed in Tobias's paper are important to the future of adaptive education via computers. First, the record-keeping functions for developing individual histories for students will become an important basis for diagnosis and prescription, key ingredients in adaptive programs. The computer can keep very detailed records of each student's preferred learning styles and achievements. It can do that better than a human can, and thus is likely to become, over time, a competent diagnostician and prescriber of adaptive instructional treatments. A second feature of the computer is its "personality." Computers are judged to be fair, patient, and to have the ability to reward regularly, contingently, and continuously those students with low self-concepts as learners. The research on the kinds of instructional materials best adapted for low-self-concept/low-ability students suggests that the computer is uniquely suited for them. Thus, research on adaptive use of computers should follow these leads to see if, in fact, the computer is well tailored to these low-ability/low-self-concept learners.

Although the future is promising, Tobias and I both heard the same promises in the 1960s. I believe the times are different and computers will increase in numbers and in the amount of time they are used in classrooms. Nevertheless, I am stilll dubious about whether adaptive use of computers will make any significant inroad into the educational system in the next few decades. Only the most sophisticated of programs will be able to do that. We do not have many under development at this time. Since we have always been able to design better texts than we now have available, better movies for instructional purposes than we have, better TV shows for instructional purposes than are in use, and so forth, I would predict that we will also have less well-designed computer programs for students than we know how to produce.

Let us turn our attention now to Klausmeier's work on school improvement. I have long been an admirer of his work. I think his formulation of Individually Guided Education (IGE) was one of the most innovative and thoughtful programs of reform at the elementary school level. The hallmark of that program was its systemic approach to school reform. It seems to me that the experience Klausmeier gained in his IGE work is at the heart of his current design for improving secondary education. As with his IGE work, there is a strong emphasis in the secondary school work he is doing on accommodating to individual differences among students. The IGE principles and the present secondary school improvement say, up front, that they are out to make adaptive education a reality. What I do not get from Klausmeier is a sense of how to go about implementing these beliefs about the importance of adaptive education. For example, he says that school reform will be concerned with "adapting the content and instructional materials to the student's capability for learning the particular subject matter." He goes on to say that the schools will use "available instructional materials flexibly, . . . especially to provide more adequately for more different learning styles and interests." He also says that the school will be involved with "using individual assignments, small-group work, and whole-class instruction to take into account individual students' learning styles and interests and also the nature of the subject matter."

My problem with these wonderful statements is that they give the same old advice every teacher has received every year in every methods course ever taken. I do not know yet how this kind of sound advice, and concern for a form of education we all admire, gets translated into any usable actions. Klausmeier's overall design is surely laudatory. But when he reports that the curriculum is designed to meet the state and district requirements, and can be adapted by the school and individual teachers to take into account differing educational needs of students, he tells me nothing different than any other school person would tell me. When he also comments that effective communication and cooperative educational efforts between the school and the community are to be carried out as part of the program of home-school-community relations, I again wonder: What's new? Klausmeier is stating a goal most educators would adhere to. What he has not given us, at least in this paper, is any sense of the strategies for implementation of these laudatory but usually unreachable goals of education.

Let me be clear about my respect for the data that Klausmeier presents. He surely has evidence of secondary school change for the better, and that is not easy to come by. Nevertheless, I do not yet know from his work the implementation strategies that make this happen. I also have a suspicion that part of the reason for school change is Klausmeier's intimate involvement with these schools. He is a committed educator with sound ideas. Such people make change happen. The real questions for education in general and for adaptive education programs in particular is: What happens when the great educator leaves a site?

The most serious problem in school reform appears to be the problem of sustaining achievements that are gained through such hard work. There is evidence that it is very difficult to sustain reform enterprises such as IGE. The key program features evaporate even when schools continue to say that the programs are great and that they work fine. An analysis by Thomas Popkowitz and his colleagues at the University of Wisconsin dealt with the myth of school reform. They pointed out, quite persuasively, that school reform is hard work and often does not last. A few years ago Robert Benjamin wrote a book about effective schools that received high praise. He told me recently that he does not think *any* of the schools he designated as effective would be so classified today. Steven Bossert and his colleagues, studying effective schools, found reliability in the form of year-to-year stability of achievement scores to be very, very low. The implications these writers draw from such data is that the big problem for educational reform is the issue of sustaining effects. There is no doubt that over a few years, with Klausmeier's attention, some of the schools he has worked with have changed for the better. My concern is whether the adaptive components of the program are at all responsible for some of the changes, whether those adaptive components are in fact implementable, and once they stop being the object of study, whether the schools will even forget what the term adaptive education means!

The next paper in this set is that of Wang, Gennari, and Waxman. It is on the adaptive learning environments model (ALEM) and includes sections on the design, implementation, and effects of the model. I also had my troubles with this paper. It was like the buildup in an unsatisfying movie, one that has a great plot until the final scene. First the background to the study is presented, demonstrating that the research literature is rich in implications for the design of the adaptive program. Then the model is presented and it is sensible. There is a section on implementation of the model, which includes some of the best data on implementation I have ever seen. The University of Pittsburgh can be proud of its work on describing implementation of treatments. William Cooley has discussed it in some of his papers, and Gaea Leinhardt has written an excellent paper on the process of documenting implementation. Now, in this study, we see in microscopic detail how a program can be run with extremely high fidelity.

Despite the buildup, when I got to the heart of the issue—the effects—I was let down. The outcome data for the adaptive educational model are very perplexing, and certainly not clear-cut. There seems to be evidence that the program is having some effect on achievement. But it is not at all clear that it is the adaptive aspects of the program that are causing the effects. For example, in looking at the causal paths presented by Wang and her colleagues, we learn a number of disconcerting things. First, the relationship between achievement measured pre and post looks exactly like any other nonadaptive program. I would have thought that an adaptive education program could in some way modify the relationship for group data between pre and post. Truly adaptive programs would affect that relationship, and in this case it does not seem that the relationship had been changed. A second issue, and more disconcerting, is that an analysis of the data in the causal model appears to show that there is no relationship between the students' prior achievement and the implementation of the ALEM model (the link between prior achievement and the block labeled instructional planning and classroom management). In addition, the statistic describing the relations between "instructional planning and classroom management" (which constitutes the implementation of the ALEM model) and "classroom processes" is negative! This indicates that the ALEM model is unrelated or negatively related to the classroom processes that we know affect achievement, such as time-on-task, distraction, waiting for teacher help, and the like. Furthermore, the direct link between the implementation of the five critical dimensions of the ALEM model and post-achievement makes no sense. Such processes should affect some intermediate event such as the students' cognitive processes, the students' time-on-task in activities related to measures, and so forth. The relationship between a teacher's creating and maintaining instructional materials, diagnostic testing, monitoring and diagnosing, prescribing, and record keeping (that is, the major elements of the ALEM model) should *not* affect test performance directly. Thus, I am questioning the causal model in its present form. Clearly, Wang and her colleagues are aware of this confusing set of findings. For me, acting in the role of critic, I would say that I have yet to see evidence that the careful work on implementation has resulted in achievement gains beyond ordinary classroom teaching. I get the feeling that this can be demonstrated, but I have not yet seen clear evidence of it.

This study is particularly perplexing for an important reason. Many people in the crazy business of educational research claim that they can produce wondrous outcomes, but cannot describe their treatments. Here we have a case of some of the best descriptions of a treatment that have ever been recorded. But at first glance, and with preliminary data analysis from the causal model, we cannot find evidence that the implementation of the adaptive aspects of the program is affecting achievement. The lesson, as always, is that it is very hard to do research on teaching and learning in schools.

In my role as critic I would like to be even more irreverent. I would like to know what is adaptive about the adaptive ALEM model. There is a lot of talk about accommodating to the students' diverse needs. I really cannot tell what diverse needs are being met besides the differences in students' rate of learning. It does look like there really is adaptation to rate of learning. But I do not see any evidence of clearly different instructional techniques for different kinds of students, or clearly different content for different kinds of student needs. Where is the concern for individual differences in anxiety, need for structure, intelligence (as opposed to speed), and so forth? I cannot even tell if the handicapped students are receiving a different program or not. It seems irreverent to ask this question, but as a critic one is allowed a certain luxury, so I ask: What is adaptive about the adaptive learning environments model? I cannot help but find it odd that these program developers say that the program is designed to "incorporate the use of intervention when needed to modify each student's capability to function under, and profit from, adaptive instruction." This actually scares me. The definition of adaptive education that I gave above requires that the schools modify their programs to meet the childrens' needs. This statement appears to require the children to adapt to the schools' needs.

I turn my attention now to Slavin's paper on team-assisted individualization. I had the great pleasure of viewing his program *in situ*. It is a very impressive program. The program is documented well, is of obvious merit, and shows adaptation to the speed of the students. At least it accommodates slower students, but because of social and structural problems in schools, the faster students are not as easily accommodated. This is not a problem of the program of TAI but a problem of the schools. For example, a teacher of fifth grade told me that the students had finished everything so fast that she had to keep them away from the mathematics curriculum for a while or the middle school teachers would be mad at her for sending students that are too well prepared! (I marvel that someone could make such a remark and think it was sensible.)

For the most part, TAI has been studied as a main effect approach, with particularly good results with mainstreamed students. This is a remarkable achievement since just a few years ago it was said that there were no systematic programs for integrating special education students into the regular classroom. It now looks like there are. Although useful for racially mixed groups and for slow-learning children, the program was designed as a main effect, individual, student-directed and student-managed, total mathematics curriculum. It is a good one, but the research has not explored the limits of individual differences and offered modifications of treatments to accommodate those differences. That is, the adaptive nature of this program is a by-product, not its "raison d'etre."

Worth pointing out is the fact that in Slavin's program and in Wang's program we have an important outcome that is a moral and philosophical concern of many educators. In both programs we see students taking responsibility for their own learning. That is a remarkable outcome of both programs and should be highlighted, though we know little about which students take responsibility and which do not, and how to adapt the instruction to promote responsibility for those who fail to take personal responsibility for their learning. That is, once again, the main effects are impressive but we know nothing about adapting instruction for individual differences with regard to this important outcome of schooling.

Let us now turn our attention to Anderson's paper on retrospective and prospective views of Benjamin Bloom's "learning for mastery." Unfortunately, I hold with Bloom himself that learning for mastery is *not* an adaptive treatment. I believe that even those who think it is an adaptive treatment actually run a learning for mastery program as a monolithic main effect treatment, and that is, in many of the schools that I have visited, somewhat opposed to the concept of individual differences. I do not think its effectiveness in many situations is in doubt. But as an adaptive program I do have my questions. In some of the programs that call themselves learning for mastery the time is actually held constant in curriculum units, destroying the one major adaptive feature that mastery has. In some of the reteaching episodes I have seen a repeat of the original unproductive instructional technique. Thus, the provision for adaptive instruction is often missing. In principle, some aspects of mastery are adaptive. In practice, I find very little that is adaptive except for learning rate. And even here we have difficulties, such as with university registrars who insist that the rate can vary any way one wants as long as everything is finished in sixteen weeks!

I think learning for mastery is simply unusually good instruction, but not adaptive instruction. Where Anderson singles out the feedback and corrective component of learning for mastery as the essence of an adaptive program, I disagree. All environments are likely to provide feedback and correctives—this is the essence of the Skinnerian argument about operants and how they are shaped or eliminated. Organisms adapt to their environment. The essence of adaptive education, however, is changing the environment to fit the organism. I believe Anderson has confused who is adapting to what.

In Wallace's paper we see a comparison of the philosophy and practice of special education with the philosophy and practice of adaptive education. He makes an important point. The *basic* philosophy of special education has always been adaptive. Built into special educators' concerns has been the provision of instructional alternatives matched to the performance of the learner. Among the most adaptive programs we have seen in American education are those designed for special students. Wallace extrapolates from this insight and asks what it would take to make special education the guiding philosophy for regular schooling. I can do no more than applaud this as a goal. I too have long felt that all teachers should be special educators. Every child is different and every teacher needs to be able to diagnose and prescribe instruction based on these unique individual qualities. The problem not addressed by Wallace is, How does one do that in classrooms of thirty, given the structural problems so characteristic of schools? Those problems can interfere with the design of special education programs. Special educators are used to working in small classroom situations, with small groups of students, and with a considerable amount of one-to-one tutorial work. Group instruction has a different characteristic. Wallace says nothing about the structural characteristics of schools in his paper. He presents a plan I can applaud, but does not present any ideas for changing schools. To follow his ideas would require that age grading be eliminated and the rate through the curriculum be opened up. Is Wallace really ready to change the Pittsburgh Schools so that some children can graduate high school at age twelve and others at age twenty-two? How are the resources to be developed to have a testing program that is not overwhelming in its quantity, but which does keep track of students through the curriculum? Who does the testing, the teachers, or will there be special testing bureaus attached to schools? Who will staff these? What are the school arrangements for reteaching students who do not reach instructional goals the first time through? I applaud Wallace's goals. I worry that without concern for the sociology of contemporary schooling these goals will never be implemented.

The last paper of this set I have been asked to review is that of Karweit on time spent and time needed in adaptive instruction. She focuses on how time is spent and how teachers control the time a student needs to get adequate instruction in three contexts: whole-group settings, within-class ability group settings, and in individualized settings. She provides an insightful look at the two time variables (time spent and time needed) that are the pivotal concepts in John Carroll's famous model of instruction. I believe she is too quick to dismiss, as too weak a variable, one of these concepts—time spent. I find it hard to discount as easily as she does the effects of allocated time, student motivation, management of time in classrooms, and so forth, on student achievement. Despite this qualification, I agree wholeheartedly with her contention that we have not given enough attention to the "time needed" variable. As she explicates the costs and benefits of time spent or needed that are associated with the three instructional contexts, we find little to assure us that adaptive education exists in important and functional ways. As a sociologist is likely to, she sees structural characteristics of schooling as interfering with the development of truly adaptive educational programs. Thus, as with the other papers, I am left uneasy about the way adaptive education would actually be implemented in the schools.

SUMMARY

The reason I see so little in the way of instructional adaptation to student differences in these papers is related to my understanding of the concept. Let me illustrate, once again, my concept of adaptive education by using an analogy to the idea of "adaptive cooking" in families. In a small family the child who is allergic to fish or walnuts is accommodated. The child who must rush to ice-skating or little league practice receives a quicker or smaller meal. The child who loves granola cookies often gets them. With one cook and four or five eaters, adaptive food service is possible. The child who is accommodated at home in the family group then joins 200 to 1000 or more students at school, and adaptive food service disappears. The child finds he or she will get frankfurters, or nothing, every Monday; that food is served between 12:10 and 12:15 everyday, or you get nothing; and the child may never get to have granola cookies in school! With the growth in size, the quality of life for the child is changed in some dramatic ways. Adaptations of all sorts seem to occur naturally in small interpersonal groupings. But in large groupings, especially institutional groupings like schools, we often see people treated impersonally, coerced into fitting themselves to a single system deemed by someone or by some group to be "the one best system." These papers did very little to help me understand how schools can function more like small adaptive family groups rather than the impersonal institutions they often become, where only a minimum concern for individual differences is shown.

The papers, as described in the conference program notes, were supposed to inform me about "the critical processes in the design, field testing, and implementation of *adaptive* programs in school settings." The papers were to present the features that make for effective adaptive instruction. There really is much to be learned from those papers about instruction, and about research on instructional processes. But, I am afraid, there is not much to be learned from these papers about *adaptive* instruction. I believe that in education the concept of adaptive education is too loosely defined, that adaptive education is not convincingly implemented, but despite these problems adaptive education is a concept that is *always* reverently discussed.

The title of this paper is: How is adaptive education like water in Arizona? My answer is: Because it is very hard to find, and when you do find it, it seems to evaporate right in front of your eyes.

B. What Is Adaptive Instruction?

Harriet Talmage

A "pendulum" metaphor has been periodically used to character-ize educational responses to critical societal issues. Such a metaphor has simplistic appeal but fails to take into consideration new knowl-edge and understandings, and the temper of the times upon which many educational responses are predicated. For the most part, individ-ualized instructional programs of the 1960s and early 1970s were caught up in the spirit of that period: self-actualization, openness, freedom to "do one's own thing"—to release some real or imagined creativity within the learner. In the 1980s, programs concerned with differences among learners are responding to a different set of societal pressures, and tend to emphasize efficiency and productivity under severe budgetary constraints. Current adaptive education is neither a forward nor a backward swing relative to previous concerns with individual differences, but a graduated upward increment that moves us beyond what preceded. As programmatic responses are now being designed to get maximum performance out of the reluctant, the energetic, the overachievers, and the low achievers, the new responses have a base upon which to build: sharpened theory, newer research findings, corrections of past errors, and adapting from the best of what preceded. Thus, a "vertical spiral" metaphor describes educational responses today more accurately than the pendulum. A vertical spiral incorporates the contributions of research and experience, all within a changing societal context.

Other important lessons have been learned from previous attempts at individualized instruction. First and foremost, those proposing adaptive instructional programs or approaches have been wise enough to select a label that avoids getting "hung up" in definitional disputation. Despite Shakespeare's dismissal of importing meaning to a name, the individualized instruction movement in the past dissipated much energy in defining itself. But how can one quarrel with "adaptive?" By the very term, adaptive can mean anything we want to call what we consciously do in the name of "good" instruction. This is the strength of the programs presented in the preceding chapters. None claims to be the definitive approach to individual differences. There is room for all well-designed programs that have adaptive components built into the design.

Five of the eight chapters represent programmatic responses to individual differences. These are Cooperative Learning (CL), Design for Improving Secondary Education (DISE), Learning for Mastery (LFM), Adaptive Learning Environment Model (ALEM), and Team-Assisted Individualization (TAI). I will first contrast the designs of the five programs or approaches presented through an examination of their selected instructional characteristics and explore briefly the place of computer-assisted instruction (CAI) in the respective adaptive instructional designs. Inasmuch as "time" and "administrative support" are critical elements in most of the programs, the issues Karweit and Wallace raise are superimposed on the programs. Next, I pose several specific questions to the authors for clarification. This is followed by a discussion of several key issues that move the discussion from an instructional delivery system level to the broader level of societal context. Finally, I return to the question: What is adaptive instruction?

COMPARING ADAPTIVE INSTRUCTIONAL DESIGNS

The adaptive programs are distinguishable from each other in the way they build or emphasize specific instructional approaches into their design components. The design components are subsumed under seven headings, as indicated below:

1. Theoretical/Philosophic Basis of the Design
2. Structural Support Provisions
   a) Organizational support
   b) Home/school/community
3. Intended Learning Emphasis
   a) Objective-driven design
   b) Domain of objectives
   c) Mastery to criterion
4. Curriculum Characteristics
   a) Basis for content selection
   b) Content sequence
   c) Size of learning increments
   d) Supporting activities
5. Instructional Characteristics
   a) Direct instruction
   b) Corrective instruction
   c) Grouping
   d) Students' role
   e) Teachers' role
   f) Time to learn and time on task
6. Assessment/Feedback Provisions
7. Staff Development Requirements

Table 14.1 compares and contrasts the design characteristics of the programs under the seven headings. Of the five adaptive approaches, ALEM and LFM appear to be more similar to each other than to the other three approaches. TAI could readily be incorporated into either ALEM or LFM as one of the corrective instruction learning activities. These three approaches share a behavioral psychology orientation, at least in their emphasis on sequencing of content, learning in small discrete steps, corrective feedback, and the role of the teacher in diagnosing deficiencies (and strengths) and prescribing appropriate learning activities. For most diagnostic/feedback/prescriptive-type programs, teacher time needed to diagnose, prescribe, and maintain

Table 14.1
Adaptive Design Components

DESIGN	ALEM	LFM	DISE	Cooperative Learning Approaches	
				CL	TAI
1. *Theoretical/ Philosophic Basis*	Alterability of individual (Bloom 1976; Carroll 1963)	Alterability of individual (Bloom 1976; Carroll 1963)	Expert opinion of effective schools	Socialization and societal needs (Deutsch 1949; Lewin 1953)	Research on learning in teams; instructional efficacy (Madsen 1967; Flanagan et al. 1975)
2. *Structural Supports*					
a) Organization	At classroom level	Not necessary	Teacher teams School organization	Cohesiveness of teachers	—
b) Home/school/ community	Yes, but outcome not reported	—	A program component, but outcome not reported as designed	—	—
3. *Intended Learning*					
a) Design objective	Micro objectives	Micro objectives	Macro: goal setting; process for program implementation	Macro and micro	Micro
b) Domain	Cognitive: skills	Cognitive: skills	Cognitive: variable	Cognitive: higher level (amenable to skill development)	Cognitive: skills
	Personal control; Self-efficacy	Acquisition of adaptive processes	Responsible self-planning	Socialization skills	Responsibility for routine management
c) Mastery to criterion	Yes	Yes	—	No, but approach will enhance mastery	Yes
4. *Curriculum*					
a) What content?	Not a concern	Not a concern	Only an adaptation to fit individual needs	Not a concern	Not a concern
b) Sequential	Yes (micro scale)	Yes (micro scale)	Global goals (macro scale)	—	Yes (micro scale)

c) Incremental	Small discrete steps	Small discrete steps	—		Small discrete steps
d) Supporting activities	Closed-ended	Closed-ended	Depends on curricular area	Fosters open-ended learning activities	Closed ended
5. Instruction					
a) Direct instruction	Yes (large & small group presentations)	Yes (large group presentations)	Yes	Yes (enhances presentations in small groups)	Yes (enhances presentations in small groups)
b) Corrective instruction	Yes	Yes	Possibly	Only if a part of a given activity	Limited
c) Grouping	Varied as needed; multiage classes	Varied as needed	Determined by overall curriculum	Small cooperative groups (heterogeneous)	Small heterogenous groups (also peer-pairing)
d) Student role	Self-management of learning tasks, assessment	Passive	Planning goals	Responsibility for self and others	Responsible for routine management and checking
e) Teacher role	Diagnose/prescribe/instruct; develop materials	Diagnose/prescribe/instruct	Advise/instruct	Facilitate/resource/instruct	Diagnose/prescribe/instruct
f) Time (to learn/on task)	Flexible time to learn	Flexible time to learn	—	Enhances time on task	Enhances time on task
6. Assessment/Feedback	Yes, built into activities; to plan next step	Yes, but built into activities; to plan next step	To plan comprehensive educational program	Group assessment	Yes, built into learning activity
7. Staff Development	Yes	Limited	Pre planning with teacher teams	90 hours	—

References:

Benjamin S. Bloom, *Human Characteristics and School Learning* (New York: McGraw-Hill, 1976).

John B. Carroll, "A Model of School Learning," *Teachers College Record* 64 (May 1963): 723-33.

Morton Deutsch, "A Theory of Cooperation and Competition," *Human Relations* 2 (1949): 129-52.

Kurt Lewin, *A Dynamic Theory of Personality* (New York: McGraw-Hill, 1953).

John C. Flanagan, William M. Shanner, Harvey J. Brudner, and Robert W. Marker, "An Individualized Instructional System: PLAN*," in *Systems of Individualized Education*, edited by Harriet Talmage (Berkeley, Calif.: McCutchan Publishing Corp, 1975).

records leaves little time for direct instruction. PLAN*, an individualized program from the previous decade, used a computer management system to perform the recordkeeping tasks. Other individualized programs of the 1960s and 1970s worked out varying forms of filing and retrieval systems. ALEM and TAI solve the paper work management by having students participate in record maintenance activities.

DISE and CL vary considerably from the others. DISE entails a reorganization of the process through which an established secondary curriculum is delivered. At the core of DISE is an advisement system to facilitate adaptation of the existing curriculum to better "fit" the needs of students than the present organizational structure permits. During the late 1950s Evanston Township High School in Illinois employed a "schools within a school" organization. Like Individually Guided Education (IGE) and the Evanston arrangement, school restructuring is a key element in DISE.

While the other programs give some attention to the processes students must undergo to learn socialization skills, CL incorporates the group process skills thought to be necessary to acquire socially constructive societal behaviors. The means are as important an outcome as academic achievement. Unlike ALEM, LFM, and DISE, CL is not a total instructional program. Rather, it is one instructional approach based on cooperative goal structuring that should supplement the other two more widely used forms of goal structuring, competitive and individualistic goal structures. TAI pays lip service to cooperative learning processes, but the data from the evaluation research studies cited in the TAI chapter do not appear to support cooperative learning practices as critical to attaining the goals of TAI.

Large computers supporting complex CAI programs and microcomputers with their supporting software have differential roles to play in these five adaptive approaches. For ALEM and LFM the computer programs can serve as one type of corrective instruction. Drill-type software could be incorporated easily and matched to many micro objectives.

Programs for managing student files are now available for many microcomputers and are easily learned by teachers and students, as

---

*Program for Learning in Accordance with Needs.

early as in the middle grades. Such software could take on the burden of tracking student progress, maintaining records, and diagnosing and prescribing appropriate activities. For ALEM, LFM, and TAI, microcomputer management system programs can readily be adapted to facilitate the types of recordkeeping necessary to sustain these approaches. These same microcomputer programs can also track advisement decisions with little modification for DISE.

For CL the open-ended aspects of programming and problem-solving potential of the computer for instruction provide natural projects for groups of students to work on cooperatively. The more exotic CAI programs under development and testing have some way to go before becoming a regular part of any of the five approaches to adaptive instruction, at least on a large scale.

The role of "time" in learning has received much attention over the past number of years. Research on time demonstrates the complexity of the concept. Time to learn as a unit of measure differs from how time is used (and the quality of the teacher-learner interactions), within a fixed period of time. In addition, attention must also be given to the value of what is expected to be learned within a unit of time.

Karweit presents one aspect of time: the ratio of a unit of time spent to time needed. This aspect of time plays an important role in how ALEM and LFM programs are structured. All adaptive programs aim toward increased time-on-task behavior as a program outcome; Johnson provides data on CL's enhancement of students' time-on-task behavior.

Increased teacher time to engage in direct instruction is another component of time important in most adaptive instructional programs. Each program directly or indirectly incorporates ways for teachers to use direct instruction, although the programs operate from somewhat different views of what constitutes direct instruction.

Arlin and Webster (1983) raise the issue of time costs in relation to time efficiency, that is, the amount of time needed in conjunction with the amount of learning. Mastery learning students come out second best in several such time-efficiency studies. We need to ask whether LFM takes too limited a view of time, a key concept undergirding LFM.

The papers on the five programs and the Karweit paper focus on "time" in relation to instruction. But any discussion of time to learn should not overlook curricular issues, especially the question of *what is* to be learned. Are the skills, concepts, and understandings worth learning regardless of the "goodness of fit" between time spent and time needed and the quality of instruction?.

Wallace holds up special education as a model for adaptive instructional programs. What he presents is a "medical model." It implies that something has to be remediated or fixed. As a consequence we have IEPs that many teachers decry as leading to rigid planning around small, inconsequential, or trivial bits of learning, so tightly structured that little room exists for individual expression on the part of students. Others, however, label the five components (from diagnosis through assessment) as "good" instructional practice.

ALEM, TAI, and LFM incorporate the Wallace model to a lesser or greater degree into their respective programs. Although the five components may be a part of ALEM, it is far from the sum of the model. CL and DISE, like ALEM, take a broader view of structuring learning opportunities than the model proposed by Wallace. These programs assume learning to be more than skill acquisition.

All the programs require some type of organizational support. For the most part LFM, TAI, and CL call for organizational support at the classroom level. ALEM requires support at the school level, and DISE is not possible without support at the school district level.

QUESTIONS FOR CLARIFICATION

Each of the adaptive approaches raises issues that need to be addressed if it is to become accepted as a viable alternative or complement to "traditional" classroom instruction.

To Cooperative Learning (CL): What provisions have been made to convince budget-strapped school districts and parents, who equate learning with competition, that ninety hours of teacher time is not too costly a price to pay in order to become competent in developing cooperative activities and in understanding team socialization skills?

To Design for Improving Secondary Education (DISE): IGE and other programs built around teachers working successfully in teams have found teamwork difficult to sustain over time. How are the problems of finding time to plan together and acquiring the social skills necessary for working together addressed?

To Adaptive Learning Environment Model (ALEM): Some low-level skills are sequential and possibly learning the various subconcepts in sequence enhances acquisition of the skill; however, is there sufficient evidence to show that learning other than the most basic skills is sequential? What about abstract concepts such as "roundness" or "peace" or "democracy?"

To Team-Assisted Individualization (TAI): Are teams a critical instructional strategy for enhancing achievement? Is the pay-off in students' time in program management sufficiently compensated in other student outcomes? Perhaps a time-efficiency study, drawing on Arlin and Webster's study, might offer an answer.

To Learning for Mastery (LFM): Does LFM dismiss too quickly that portion of individual differences that we call innate ability by setting a ceiling low enough to give a false impression of egalitarianism?

REVISITING PERSISTENT EDUCATIONAL ISSUES

Regardless of the efficiency of instruction or its effectiveness in enhancing achievement, every instructional program must examine the persistent educational issues.

1. What goals are uppermost, self-actualization of each individual or the larger societal goals? Can instructional approaches accommodate both or are they mutually exclusive? A single societal goal, pertaining to acquisition of basic skills, appears to loom large in at least three of the five programs. All the approaches give some attention to the learner assuming responsibility for some portion of the learning. CL goes a step further than the other programs in acknowledging the importance of socialization skills in order to function in society.

2. Is the subject matter worth learning? None of the five approaches addresses this curriculum concern in any depth. DISE rearranges the curriculum within the constraints of the state's educational mandate. The other programs accommodate instruction to the ongoing curriculum. But can any program or approach ignore the worth of what it intends the students to learn?

3. Other than the basic skills, can we prescribe *how* the learner is to learn? Or is learning idiosyncratic? Herman Melville had a word to

say on this: "From without, no wondrous effect is wrought within ourselves, unless some interior, responding wonder meets it. . . ."

WHAT IS ADAPTIVE INSTRUCTION?

If these five approaches are representative of adaptive instruction, we can surmise what it is and what it is not from the persistent issues left unanswered.

What is it? It would appear that adaptive instruction is whatever a developer decides it is so long as it incorporates direct instruction, provides some form of assessment and feedback, focuses principally on cognitive learning, gives some attention to building self-direction, and makes some attempt to involve the learner in the planning or management of the learner's progress. It can be a total system of instruction (ALEM and LFM), a comprehensive plan for rearranging an individual's educational program (DISE), or instructional strategies for augmenting ongoing instructional practices (CL and TAI).

By its very nature, there should never be *the* instructional program. The more we learn about learning and about instruction, the more we will need a variety of ways to be adaptive to individual learners.

One thing present-day adaptive approaches hold in common: all have built on past research, thus nudging us one small increment in the upward spiral. Hopefully this is leading to increased learning through improved instructional practices.

REFERENCE

Arlin, Marshall, and Webster, Janet. "Time Costs of Mastery Learning." *Journal of Educational Psychology* 75 (March 1983): 187-96.

PART III

Epilogue

CHAPTER
15

Adaptive Education in Retrospect and Prospect

Margaret C. Wang
and Herbert J. Walberg

Several prominent psychologists of the early twentieth century such as Freud, Piaget, Thorndike, Skinner, and Watson, as well as leading educational psychologists of today such as Bloom, Bruner, Carroll, Cronbach, Gagné, and Glaser, have pointed explicitly to the educational implications of learner differences. Yet providing instruction that effectively accommodates differences in the learning characteristics and needs of individual students poses a continuing challenge to educators. Every class contains students with different interests, problems, and talents; and most educators realize that whole-group instruction lessons geared to the "average" student are bound to be too difficult for some learners in the class and too easy for others.

The preceding chapters of this book show a number of possibilities for adapting instruction to individual differences. These include mastery learning, cooperative learning programs, individual assessment and prescription, and flexible time allowances for each student or groups of students. Several significant developments and findings related to the design and implementation of adaptive instruction in school settings have been noted. In this concluding chapter we highlight in retrospect, and as an indication of prospects for a future agenda for research and development, such topics as designs of adaptive instruction, new views of learner differences and roles, and definitions of learning environments.

PROGRAM DESIGN AND GOALS

Recent programs of adaptive instruction often combine a number of components that have been found to be effective (for example, flexible scheduling, individual diagnosis and prescription, mastery learning, cooperative learning) into flexible educational systems. Although implementation of such programs is more complicated and challenging than traditional whole-group teaching, extensive evidence reveals successful implementation under a wide variety of circumstances. When students in these programs are compared with control groups, for example, their scores on achievement tests on average are found to be moderately better (see Chapter 1).

Of course, averages can be misleading. Students in adaptive instruction programs sometimes fail to achieve as much as those in control groups; often they do about as well; and sometimes they achieve considerably more. This variation suggests that further research is required to determine the circumstances under which adaptive instruction has the most beneficial effects in terms of a range of student outcomes.

Achievement, however, is not the only educational goal or criterion for evaluation. Standardized achievement tests may not reflect either the intended district curriculum or the learning goals of particular teachers and students. Thus, active engagement in tasks, cooperation among students, a variety of activities and learning experiences, opportunities for student choices, and continuing motivation must be considered. The chapter authors have shown that, based on these criteria, a spectrum of adaptive instruction programs stands up very well to traditional teaching.

THE TEACHING AND LEARNING PROCESS

Jackson (1968) found that teachers in traditional classrooms engage in 200 to 300 interpersonal exchanges an hour and that their language reveals "an uncomplicated view of causality; an intuitive, rather than rational, approach to classroom events; an opinionated, as opposed to an open-minded, stance when confronted with alternative teaching practices; and a narrowness in working definitions assigned to abstract terms" (p. 144). Rosenshine (1982) argues that expert teachers can go far beyond these kinds of simple expressions, but that such expertise may be rare and may take years, if not decades, to acquire.

As a consequence, students in conventional classroom settings often receive inconsistent or vague information about learning goals and uninformative mass-processed feedback about their performance (Doyle 1977). They are also made to wait. Jackson (1968) found that delay, denial, interruption, and distraction typify classroom life; patience seems to be the greatest virtue.

On the other hand, Shimron's (1976) research has shown that students who were allowed to work at their own pace on individualized materials spent twice as much time on-task, completed three times as many units, and found the experience of a faster pace more varied and interesting. Similarly, synthesis of research on open education, in which some authority for planning and conducting learning is delegated to students, has shown nearly equal gains on standardized achievement tests, but higher levels of creativity, positive attitudes toward school, independence, freedom from anxiety, cooperation, and other socialization outcomes that educators, parents, and students hold more valuable than conventional test results (Peterson 1979).

Cognitive psychology and the research on classroom teaching suggest the importance of organizational support and management practices in the implementation of new programs, as well as the need for more effective integration of unique program components with the operationalization of complex systems such as adaptive environments for school learning. Research points to the cognitive complexity of teaching, the difficulty of suitably accommodating individual differences, and the need to attain efficient time use while increasing the overall efficiency and productivity of education.

CURRICULUM MATERIALS AND OTHER RESOURCES

In adaptive learning environments, students are encouraged to use a variety of resources (for example, time, curriculum materials, instructional help from teachers and peers) to facilitate their schooling tasks. Even in traditional classrooms where this is not the case, successful learners have been found to seek out and use supplementary resources. For example, in situations involving large-group instruction and where the only form of in-class presentation is the teacher lecture, successful students make adaptations such as seeking supplementary reading sources, discussing lesson content with fellow students, spending more time on a task than they ordinarily would feel necessary, and arranging for personal conferences with the instructors.

Quite obviously, the difference between adaptive and more conventional learning environments is the built-in provision for assisting students in making these types of adaptations (for example, by making alternative materials available, using alternative procedures, allowing varying amounts of time for individual students to learn and receive additional information). Descriptive studies detailing the nature and pattern of the use of various adaptations are likely to provide data for furthering understanding of how students' abilities in effective selection and utilization of resources contribute to the adaptive instruction process.

ROLE OF THE LEARNER

Much research on the adaptive process in classroom learning has focused on subject matter. The goals of schooling, however, include learning in areas other than subject-matter achievement. Adaptive environments not only may facilitate subject-matter learning, but they also appear to be conducive to the development of positive attitudes toward learning, motivation for life-long learning, independence and responsibility, and a host of related learner skills.

Recent research on learning suggests a change in our conception of the role assumed by students in the learning process. Essentially all learning involves both external and internal adaptation. External adaptation occurs in the ideas and content that are to be learned and in the modes and forms in which content is presented to the learner. Internal adaptation takes place in the mind of the learner as new content is assimilated and mental structures are modified to accommodate the new content (Wang and Lindvall 1984). Thus, the learner is viewed as an active information processor, interpreter, and synthesizer. Furthermore, the learner is the ultimate agent of adaptation.

Individual learners not only are able to take greater responsibility for managing, monitoring, and evaluating their learning, but they also can be instrumental in adapting the learning environment (for example, identifying and obtaining learning resources to fit their needs and goals) and adjusting themselves to the demands of the learning process (see, for example, Brown 1978; Flavell 1979; and Glaser 1984). Major differences between more proficient and less proficient learners are believed to include the ability to assume an active role in learning and a perception of self-competence for performing the role. Teaching students to adapt to various environments, moreover, may be as important as suiting environments to students; and exposing students to variety may produce long-range benefits.

REFERENCES

Brown, Ann L. "Knowing When, Where, and How to Remember: A Problem of Metacognition." In *Advances in Instructional Psychology*, vol. 1, edited by Robert Glaser. Hillsdale, N.J.: Lawrence Erlbaum Associates, 1978.

Doyle, Walter. "Paradigms for Research on Teacher Effectiveness." In *Review of Research in Education*, vol. 5, edited by Lee S. Shulman. Itasca, Ill.: F. E. Peacock, 1977.

Flavell, John H. "Metacognitive and Cognitive Monitoring: A New Area of Cognitive-Development Inquiry." *American Psychologist* 34 (October 1979): 906-11.

Glaser, Robert. "Education and Thinking: The Role of Knowledge." *American Psychologist* 39 (February 1984): 93-104.

Jackson, Philip W. *Life in Classrooms*. New York: Holt, Rinehart & Winston, 1968.

Peterson, Penelope L. "Direct Instruction Reconsidered." In *Research on Teaching: Concepts, Findings, and Implications*, edited by Penelope L. Peterson and Herbert J. Walberg. Berkeley, Calif.: McCutchan, 1979.

Rosenshine, Barak V. "The Master Teacher and the Master Developer." Unpublished paper, University of Illinois at Champaign-Urbana, 1982.

Shimron, Joseph. "Learning Activities in Individually Prescribed Instruction." *Instructional Science* 5 (October 1976): 391-401.

Wang, Margaret C., and Lindvall, C. Mauritz. "Individual Differences and School Learning Environments: Theory, Research, and Design." In *Review of Research in Education*, vol. 11, edited by Edmund W. Gordon. Washington, D.C.: American Educational Research Association, 1984.